Under the
Southern Sun

✳

ALSO BY PAUL PAOLICELLI

Dances with Luigi

PAUL PAOLICELLI

Paul P......
7/22/03

Under the Southern Sun

❋

Stories of the Real Italy and the
Americans It Created

THOMAS DUNNE BOOKS
St. Martin's Press
New York

THOMAS DUNNE BOOKS.
An imprint of St. Martin's Press.

www.stmartins.com

Design by Kathryn Parise

LIBRARY OF CONGRESS CATALOGING-IN-PUBLICATION DATA

Paolicelli, Paul.
    Under the Southern sun : stories of the real Italy and the Americans it created / Paul Paolicelli.
        p. cm
    Includes bibliographical references.
    ISBN 0-312-28765-8
        1. Italy, Southern—Description and travel. 2. Paolicelli, Paul—Journeys—Italy, Southern. I. Title.

DG821 .P36 2003
                                                                        2002034793

ISBN 0-312-28765-8

First Edition: March 2003

10   9   8   7   6   5   4   3   2   1

CONTENTS

IN THE SOUTH,
THEY CALL IT MACARONI . . .

Contrary to popular mythology, Marco Polo did not bring macaroni to Italy. It has been eaten on the Italian peninsula since before Roman times. It was probably first concocted during or before the period when the Greeks occupied what is now Southern Italy and Sicily. Some say that the modern Italian word *maccheroni* was originally Arab. But wherever the origins, it was definitely from the South, where all of Italian civilization began.

This book is dedicated to, and about, the people of Southern Italy. Those who stayed and those who left. It's for a generation whose sacrifice made a better life for all of us, here and there. People of il Mezzogiorno, where the Southern sun blazes bright.

Of those who left, a high percentage came to America—Italian immigrants overwhelmingly from the regions of Campania, Abruzzo, Calabria, Molise, Puglia (Apulia), Basilicata and Sicily. The poorest regions of Italy at the time of their emigration, they remain so even now. But once they formed the cradle of modern society.

The immigrants were forced by circumstances and bad timing to move, adapt, adjust and dramatically reinvent themselves and their lives. They did this for their children, for survival. But unlike other immigrants at the time, they were slow to break completely with the old world. Many communicated a strong sense of shame for their poverty and general lack of education. They never blamed their situation on the governments or social systems that had clearly failed them. They sought only opportunity in their new home, taking pride in the fact that they could now provide for their own. Many hoped one day to go back, but as they prospered, married and raised their American children, they became the bridge from the Old World to the New.

Who knows how many dreams were abandoned so that their children might fulfill theirs?

The first generation talked little of their losses; they put their hopes into the future and ignored the disappointments of the past.

What they did keep of the Old World was a sense of who they were. A system of values, what the anthropologists would call an *ethos*. A system of right and wrong. A way of doing things. They watched their children become Americans, though they never fully made the same transition.

Most of all they kept and handed down *the food*; the one continuing enjoyment from the Old World and old life. The food reminded them of things they had learned from their own parents. Evening meals were always the part of the day—no matter how hard the times, scant the crops, or bad the government—that brought them together in physical and spiritual nourishment.

It was at the tables here, and in the Old World, where the stories were told. Their food was an entrée into American society, the welcoming into their homes. Their cuisine helped them gain acceptance as a civilized culture in their new land, despite the lack of formal education or proper language skills.

These people, these Southerners, never used the word "pasta." Even today, only Northerners in Italy call it that. Ask a Northerner to define "macaroni," they'll tell you it's a type of pasta.

Ask a Southerner, and they'll say macaroni *is* what others call pasta.

To call it anything other than macaroni is putting on airs, acting snobbish.

While that first generation was willing to make any sacrifice for their family, willing to try and learn English and American ways, some even willing to change their names so that their kids would fit in, assimilate, they kept their food and the family notions that went with it. They kept their eyes straight ahead, kept silent about their aching backs and dashed dreams, kept focused on their family's future. They set the table, invited the neighbors over, served the supper, and called it macaroni.

If there is a central metaphor to describe the differences between the North and the South of Italy, then "macaroni" is it. It's not so much a food as a philosophy born of hardship, exploitation and poverty. It's the contrast between wealthy people who can establish self-determining governments, or a clearly defined canonical and religious structure of power in the Church, as opposed to a people eternally oppressed by outsiders who owned their land and controlled their destiny. Macaroni was their heritage as well as their nourishment, and they carried it with them into the New World.

FOREWORD

THE LONG VOYAGE SOUTH

I stood at the prow of the gigantic ferry as it lumbered across the dark water of the North Sea. Alone and completely isolated from friends and family, I watched as the boat churned the black-green water into brilliant white spume. I tried to imagine what it must have been like for my grandfathers crossing another sea nearly a century before. What laments or regrets did they feel as their ships got farther and farther away from their native land? What hopes and curiosity did they have as they neared their new world? What had that great green crossing ended, as well as begun?

I was lost in thoughts of future and past as the ship worked its way southward. I could picture my grandfathers standing on distant decks, wondering if the coming confluence of ship and shore would enlighten, fulfill or turn a daunting dream to dust. It was the immigrants' gamble and the foundation of the American experience.

My journey now was really about their journeys. Their lives had, in some very significant ways, taken over my life during the previous decade. And, like all great odysseys, I'd thought my work had ended when it had really just begun. It was only now that I was coming to realize fully the effects of history and government on their migrations;

the nature and extent of the land where they had been born; and the very strong influences that land had left on them and, through them and their children, on me. I was the end of the line—the last American generation to have direct memory and ties with the great diaspora from Italy during the end of the nineteenth and early part of the twentieth centuries.

And I was learning how inadequate the word "Italian" was to describe the experience.

My grandfathers were from Abruzzo and Basilicata. *Southern Italy.* A breed apart from the rest of the Italian peninsula. They knew of Dante, Machiavelli, Da Vinci, Michelangelo, of popes and of Garibaldi. They knew of the Renaissance, and of papal wars. But their parents would have thought of those names and events as being from another country— one that spoke a language similar to, yet different from, their own, and with a different form of government and society. My grandparents and the overwhelming majority of Italian immigrants to the United States during the great migration hadn't been tanning in the Tuscan sun. They and their ancestors, since the fall of Rome, had been broiled by the Southern sun of il Mezzogiorno, the "high noon," "middle-of-the-day" region of Italy; the *South.* The places that even now the tourists seldom find.

The concept of "Italy" had only occurred in my great-grandparents' lifetimes. There was no "Italian" nation prior to the middle of the nineteenth century. More important, the supposed unification of the Italian peninsula never included the South of Italy as an equal partner. Its inhabitants were from a different land that could be obscured and ignored from the distance and relative comfort of America.

And so it was.

Most of my generation of "Italian-Americans" grew up with the notion that our families had emigrated from a country much like our concepts of England or Germany, or even Poland, while nothing could have been further from the truth. The only thing that had unified Italians at the time of my grandparents' departure was a tenuous paper legality. In fact, it was because of this huge fissure between North and South that the overwhelming majority of Italian-Americans are, in fact, *Southern* Italian-Americans. Distinctions that were never made during my youth, history that had never really been discussed.

Over the course of the previous couple of years, as the result of my first book on the subject of Italian heritage, I had received hundreds of calls, letters, faxes and e-mails and spoken with still hundreds of others at book signings and talks. Virtually every person I communicated with wanted to share the same thought; they'd also been quiet or confused about their own family stories and now wanted to find appropriate ways to learn more, celebrate and annotate the experience. There had been something in all of us that had kept the story muted, yet something else that had kept it strong in our imaginations.

It also seemed to me that there was a strong sense on the part of those who contacted me that *finally*—to steal a line from Arthur Miller—*attention was being paid.* I learned that many felt the stories of *Southern* Italian families had been ignored in the popular media for a very long time, that the stories had never really been told with the same fervor and with the same distribution as many others.

I started looking deeper into the subject. In my previous work, I had dealt mostly with my own family's experiences. Now I researched the scant resources I could find to explain the much larger picture of Southern Italian emigration.

Finding specific references for Italian-American history and the history of their American immigration wasn't easy. Even the most respected of American historians can sometimes have blind spots when it comes to the Italian-American experience.

No less than eighty-three percent, or over eight Italian immigrants out of ten during the great migration between 1880 and 1920, were from "il Mezzogiorno," Southern Italy and Sicily. Remote towns and provinces not known to their Yankee interviewers at Ellis Island or other ports of entry, and places that, even today, remain generally forgotten in family Bibles and faded documents.

Yet most of the popular books written about Italy, both contemporary and older, deal with the North. Rome has long held a central place in literature about Italy. Rome was a relatively small capital of around one hundred and fifty thousand inhabitants at the time of Italian unification. Rome's power had been centered in the pope and the Roman Catholic Church for centuries, not a secular or national political state.

Contemporary writers, myself included, "discovered" the Roman ambience or the Tuscan countryside. And, enthralling as they are, they are not the atmosphere from which so many escaped in the early part of the last century.

Nor were the majority of the relatives of current Italian-Americans fleeing Venetian gondolas or French-speaking Alpine ski resorts. American writers such as Henry James or Edith Wharton spent thousands of words on the essential Roman construction of the nobles' gardens in the environs of Rome or the intricate interrelationships between foreign men and women in Venice. Again, not a shared experience of most who left to find another life.

When James does focus on the Italians themselves, he writes of the disdain in which Italian immigrant workers were held in American cities.

English writers, George Gissing and Norman Douglas in particular, did go into the South of Italy and did attempt to paint a contemporary picture of the country for their readers. But neither came from the culture or had any genealogical or emotional links to it. Both men related the Southern Italian culture in English school classical terms.

Gissing writes with a sense of looking down at the "wogs," and a nostalgia for the higher civilization of the Greeks.

Douglas, more of a linguist, chuckles over the colorful peasantry and their barely articulate forms of communication. He does write faithfully of the major historical developments in "Old Calabria," much of which was actually Puglia and Basilicata, despite his obvious sense of British superiority.

Neither man defined Southern Italy as such, but only as an ancient historical region. The major political and social turmoil that was going on in that very land at the time of their writings is oddly absent from their narratives.

There's still great confusion and debate among both contemporary Italians and Italian-Americans as to the exact definition of Southern Italy, even today. While preparing for this work, I wrote to several friends and asked a simple question: "How do you define the Mezzogiorno?"

I got back as many responses as people I had asked.

When the American author Joe McGinness went to Italy a few summers ago to cover the spectacular season of an obscure Abruzzo football team, he was amazed by the very little, and very antiquated, information he could find on the area. Even more surprising, most of the descriptions he'd read of Castel di Sangro, just down the mountain from my own grandfather's birthplace of Gamberale, were negative and judgmental in nature. McGinness was surprised by the beauty of the countryside, surprised by the warmth of the people, surprised by the lack of information and knowledge about the region, even among the Italians themselves.

In the States, the misinformation about Southern Italians began almost as soon as they arrived. By 1910, John De Ville wrote in the *Catholic Encyclopedia* that "the Latin type is ethnically predominant among them, since the Northern Italians, as is well known, have a considerable Teutonic element in their composition."

De Ville plainly favored those "Teutonic" virtues and claimed that the Southern "element has not contributed [economically] as largely to the progress of the United States as have other races. They have, however, enjoyed their share of American prosperity." De Ville was writing at a time of near hysteria over the "sullying" of the Anglo-Saxon society by swarthy Southern types. His writings, as clearly skewed and biased as they were, and many like his, became the foundations for future historians.

In contemporary times, Thomas Sowell of Stanford is considered one of the foremost experts in cultural migrations to this country. Yet even he, when writing about the Italian-Americans, seems sometimes unfamiliar or uncomfortable with the subject of *Southern* Italians. He points out that it was the Northern Italians and the government of Italy who demanded that the distinction between the two regions be made on the Ellis Island registries, but then wanders into stereotype when he describes their contributions to this society.

Sowell says that Southern Italians "brought *no tradition of individual initiative* as employees, being from a society where such initiative was considered offensive by employers and others above them on the social scale."

Then, seemingly without noticing, he contradicts his own analysis. Sowell goes on to describe how Italian immigrants in South America quickly became key players in both the political and economic structures...those same people without the tradition of individual initiative. He does add that, in America, "...Italians were noted for their diligence and sobriety—the latter often contrasted with the drinking of the Irish—but also for *a lack of initiative* that required them to have considerable supervision."

Sowell—a descendant of African-American slaves—does, however, write with compassion and almost poetry in summing up the Southern Italian immigration experience. He points out that, of all of the immigrants from the great wave of European immigration, the Southern Italians were mostly what he calls "sojourners." He defines sojourners as men working in the States to alleviate the desperately poor conditions in their native land. Men who denied themselves physical comfort, living in virtual squalor, while saving every possible penny to send "home" and protect their families. He describes the first waves of immigrants as "...*heroic in their quiet tenacity and self-sacrifice for their loved ones back home. Too proud to take charity, they were not too proud to wear rags and to do the hardest and dirtiest work spurned by others*—all the while sending money home from foreign countries to fulfill their family responsibilities."

And then Sowell tells the story as most Italian-Americans know it:

The time that Italian-born men were away from their wives and children ranged from several months for migratory workers to several years for those who slowly accumulated the money required to bring their families to join them in a foreign land. That such human dramas were re-enacted literally millions of times in the far reaches of the globe is not only a tribute to the Italians, but also *an inspiration as showing what the human spirit is capable of—and perhaps a rebuke to those who whine over much less formidable problems.*

Sowell describes men I knew, was related to, or had heard of—men willing to sacrifice everything to provide for their families. My paternal grandfather died a young man on a steel-mill floor doing just that—anything he could to protect and feed his family. Virtually everyone I know of Southern Italian origin has a similar story.

Latin types?

Teutonic elements?

It's that type of bias and nonsense that can and did lead to specious stereotypes.

Based on my mail and other communication, I believe a great many contemporary Italian-Americans—those of us in the third and fourth generations—are dedicated to learning more about, and coming to terms with, those who became what Sowell called the sojourner.

Dr. Jim Mancuso, professor emeritus of the University at Albany of the State University of New York, describes the same experience as *l'avventura*, a wonderful combination word describing adventure and daring, and echoing Joseph Campbell's' writings on the "adventurers" and the spiritual wealth that those willing to dare great risks bring back to their culture. We are all descendants of those risk takers.

Much Italian-American writing has focused on the successes of the American part of the equation. There are countless books on the lives of successful Italian-American athletes, entertainers, artists, writers, film directors, scientists, actors, bankers—you name it. In short, there is an endless celebration of the *American* side of *l'avventura*. But the literature, poetry and fiction describing the influences that led the ancestors of these American success stories to come here in the first place are strangely not part of the Italian-American or general culture.

Far too many of us have realized that we didn't ask the right questions or were otherwise preoccupied when we had the chance to get straight answers, and that first generation was so reluctant to...as Professor Sowell said...*whine*.

And what is it we're searching for?

Possibly an attempt to help define ourselves by learning what formed the old ones, the grandparents and great-grandparents who first came here. The ones who spoke with marvelous accents and expressed themselves so differently, so much more clearly in many ways, than many of the others we knew who were fluent in American argot. They dressed differently, looked at the world in a way we could only imagine. They left their birthplaces and little towns and hamlets, often left parents, sisters, brothers, came to America and started anew, far away from the malarial cities or flinty fields and sometimes scanty crops of il Mezzogiorno.

In their new land they kept the things that had framed them in the old, and they passed those on: a sly skepticism of the outside world; an equivocal relationship with Church religion; a demand for excellence in their work and play; a profound sense of family and of commitment to their children and their God as the center of their inside world; a sense of humor, irony and artistry that allowed many to succeed in the creative fields; their *macaroni*; a diet that either instinctively or intuitively comprised both the most tasteful and one of the most healthy in proportion; and a smiling sense of optimism and good cheer.

And when they finally left us, after lives of hard work, laughter and philosophizing, and offering us only fleeting, ineffable insights into their times and world, there was a void for those left behind that could never be filled. A connection that could never be made again, except in reminiscence and in dreams.

It's taken me a long time to get here, to try finally to appreciate what it was my parents and grandparents provided for me. How easy it was to simply assume and accept the fact of their lives, to find my grandparents' accents amusing and comical, and never fully comprehend the many miles and sacrifices and struggles that their speech and their lives were really all about.

I grew up as an American, plain and simple. But I also had this blood called Italian running through me that, as my life progressed, piqued more and more curiosity, until now the issue has all but consumed me.

It is the *Southern* Italian sensibility that I am in search of.

The more I learned about this culture, *my* culture that I had come to embrace so late, the more I realized that my experiences, my family's experiences, fit into an entire grouping of people from Southern Italy. People who had learned from the cradle to develop relationships in a series of ever-expanding rings. The center of the rings is the most important, the outer rings, the least: nuclear family, extended family, village, church, province, region, state.

This order or hierarchy is in the blood.

It comes from centuries of experiences with bad governments, sometimes hypocritical clerics, malicious politics and marauding strangers.

And while those of us fortunate to have been born in the United States respect our government and value our citizenship as a very basic part of our identity, we are still somehow carried forward with the notion that we didn't and couldn't share too much about family with the public at large. We kept things intuitively at the "inside, outside" levels, despite our determination to be exemplary Americans.

From the top deck of the ferry, I could see Germany ahead. I was southbound. My self-created voyage would take me down the length of Europe to the most remote corners of the Italian peninsula in search of that history and those people of the South. It was the continuation of a journey I thought I'd completed several years before. It was to be both daunting and illuminating and, as with all such journeys, life-altering.

As the boat docked, another adventure began. This book is the result of that adventure. It is an attempt to explore those Southern roots and influences in all their myriad contradictions and colors. It's an attempt to explore the land and learn of the people from whom most of us who call ourselves Italian-Americans originated. To celebrate and evaluate the continuing but waning ties. It is not a pure history book, but more in the tradition of a travelogue, somewhat like the last-century musings of Norman Douglas or George Gissing. But unlike those men, both British, I have not visited a strange culture somehow not quite up to Northern European standards.

This story is often personal; it deals with the origins of my own family and the influences that led them to America; but it also represents the people of the South and all the Southern families who went through similar experiences and formed the large body of contemporary Italian-

Americans. I am not a historian, nor do I consider this work journalism, but rather as "journaling"—observing and storytelling. Southern Italy is rich in people, landscape and inspiration for this sort of excursion into prose.

I pray my words will be equal to the journey.

Viterbo

ROME

Tivoli

L'Aquila

Pescara

ABRUZZO

Lanciano

Avezzano   Sulmona   Vasto

Castel   Gamberale
di Sangro

MOLISE   Campobasso

Cassino   *PUGLIA*   Bari

CAMPANIA

Gaeta   Caserta   Altamura   Gioia del Colle

Naples   Salerno   Potenza   Matera   Castellaneta
                                                             Taranto

Paestum   Miglionico   Metaponto

Agropoli   *BASILICATA*

Sala
Consilina

Castrovillari

Ferramonti   Rossano

Cosenza

Amantea   *CALABRIA*

Catanzaro

Vibo Valentia

Palmi   Gerace
Milazzo   Siderno
                              Locri

Palermo   Cefalù   Reggio di Calabria

Trapani   Taormina   Messina

Marsala   Corleone

Castelvetrano   Bisacquino   *SICILY*

Agrigento   Catania

Syracuse

Adriatic Sea

Tyrrhenian Sea

Ionian Sea

Mediterranean Sea

1

Il Mezzogiorno

DOWN THE AUTOSTRADE AND INTO HISTORY

South of Rome, the scenery changes. The landscape becomes dramatic and even dangerous. The soft rolling hills of Tuscany, the incredibly sprawling plains and gentle knolls of Lazio become the jagged and rugged mountains, ravines, cliffs, and the near deserts of Campania, Calabria, Basilicata and Puglia. Driving down the single autostrada along the western coast that leads to the deep South, all of Italy's history passes by with the terrain.

Monte Cassino dominates the terrain where the Germans drew their line of defense in 1943 during the Second World War. The Allies fought for every inch of earth in the valley. The rebuilt abbey sits solidly and majestically atop its mountain, a silent and stately reminder of thousands of lives lost, including hundreds of Italian civilians caught in the deadly crossfire, while still others starved to death attempting to hide in the hills during that terrible winter.

The abbey had also been destroyed by the Longobards, Saracens and an earthquake over the fourteen centuries before the Allies advanced. We don't know the death tolls from those particular events. The Goths sacked the place before St. Benedict founded his monastery on the remnants of a Roman fortification. The Romans fought in this region against rebelling native tribes.

Blood is in the soil here.

Yet the abbey remains and endures.

A few kilometers farther south, Vesuvio broods over Naples, a unique emblem of indifferent power. It was on the hills of this volcano that Spartacus hid from the Romans, its fertile soil, rich with fruit and grain, feeding and protecting his rebellious slave army for a time.

Less than a century later, Vesuvio's deadly eruption killed thousands more when it destroyed Pompeii and Herculaneum. The relics from that ancient tragedy give us a direct and fascinating look at the objects and organization of daily life two thousand years ago, household items that are still stylish and functional and a haunting reminder of how quickly life can be taken, cities destroyed.

Driving through Italy is driving through time.

Driving through Southern Italy is driving through the geography of the entire sweep of Italian history. This is where Italy began. In fact, it was the tribes here who were first called "Italian." Early populations in the North were a mixture of Gauls, Goths and various other migrations until late in the Roman era.

Nearing the shores of Southern Italy, one goes from driving through ancient Italy to driving through ancient Greece, for the majority of the coastline of the South, from Sicily and up to and including Naples, was known as Magna Graecia. The natives of this region, the Etruscans ranging south throughout what is modern-day Campania, the Brutians in Calabria and the Lucani in Basilicata, began trading with the Greeks at the dawn of modern civilization. Centuries later, as Greece struggled with overpopulation, she established her first colonies along the shores of modern-day Sicily, Puglia, Basilicata and Calabria—the bottom of the "foot" of Italy.

It is Southern Italy and Greece where modern civilization began.

And it is here, too, where the confusion over Italian history, and ultimately Italian-American history, begins...who were these people and who are they now?

My own confusion had begun several years before. I was on the floor of the Democratic Convention in 1984, when Mario Cuomo, then governor of New York, made his now famous and often quoted speech about his father's life in America—a man who had been born not far from Naples. Cuomo talked of what he had learned from his father's struggle. It was, of course, an Italian-American experience which Cuomo related so eloquently that evening in San Francisco. His story demonstrated the innate dignity and achievements of his father's generation. He described his father as "a man who came here uneducated, alone, unable to speak the language, who taught me all I needed to know about faith and hard work by the simple eloquence of his example...." And, describing his childhood, Cuomo said, "I learned about our obligation to each other from him and from my mother. They asked only for a chance to work and to make the world better for their children...."

It was a personal and stirring speech, delivered in the Moscone Center, which was named for still another Italian-American of political achievement.

And it was a speech I found strangely troubling.

I was not there as a cheering Democrat, but as a member of the huge press corps covering the event. Also, I was most definitely not there as an Italian-American, but as a professional journalist helping to report on the American political process. I had never mixed the two—my profession and my family—and was uncomfortable that Cuomo had. I never talked about my father's or grandfathers' experiences in public. I barely talked about them at all. Cuomo's stories of his father's principles and hard work was just not the kind of subject I thought appropriate for public discussion.

If pressed to describe my poorly defined attitudes toward my ethnic identity from that time, I would have probably paraphrased Herman Wouk's title from his novel dealing with Jewish ethnicity in conflict with public personae; I had lived mostly in an *Inside, Outside* world. In my "inside" world—the world of family, close relatives, the same blood—I celebrated the accomplishments and mourned the losses of my own relatives, especially that first, largely uneducated and hardworking generation, like Cuomo's father, who had made our American lives possible.

At the level of "outside" world—school, the church, workplace, society in general—I went about my life in the way I believed the "average American" would go about it. While I certainly felt no shame over my origins, I did not want to be identified as a representative of any particular group other than my chosen profession. I belonged to no political or fraternal organizations, had no strings to any societies or groups of any sort, either religious, ethnic or social, and believed that lack made for a more objective journalist.

Yet I recognized the ring of truth in Cuomo's speech that night. I identified with the powerful metaphors he used for a generation capable of self-sacrifice and spirituality, the same qualities I admired in my own family. I remembered similar feelings from my own childhood and the stories of my parents' early experiences. Cuomo talked about the "simple eloquence" of his father's example—a man uneducated and inarticulate in English who taught the future New York governor "all I needed to know about faith and hard work."

The words stayed with me for a long time, and it was longer still until I came to an understanding of why they troubled me.

I didn't know it at the time, but I was reacting culturally—exactly the same way my relatives and ancestors would have reacted—as a *Southern* Italian. *Keep your business to yourself. Don't talk about personal things. Tell the government or those who represent it what they need to hear. Volunteer nothing, be polite, move on. Smile, invite them to dinner. Never share your true feelings unless you can trust, and you can only trust blood, the inner circle; the rest might never understand, so don't waste time trying to tell them.*

No one had ever spoken those actual words to me, but they were what I believed and what I would learn an entire culture believed: the *Southern Italian* culture, the majority of whom came to America from the relatively new country called "Italy" to find the life that Cuomo had so passionately described.

It took longer still for another question to arise in my mind: If Mario Cuomo had learned all he needed to know about truth and values from his father, a hardworking but poorly educated immigrant, *where had his father learned those values?*

And, in a broader context, how could the Cuomo family, in a single generation, produce a major American political figure? Obviously, Cuomo had learned some important lessons from his immigrant family. What about people like Frank Capra, whose family came to America with little formal education and poor language skills, yet, within twenty or so years, Capra was helping define America through his films? Or the poet John Ciardi, or composer Henry Mancini, or businessman Lee Iacocca, all sons of Southern Italian immigrants, along with countless athletes and entertainers. The examples of Italian immigrant families who had, in less than a normal life span, produced great American success stories such as artists, musicians, actors, scientists and bankers were endless, and the overwhelming majority of them had been from Southern Italy and Sicily.

Surely there was something in the Southern Italian experience that could explain that success.

A Trip Through Time...

Driving down to Italy from the north through the countries of the European Union, one can't escape the obvious remnants of the nation-state system so prevalent during the eighteenth, nineteenth and twentieth centuries. In order to visit with friends in Switzerland, a country with roughly the same population as the Los Angeles region, I had to stop at the border for a customs check, show my passport and pay a road tax (good for one year).

Just ten years ago this was the process for most Western European countries and all of Scandinavia, and is still the process in what is now the collection of independent states that was once Yugoslavia.

Today's relative ease in driving about Europe reflects an attempt on its part to diminish outward claims of sovereignty and the long legacy of nationalism. Europe has been in a constant state of political change from the end of ancient feudalism through the Reformation, the Age of Enlightenment, the rise of the concept of nation and the struggle, often bloody, through various social experiments and "isms" ranging from Communism to Fascism to Nazism to Socialism in an effort to determine individual and governmental balance.

My reading of this history always returns my American thoughts to Abraham Lincoln. I believe it was Lincoln, more than any other American, who clearly saw the weakness in this sort of small state system, and saw his own times for what they were. It was Lincoln's deep belief in union, that the whole is greater than the sum of its parts, that was at the core of his thinking when he chose the terrible and bloody American Civil War over the concept of individual state's rights to secede.

Lincoln, and only a handful of others, understood in the mid-nineteenth century what would happen to the United States if they weren't united; essentially what occurred in Europe over the following century. On the Continent, there was an incessant and often violent attempt at domination and subjugation of others by one national entity or another, unending political and diplomatic intrigue, and a constant changing of borders—much like malignant cancer cells migrating into strange and ultimately fatal masses. During this same period Americans were saved, directly as a result of the Civil War, from the upheaval and madness of Europe, which continues in some parts of the continent to this very day.

The Balkans are the purest example of this remnant of European nation-state philosophy.

In 1992, I visited Ljubljana, Slovenia, on a consulting trip for the Independent Media Fund. I took the fast train from Rome to Venice, where I transferred to the Slovenian train. At the border, we came to a halt. Two heavily armed soldiers came through the car barking orders in what I assumed was Slovenian. One guard, a thick, heavyset woman with her hand on an automatic rifle, demanded to see my passport, then motioned for me to leave my possessions on the train and report to an office in the station.

A fellow passenger saw my confusion and explained, in Italian, that I needed to obtain a temporary visa in order to continue the journey—a visa I had to pay for with Slovenian money, which further complicated the transaction. And this was a benign experience—Slovenians had no objections to Americans visiting their country. Just five years before that journey, I would have been subjected to even further scrutiny, since the Iron Curtain would have been still very firmly in place.

Slovenia has two million inhabitants, give or take a few. Yet it maintains a separate government, currency, flag, national anthem, national border, requires visas of visitors, has a separate official language from the rest of the peninsula and is a sovereign and wholly separate nation from the rest of the Balkans and Europe. It takes a little more than an hour by car to cross the entire east-to-west span of Slovenia, and then there's another border. This time it's Croatia, which also has its own official language, currency, requires an entry visa and so on. And thus it is down the length of the Balkan peninsula.

Imagine going on a trip of around one hundred miles from Erie, Pennsylvania, to Cleveland, Ohio, and having to stop at a state border guarded by heavily armed soldiers, apply and pay for an entry visa, exchange money, buy a dictionary in order to read Cleveland menus and negotiate hotels, be subjected to a search of your body and possessions and see more armed men and women guarding all of the main entry points into the city.

Now consider this: Cleveland is more than twice as big as the capitals of Slovenia, Macedonia, Croatia or Bosnia-Herzegovina—all of which impose these impediments on travelers, as well as having separate languages or dialects, flags, anthems and sovereignty. (And there are almost as many Slovenians in the Cleveland-Pittsburgh corridor as there are in Slovenia proper).

In his fascinating work, *The Myth of Nations, the Medieval Origins of Europe*, UCLA Professor Patrick J. Geary writes,

> …there is nothing particularly ancient about either the peoples of Europe or their supposed right to political autonomy. The claims to sovereignty which Europe is seeing in Eastern and Central Europe today are a creation of the nineteenth century, an age which combined the romantic political philosophies of Rousseau and Hegel with "scientific" history and Indo-European philology to produce ethnic nationalism. This pseudoscience has destroyed Europe twice and may do so yet again.…

Today's European Union is an attempt at a United States of Europe, which hopes to eliminate the very political conditions that have been choking Europe and causing many of its social, economic, religious and political problems since the end of feudalism.

Italy's role in all of this is unique.

The Northern states of Italy, from the twelfth century on—most notably Venice and Florence—were independent, and vastly influential throughout the then-known world. They were essentially city-states dominated either by royal houses of extraordinary wealth and great influence over the Roman Catholic Church (the Barberinis, Medicis, et cetera), or the doges of Venice, who were the first major international businessmen and government leaders.

The North of Italy meant (and still means) wealth, education, sophistication and relative comfort, the epitome of each in all of Europe at the time. Commoners could farm, learn trades, apprentice in the arts and go into the lower clergy or domestic service. Aside from the plague, which swept through on a nearly generational basis, life was on the whole quite tolerable and even enjoyable.

John Milton, the English poet and civil libertarian, went to Italy to confer with Galileo. Mozart studied the Italian masters. Tintoretto was hired to do the artwork in churches throughout Germany. Shakespeare set several of his plays in Northern Italy, obviously fascinated by its geography and government. Venice negotiated prices and trade for the entire middle section of Europe and the Adriatic region. Northern Italy was the cultural head and heart of Europe.

Immediately to the south of Venice and Florence lay Rome and the Papal States, an independent patch quilt of territory run by the Roman Catholic Church and controlled directly by its clergy. The popes were the major political players of this period. When England's Henry VIII demanded a divorce from Catherine of Aragon, the pope refused. Not because of any spiritual or religious consideration, as we were taught in Catholic schools, but because Aragon and Spain were far more important politically to the pope's aims than the relatively unimportant island of England. Permitting the divorce would have alienated the Spanish nobility related to Catherine and several popes.

The pope's influence was a dominant and often determining factor in forming the political coalitions and rulers of Europe. It was the pope who crowned the first Holy Roman Emperor, Charlemagne. It was the pope who first sanctioned and blessed the Norman rule of Southern Italy and continued to play a key role in Southern rule. It was the pope who took offense at Napoleon's insistence that he crown himself. And it was the pope who had been involved in every political movement in Western Europe until this very day with a Polish pope largely credited with helping bring down the Iron Curtain.

Not surprisingly, popes and their clergy have been adamantly, and sometimes violently, opposed to the rise of both nation-states and democracies. The concept of self-determination flies in the face of what the Church saw as its own role: to interpret government through its clerical and spiritual filter.

Now, finally, we come to the South of Italy; the last of the regions of Western Europe to emerge fully into the Age of Enlightenment. Or, more accurately, to miss the Age of Enlightenment entirely and find itself in the twentieth century without an intervening period of transition from feudalism (which was, in fact, a remnant from Roman times) into a period of democracy and self-determination. The very concepts of self-rule and economic parity were as difficult to implement in Southern Italy in 1920 as they would have been in 1020 or 20 B.C.E.

This was the intellectual, social, economic and political landscape into which most of the great wave of Southern Italian emigrants to the New World were born.

As Americans, we tend to look at European history in truncated form. We gloss over the enormous effects the creation of our extraordinary form of government had on Europe.

When Thomas Jefferson wrote the main body of text for the American Declaration of Independence, he was writing for a specific audience in Philadelphia and a united thirteen American colonies. When he wrote that men were created equal, with "unalienable rights, among them life, liberty, and the pursuit of happiness" (words based in part on the writings of an Italian, Filippo Mazzei), he changed not only what was to become the United States of America, but the world as well. Those words affected the thinking of every ruler, politician, thinker, reader, pauper and priest.

Our experiment in creating a democratic republic was the first since ancient Greece but, unlike its antique predecessor, was based on a sequence of historical events coming down to the United States through both the folly and enlightenment of European existence, among them the Magna Carta, English common law, the Renaissance, the Reformation, Counter-Reformation, countless civil wars, the plague, the evolving of modern science and geographical discoveries only dreamed of in ages past. In short, we wanted to do things differently. We tend to forget, or have never quite realized, how that energy and excitement affected and, in some cases, infected, the rest of the world.

It was the United States, both conceptually and legally, that hastened changes in modern Europe, fed desires for individual property rights; concepts of individual will and destiny separate from the church and state; ground-breaking notions that government should be completely secular, independent from any monarchy or formal religion; and the truly audacious concept that the press should be independent and free from every government and religious institution.

America's gamble, its experiment in individual freedoms, upset a very old and very dilapidated apple cart.

Nowhere was this more the case than in what we now refer to as Italy. At the time of the signing of our Declaration of Independence, Southern Italy was comprised of a grouping of regions and peoples under the political umbrella called the Kingdom of Two Sicilies and ruled by the Bourbon dynasty.

If we traveled backward to the middle of the nineteenth century, the people in the few major cities and thousands of small towns and villages of Southern Italy would not refer to themselves as "Italian." They thought of themselves as Sicilian, Calabrian, Puglian and Neapolitan;

more specifically, they were Abruzzese from a particular mountain range or valley, Basilicatan from a name that would indicate inland or coastal origins, Lucania natives or Reggio di Calabria citizens. The concept of "Italy" was as foreign to those people of the South as was the Piedmont House of Savoy, then ruling the newly unified country and unable to speak basic Italian.

In fact, in Sicily, Greek was the most common language until the Napoleonic era, while the dialects that dominated the Southern regions were, and remain, as equally incomprehensible to Northern Italians as the Sicilian Greek of the eighteenth century would have been.

The South of Italy had been essentially static for the better part of fourteen hundred years. There were few changes in the way of life for the people in the South from the fall of Rome until the nineteenth century. Governments changed on a regular basis, but the control of the people and their repression remained basically unchanged. Families mostly farmed portions of large foreign-owned estates for subsistence and little personal profit. This was the case of the *latifundium* in Roman times, and *latifundia* in subsequent periods—there was little or no private ownership of land. Church and Church property were the only areas for public use and gathering. Low literacy and education rates persisted, and a basic peasantry and very small merchant class made up the overwhelming majority of the population.

During those many centuries, as the South remained unchanged, its rulers were mostly sanctioned by the popes, attempting to maintain a delicate balance of power. The Church struggled to keep its political and religious authority over the major Western European countries—an authority finally challenged in Italy in the nineteenth century by the developments in the North of Italy, and the war to unify the Italian peninsula. Yet, the more the North changed, the more the South stayed the same.

Religious mysticism and piety were all that the South of Italy represented to the rest of the world; military, political and religious leadership all formed in the North, even after the supposed Italian unification. In the South, to this day, one would be hard-pressed to find a statue or monument to a war hero, scholar or politician.

In the end, it wasn't a unified Italy that changed Southern Italy in the latter part of the nineteenth century.

It was America.

It was the idea of America, the concept of individual freedom, of open job markets, an economy in which everyone could participate, that radically and forever changed the nature and structure of the South. It was nothing that had been done politically or legally in the North of Italy, which still dominated the Italian peninsula, nor was it anything on the continent of Europe that affected the South as much as the New World, and specifically the United States.

In fact, it was the failure of Northern policies toward the South that prompted the great migration to the New World. The changes for both the Old and the New World were sweeping, irrevocable and breathtaking. And yet, to this day, the details of that era are generally unknown or misunderstood by most of us with vowels at the end of our names who claim an Italian heritage.

That is not to say Southerners couldn't communicate because of dialects and regionalism. They could, and powerfully so. But not in the argot or with the same degree of literacy as their cousins in the North. Theirs was an oral tradition, the passing down from one generation to the other, since Grecian times, of the sayings, observations and values that had held them together as families and regions despite the constant dominance of foreign governments and ruling strangers.

The family was the center of this ancient society, and the father was the head of the family, the mother its heart. It was the Southern Italian parents who over the many long centuries kept their identity as a people and culture intact. They didn't pass this down to their children in books or written form, but rather in words and, most important, by actions.

It is a culture that knows itself but says little to the outside world. A culture rich in ancient lore and knowledge, but poor in textual or academic foundation. Having kept its ancient traditions until modern times, it could jump from feudalism to the New World and produce American politicians, motion picture directors, athletes, bankers, actors and leaders within a single generation. The South had been a financially impoverished region, but its people were not lacking in instinct, morality, values and stunning human insights.

How else could you explain Cuomo's words about his father: "all I needed to know about faith and hard work by the simple eloquence of his example."

It was to this place, the South, where I was bound. Specifically, to Matera in the heart of Basilicata. The town where my paternal grandparents were born....

2

The City of the Sassi

MATERA

I sat at the edge of the main square near where the death notices are posted each morning and watched the nationally televised talent spectacular. Youngster after youngster walking down a small flight of stairs as they lifted their arms above their heads and brought their hands together in a theatrical clapping motion to encourage applause from the crowd. Youngster after youngster straining on the high notes in dramatic fashion as they sang ballads of haunted or fated love, slick modern lyrics dealing with hip modern relationships.

The technical part of the program was sloppy; obviously too quickly and poorly put together. Microphones were in constant feedback or, worse, silent when the singers sang. The embarrassed emcee, a tall and thin young blonde with an ample bosom and elaborately coiffed hair, tried to make light of the malfunctioning mikes, smiling broadly and joking in her Northern accent.

The lighting grid didn't light what it should; performers stood in shadow. A giant television screen, designed to show the large shoulder-to-shoulder crowd intense close-ups as the singers strained in musical passion, was poorly canted and cut off half the picture from the huge crowd in the Piazza Veneto. Not the usual performance for the people who invented modern music, or for the television network owned by the prime minister of Italy.

Each contestant in the talent show was a local youngster, recruited from the region to compete in the program. The broadcast was one of a series produced in several regions around the country as part of the summer TV fare.

All of the contestants descended the stairs at the back of the stage to the theme of "Rocky," a tune from the American movie, but not one casually chosen here in Matera. Gioia del Colle, a tiny Puglian village a few kilometers away, is the hometown of the Sylvester Stallone family. The actor's father was born there. Everyone in this crowd knew the relationship between the theme music and their native geography. Everyone in Southern Italy knows who was born where, especially famous American film stars or their families.

The final contestant sang "New York, New York"—"I wanna wake *ap* in a *ceety* that *niver slips*." Many in the crowd sang along. New York became home to thousands of their ancestors; they feel an obvious tie.

The crowd, as many summer crowds in Southern Italy these days, was mostly young. Thin kids with perfect bodies and straight white teeth, perfectly groomed and dressed in the latest styles with bright smiles as they joked with their friends. A far cry from the badly nourished youngsters who would have been in this very square only a century ago. And a century, especially in Matera, is less than an eye blink.

There is a plaque on a wall facing the square dedicating it to the former Italian king and prince of Savoy, Umberto I. The plaque was put up in 1904.

There had probably been a ceremony, with a brass band, a platform, speakers shouting into megaphones. I can imagine my grandfather attending that dedication—he was possibly here in 1904—an eighteen-year-old. I can picture him clearly in my imagination. I see a lean frame much like the photos I've seen of my father at eighteen, much like my own lanky eighteen-year-old frame, standing in this same square in a very different time, long before television. He could very well have been here watching honors being paid to a dynasty that did little or nothing to alleviate the lack of opportunity that led him to America.

Umberto I was probably memorialized by the local government in an attempt to curry favor from Rome. The plaque refers to him as an heroic model, a valiant warrior. He had been assassinated by an anarchist in 1900 in the Northern city of Monza. But Umberto had never been here. The Savoys didn't really know the South. Umberto's father, Vittorio Emanuele II, Italy's first king since before the founding of ancient Rome, didn't even speak Italian.

And even if the Savoys had visited, they didn't know how to fix the problems here. They never understood or cared to understand the region, its economy, history, geography, or its people. They didn't trust the Southerners. Instead, they represented a government that allowed the South's lifeblood and energy to slip away to the Americas without so much as a whimper. The Savoys and all in power at that time told my grandfather, and thousands like him, that his problems weren't any of their business. They let America fix the problems with the Southern economy. It was too much for a united Italy, which was really the unification of the North of Italy—never the South.

And we—those of us who still maintain a fading and hyphenated identity with these towns and villages—we are the legacy of all that escaped youth and energy, now coming back and sitting in the square by the death notices where few seem to notice the passing of the thirty-four-year-old sanitary worker Cinzia Camerlengo or the eighty-seven-year-old tailor Francesco Paolo Morano. It is now microphones and lights that interest this new generation in a completely new country.

Time is still passing on the cold white stones of Piazza Veneto.

The Italy under the Southern sun is on the move...

My paternal grandparents were born in Matera, now the capital of the province of Matera in the region of Basilicata. Until recently, this region had the distinction of being the very poorest and most unknown of all the Mezzogiorno, and thus, all of Italy.

When my grandfather emigrated to America, there was no province of Matera; the only province in the region was Potenza. My father's family always claimed Potenza as our place of origin, since it was the only place listed on the few formal documents we could find. My grandfather had died a young man in a steel-mill accident in Clairton, Pennsylvania, and there had been no firsthand accounting of his travels. No one knew very much about Matera, it wasn't a town or a name that brought any sense of recognition on the part of either Americans or other Italians.

Thanks to modern technology and the Ellis Island Web site, I had found my paternal grandfather's entry records into the United States. His first recorded entry in 1909 did list Matera as his place of origin. By 1911, when he returned for a third or fourth and final time, he was then recorded as "Southern Italian." The listing was no longer simply "Italian." The distinction had been demanded by the Northern Italians and was backed by Rome, to separate Northerners from those they saw as inferior. And the records no longer listed his actual birthplace, only his province, which is what led to some family confusion. The name Matera had remained obscure for most of our life, until my research in the early 1990s found a definite link, a decade before the Ellis Island technology became available.

While in the North, preparing to go South, I told a friend, an American woman who had lived in Rome several years, I was on my way to Matera.

She wrinkled her nose. "Why would anybody want to go *there*?" she asked. She meant it as an honest question, in the same way most of the Northern Italians I know would have asked.

I went into my usual litany....

Matera is, most probably, the oldest city in all Europe.

Matera was an old city when Athens was founded, an ancient city when the Greeks first began to colonize nearby Tarus—now Taranto—and Metaponto, where they minted the coins for Magna Graecia and where the Greek philosopher and mathematician Pythagoras ran his academy.

Matera was ancient at the time Kind David was organizing Jerusalem and building his temple there.

It was an ancient place of civilization when whoever built Stonehenge was dragging its massive monoliths into place.

Man has lived continuously and in a structured manner in Matera proper for at least seven thousand, but more probably ten thousand years, and in the region since at least the early Paleolithic era, or the Stone Age, which began about 10,000 B.C.E.

Matera played a major role for the Roman Catholic Church in Southern Italy, with dozens of monasteries and convents throughout the area and an entire cult of monks who lived in the caves in Matera's surrounding cliffs.

In fact, there's substantial evidence that Matera had been a religious center since the dawn of organized religion.

UNESCO has declared Matera a City for Humanity and a place to be preserved so that future generations can better understand the past. It refers to the city as an international "cultural treasure," and shares this recognition, in Italy, with only four other and far more famous cities: Rome, Venice, Florence and San Gimignano in Tuscany.

And yet, Matera is probably one of the least-known places in all of Europe today, not well known in Italy itself, and was all but completely unknown to most Americans, like my own family, who are, in fact, the diaspora of this ancient and amazing spot on the map. It is the Rodney Dangerfield of cities—it doesn't get any respect.

MOVING IN

I had decided early on in my planning that I would live in Matera and use it as my home base during my travels about the Southern regions.

I hadn't anticipated the difficulty this decision would cause; finding a short-term lease for a furnished apartment was not easy. It is just not the way things are done in the South; this is not Rome, with strangers coming and going every day. It took all of my attention and several people helping me in the effort to realize my wishes.

In the end, however, I found the perfect place—an old apartment building directly across from the open and very old market square. The building sat just a block off the Piazza Veneto on Via A. Persio and, most important to me, the same building had been there when my grandmother and grandfather lived in Matera as children. They had to have passed by this building to get to the cathedral where they'd both been baptized. If they had entered the city from the southeast—the direction where they both had moved to a small village, Miglionico, before marrying and emigrating to New York—they had to have walked down the Via A. Persio. I could picture them, small children my daughter's age, passing by as I stood at the balcony. Except for the modern cars and lack of working animals, I saw the same buildings they would have seen, the same passageways and street. I wanted to have that sense of connection with them, that geographical tie in my life, even if only for a few months.

At the time they lived in Matera, nearly eighty percent of the men in the area, and in all of Southern Italy as well, would leave to find work in other places. Many, like my grandfather, would cross an ocean and work in New York City, live in hovels, and save every possible penny, then commute back to Italy several times over the incredible distance.

My grandfather, like so many of his generation, came back and married a girl from his village. After the wedding, he stayed in Miglionico for a while, then left my grandmother pregnant with their first child and returned to Greenwich Village. A year or so later he returned to Italy, saw his son, my Uncle Bill, left my grandmother pregnant again, and departed once more to the States for work. Another year later he, like many of his *paesani*, had saved enough for the entire family to resettle in their new country. In my family's case, they moved from a small ancient village along the Roman Via Appia to Manhattan, and a spacious apartment near Washington Square. My grandfather's story was typical of the stories of so many young men of his generation. And that generation would have been passing below my Matera apartment in the latter part of the nineteenth century. The old building with its balcony overlooking the old market helped me feel close to them.

The apartment was sparsely furnished. I had to fight and wait for a telephone to be installed, but the place was very large, had a modern bathroom and shower stall, and provided a wonderful cross-breeze in the hot summer evenings. I loved shopping in a market where my grandparents and great-grandparents had undoubtedly shopped, loved hearing the noise in the streets below as the youngsters passed by at night on their late-hour return from the piazza. I would awaken early in the mornings to the pre-dawn shouts of the men setting up the market across the street. I enjoyed the wake-up calls, they gave me an insight into the way life has been conducted in this town for a very long time.

I even learned to enjoy the two sets of church bells, which went off every fifteen minutes, every hour, every day. The first bell chimed the hour, the second rang one, two, or three times to indicate the quarters of the hour. Two sets of these bells rang about forty-five seconds apart from each other. I found it oddly silent when I stayed away from Matera and didn't hear regular chiming. In fact, the bells are such a prominent part of the Southern way of life, there's a word, *campanilismo*, which describes the Southern Italian people as belonging to communities within the range of their village church bells. Outside the range of their own bells is foreign territory to many in the Southern psychology. I was amused later to read of an Italian immigrant to New Jersey who found the absence of hourly bells the oddest thing about America. The bells represented much more to these villagers in long-ago days than the mere passage of time; they rang out a sense of community, centrality, prayer and of knowing where and who you were.

It had been two years since I'd been in Matera and over seven since I'd spent any real time there. The progress was apparent; the UNESCO proclamation was a source of great pride and new tourist agencies were sprouting up around the town. What was once a ragtag lot of young men and boys offering visitors tours of the Sassi was becoming professionalized, though the use of foreign languages seemed to be coming ever so slowly. It was still not easy to find guides fluent in English.

Wrinkled noses are common in Matera. The second a stranger speaks a single word, the natives recognize a foreigner. It's not that they're inhospitable, but that centuries of wariness have been bred into them.

Not long after arriving, I walked into a camera store to have some photos developed. Upon entering, I said hello and two Italian words, "*per sviluppare*," or, "to be developed."

"*Il suo nome?*" asked the young woman behind the counter—your name?

I told her.

She raised an eyebrow and said in the Matera dialect, "You have a name very much from here but an accent absolutely from somewhere far away." She said this on the basis of two words. And she did not have unique or especially sensitive hearing; her reaction, I was to learn, was common.

My name, however, *was* another matter. It was a name from the town, and, more important, a respected name. There was a count, a doctor, of the same name from the eighteenth century buried in a side chapel in the Church of San Francesco, one of the two largest churches in the town. He had been a noble and had apparently won the hearts of the people. He is one of only three people buried in the church, a high honor at any time in history. It helped, I found, to have a name that was recognized, even if my accent was strange.

Early one morning, just after arriving in Matera, there was a loud knock at my apartment door. I had been sleeping. I tossed on some clothes and found two men wearing T-shirts and bright orange pants demanding access to my apartment. They were TIM employees, telephone men. I had trouble understanding them and they didn't seem too happy to be meeting a foreigner. I found the exchange especially difficult without coffee or a bath. They'd come to make sure the line was working and demanded rather gruffly that I show my documentation before they could proceed. I grumbled in English and shuffled about the apartment, only half-awake, looking for my things. I handed the tallest fellow my passport.

Instant attitude change.

"Your name is a name from this place, this town," the man said in amazement. He showed my passport to his partner, who seemed equally impressed.

"My grandfather was born here," I said.

"You are from here. You are *materano*." He was almost gasping. "My sister has married into this family." His wonder was sincere. Within minutes my phone was working and both men were giving me their personal home- and cell-phone numbers.

"If you need anything at all while you're here," the tall one said, "you call me. We are in-laws."

NICOLA NICOLETTI

One evening I strolled through Via Ridola, past the seventeenth-century Chiesa del Carmine, an ancient seminary complex now being reconstructed by an engineer with the same family name as mine. It abuts the little lookout of Piazzetta Pascoli. The small deck of the piazza offers a wonderful view of the Sasso Caveoso, one of the two main hillsides completely beehived with now deserted houses originally dug into the cliffs as caves. It was in the Sassi that most of the common people of Matera lived from thousands of years ago until just after the Second World War, when the homes were condemned by the Italian government and the people moved to government-built housing.

On that evening, like most evenings, there were groups of local men standing about in animated conversation, looking out over the Sassi and occasionally pointing or arguing. One of them turned to me and asked if I was Italian. I told him I was American, but that my family had originally come from Matera. He seemed surprised and introduced himself.

"I am Nicola Nicoletti."

I told him my name. His eyes widened. "That is truly a name from this town," he said. "There are Nicolettis and Paolicellis on the war monument in Piazza Veneto." We began a long discussion. The man seemed delighted that I was a returned son of Matera.

"You see that house, over there on the hillside?" He was pointing to the hill opposite our lookout point.

I nodded.

"I was born in that house and grew up right there in the Sassi."

"Was it as bad as Carlo Levi says it was?"

"We were very poor then. Most people kept their animals in the houses with them. Things were very bad here. Like you see in the old photographs."

I had often wondered how a city could have lasted nearly ten thousand years, yet could have been in the terrible shape the old photos seemed to show, or what Levi described in *Christ Stopped at Eboli.*

"Why were the animals in the house? Surely your parents knew about disease?" I was referring to the pictures I'd seen in the museum showing the worst of the times in the Sassi at the end of the war. People in rags sat in front of hovels, their animals in close proximity; children were filthy, barefoot and in tatters.

"It was the times," he said vaguely, and told me that he was sixty-three years old and had been a young boy during the Second World War, that there had been little food and no luxuries, but it still didn't explain the horrible sanitation I'd read had existed here.

Nicola invited me to stop by the Duni Music Conservatory, the town's most famous school, the next day. He wanted to take me to a special balcony where I could get an exceptional view to take pictures of the back of the Sassi where the original dwellings had been built. He was an energetic and friendly man and seemed impressed with my interest in the city.

I arrived at the conservatory around midday the following day. Nicola said he'd been expecting me and thought I'd forgotten our appointment. He is a guard and concierge at the school. He introduced me to a female co-worker.

"He is *materano*," he said to the woman and told her my name.

Nicola seemed truly happy to see me and took me up to the promised balcony for my shots. I was especially conscious of my lack of language skills that morning, for some reason stumbling over every word I tried to pronounce and embarrassing myself by having to take so much time thinking about how to phrase what I wanted to say. I hadn't tried to speak Italian at any depth for nearly seven years and I hadn't studied it until just ten years before. I was tiring of the verbal battle and apologized to Nicola. He seemed to understand, yet continued to speak very rapidly about the conservatory and the local composer Egidio Duni, who had been fairly well known throughout Europe during the eighteenth century.

I then made the mistake of turning my camera toward the castle turrets looming over the southwest side of the city.

"Ah," he said excitedly, "*il nostro castello*"—our castle. "Come, let me show you the best place to take pictures." Without waiting for a response, he was off.

Along the way he explained that the three-turreted castle had never been completed. It had been started by Count Tramontano in the later Norman period, but the count had been assassinated in a plot by local nobles. He was murdered in a small street near the conservatory, the Via del Riscatto, or the Street of Vengeance or Repayment. The people didn't want to pay the extra taxes for the castle in any event. But the citizens did have to pay a sum of money to the King of Naples for the count's murder.

Before I knew what was happening, I was jogging to keep pace with an alleged sixty-three-year-old who sped the mile or so, all uphill and in the searing heat of a Southern Italian summer, to the spot he deemed best to take photographs. I was completely saturated with sweat and gasping for breath. My older friend hadn't broken a bead of perspiration.

I had never been this close to the castle before. It was surrounded by a chain-link fence, but it was clear the fence could be crossed by the amount of graffiti on one of the turrets.

"Who does this?" I asked Nicola, pointing at the inscriptions, which looked exactly like the ones on New York subway cars. "It seems like there's an international school for graffiti artists."

Nicola shook his head disgustedly. "*Maleducati,*" he spat. The badly raised.

We walked about the entire circumference of the castle.

"What you are doing," Nicola said, "is very important. I will do anything I can to guide you."

He went on to say he wanted to help write the story, or was it history?—in Italian I'm never sure, since the word is the same—of "*our* city." He made me promise to call him and that he would then take me to the original Sassi south of the city to take photographs there. I agreed to another meeting but secretly vowed to allow enough time to recuperate fully.

THE LEVI LEGACY

The history of Matera would be an enormous work. There are references sprinkled throughout ancient literature. The most famous description comes from the early fifteen hundreds. A Dominican friar named Leandro Alberti traveled through Basilicata and stopped at Matera. His journal is one of the most poignant records of that age. He came upon Matera at sunset and described hundreds of small lights that had been lit each evening, for centuries, on the town crier's signal....

> *Walking twelve miles along the Apennines, one comes upon a lovely valley containing the city of Matera. Parts of it lie in two deep valleys, and the third part on a height which dominates the above-mentioned lower valleys. This allows the inhabitants to simulate (at will) a beautiful, clear sky adorned with bright, shining stars. Thus it appears to those in the third part of the city atop the hill to see spread out at their feet a starry sky in which various figures are distinguishable, as astrologers might see them, such as Triton, the Hyades, the Pleiades, Ariadne's Crown and other like figures.*

The lights are now electric and illuminate the mostly empty Sassi each night, still with evocative effect. They are designed to reproduce the shades of so many ancient torches reflecting off the gray-white stone. What is missing now are people, though there is currently a major resettlement effort underway in a refurbished section of Sassi with modern utilities and sanitation. Still, the soft electric glow lends an ageless cast to the stones; it's not hard to imagine the town described by Friar Alberti.

The twentieth-century story of this place has seldom been told, either in or outside of Italy, and is diametrically opposed to Alberti's poetic descriptions.

Throughout the city, in *trattorie* and cafés, in the library and museums, there are constant reminders of Carlo Levi, a medical doctor, artist, and writer from Northern Italy whose Jewish faith and political beliefs led to his imprisonment by the Fascist government. Posters with Levi's artwork are prominently displayed throughout Matera; at least two restaurants have photographs of Levi greeting guests or the proprietor. He is an inescapable, omnipresent figure. His book *Christ Stopped at Eboli* was first published in Italy and the United States just after the Second World War and received a large readership. It details his house arrest by the Fascists and his exile to the heart of Basilicata.

It should say enough about how Mussolini and his government related to il Mezzogiorno by the very fact that they sent their political enemies into exile in the Southern provinces. Basilicata was the most remote of the remote. Mountainous, poor, few roads badly maintained, forgotten by time. Even the Mafia and its mainland branches ignored this place. There was just nothing of value worth exploiting.

In his book, Carlo Levi devotes a mere six pages to Matera. Yet those six pages are one of the few modern documents written about the city during the twentieth century in international contemporary literature. And those scant paragraphs describe a place of unrelenting poverty and filth.

This is the legacy that Levi gave to Matera. It is written mostly in the words and through the eyes of Levi's sister, also a medical doctor, visiting Levi during his imprisonment and describing what she had seen at Matera on her way to nearby Gagliano.

In these dark holes with walls cut out of earth I saw a few pieces of miserable furniture, beds, and some ragged clothes hanging up to dry. On the floor lay dogs, sheep, goats and pigs. Most families have just one cave to live in and there they sleep all together; men, women, children, and animals. This is how twenty thousand people live ... I have never in all my life seen such a picture of poverty ... I never even dreamed of seeing a sight like this ...

Hardly the city of lovely lights described in medieval times. Dr. Levi called the Sassi "A schoolboy's idea of Dante's *Inferno*." It was this image of Matera from Levi's book that most modern Italians recall when thinking of the town. For many *materani*, it was Levi's writings that helped the new government after the war to address at last some of the terrible conditions in the South. The current citizens are proud of the accomplishment.

But other voices are now being raised. Paolo Laurita, a journalist, editor and publisher in Potenza, has published a book, *Oltre Eboli*, or "Beyond Eboli," by Antonio Motta. Laurita says that one of the problems with Levi's book is that Levi was a Northerner. He saw the South through Northern eyes and repeated many of the stereotypes he'd expected to find.

The prose picture of Matera made by Levi, while ultimately beneficial to the city by drawing attention to its plight, was a verbal snapshot taken during the worst poverty of modern times and possibly in the city's long, long history. Italy had been in the throes of an economic depression accompanied by a population explosion prior to the Second World War, but the South had been far worse off than the North.

The country was in the depths of depression when Levi's physician sister stopped by to get her papers issued. Because of a series of nearly unbelievably repressive laws promulgated by the national government, subsistence farming had declined. A ridiculous tax structure demand-

ing a head payment for each farm animal adversely affected the Southerners far more than their Northern counterparts. In addition, birth-
rates had skyrocketed at exactly the time when the social services and
basic necessities of life were least available. The overcrowding led to
people's sharing spaces with work animals in what had been the animals' stables. Others attempted to hide their animals in their homes to
avoid the tax.

It was a vicious and downward-spiraling cycle, mostly the result of
bad government in Rome, that Levi had found and recorded:

> The young men of promise, even those barely able to make their way, leave
> the village. The most adventurous go off to America, as the peasants do, and
> the others to Naples or Rome; none return. Those who are left in the villages
> are the discarded, who have no talents, the physically deformed, the inept
> and the lazy; greed and boredom combine to dispose them to evil. Small
> parcels of farm land do not assure them a living and, in order to survive,
> these misfits must dominate the peasants and secure for themselves the well-
> paid posts of druggist, priest, marshal of the carabinieri, and so on. It is,
> therefore, a matter of life and death to have the rule in their own hands, to
> hoist themselves or their relatives and friends into top jobs. This is the root
> of the endless struggle to obtain power and to keep it from others, a struggle
> which the narrowness of their surroundings, enforced idleness and a mixture
> of personal and political motives render continuous and savage....

This is how Levi described Basilicata for Italy and the world. And it
is that portrait to which, not surprisingly, some modern journalists and
writers, like Laurita, now object. After all, if only the lazy, deformed or
those lacking in talent remained in Basilicata, the people now living in
the region are their sons and daughters. Could the present-day Basilicatans truly be comprised solely of progeny of the unskilled and inept?
This is exactly the sort of negative stereotype of the South that has per-

sisted in the Northern mentality since before the time of unification: the South as incapable, inept, incompetent, a watered-down gene pool; the descendants of the lazy or deficient.

COSIMO DI PEDE

A few years ago, I passed through Matera with a writer friend, John Keahey, on a photographic mission for John's book, *A Sweet and Glorious Land*. We spent one night in town during an exceptionally cold period. Before leaving the next morning, I stopped by a local hardware store to buy an electrical adapter. A fellow talking with the proprietor overheard my accent and asked if I was an American. He was excited to learn that I was a "son of Matera" and said I must come with him and meet his father, who had lived in America for several years.

Michele Di Pede, a diminutive man of about sixty with a thinning hairline and a slight paunch, introduced himself as the owner of an electrical appliance store just a block away. By chance he had been visiting his friend's shop in search of some electrical gadget or other. During the short walk to his own store he managed to tell me half his life story—he had had a heart attack and bypass surgery not too long before, that he spoke no English and had spent his entire life in Matera. His father, however, who was in his nineties, loved to speak the language and enjoyed meeting visiting *americani*.

John and I greeted the old man and greatly enjoyed our chat. Signore Di Pede's English was enchanting and sounded frozen in the 1920s—the period in which he had learned it. Michele, meanwhile, collected our business cards and showed us a drawerfull of other cards from Americans who had stopped by, mostly to have something interpreted by his father, the unofficial English translator for the town.

More than two years later I walked into the store and reintroduced myself. Michele remembered me and even my last name. He immediately went through his little cluttered drawer and produced my business card, all the while chattering away about his health, his father's health, the intense heat and Italian politics in general.

Cosimo Di Pede, Michele's father, would be one hundred years old in a few months. *A centenarian.* And Michele said he still came to the shop each morning, fully dressed in a suit and tie, no matter the temperature, and took up his seat of honor at the back of the shop, facing the street from the deep shade.

The next morning I stopped by to say hello. The old man was remarkably healthy. He was quite trim and had a reddish glow on his cheeks, his pale eyes the only sign of his advanced age. Signore Di Pede's English still held a tinge of a New Jersey accent.

Michele sat at his father's side behind the shop's only desk and smiled approvingly as I talked with the old man. Michele seemed to have aged more than his father during the past two years, his hair a little thinner, his face a little more drawn. His lively eyes, however, continued their active dance.

I asked the elder Signore Di Pede to elaborate on his experiences in the States.

He told me he had gone to America in 1918 with every intention of staying. He went through Ellis Island, lived in New York for a very short time and within a few weeks was in New Jersey working as a weaver.

"Where did you learn your English?" I asked. "Did you study it here in school?"

"No, no," he replied. "I didn't know a word of English when I left here. When I got to New Jersey, an Italian fellow ran the factory where I worked. I spoke with no one but him. Each day a big, burly German supervisor would stop by my position and smile at me. I thought he was making fun of me. After a while I got tired of his looking down on me, so the next time he stopped by with his big grin, I hit him with a spindle."

Signore Di Pede laughed at the memory.

"Well, the boss, he came over a few minutes later and wanted to know what had happened. He couldn't believe that I would be fighting with another worker. 'He's making fun of me,' I said, and pointed to the German. 'I don't like to be made fun of.' My boss told the German in English what I had said. The German was surprised and told the boss that he wasn't making fun of me at all, that he was so pleased by how fast I could work, it made him smile. He said I was the fastest learner he had ever seen and it gave him great pleasure to watch me work.

"Later that day, the German came back and told me, through my boss, he was my friend. He took me to lunch and said he was going to teach me English, that I could never be an American until I could speak the language.

" 'Here's what we're going to do,' he said. 'I'm going to tell you how to say everything in English and you're going to teach me the Italian word for the same thing.' And we got to work. We started with 'Salt—*sale*, fork—*forchetta*, floor—*pavimento*, smile—*sorriso*, and went on from there."

Those lessons with the burly German so many years ago had made Cosimo fluent in English, who, it turned out, never had a single day of formal schooling. He was one of the sons of Basilicata Levi had written about, one of those who escaped to America, but one who ultimately returned.

I asked Cosimo about his childhood, about the Sassi, if things were as bad as Levi had written. But the old man was clearly more interested in telling me the story of his English lessons and of his family. It seemed that once his mind focused on a story, it was difficult to change the subject.

Cosimo continued his story. He, like my grandfather and so many others before them, returned to Matera with the intentions of marrying and returning to the States.

But it was bad timing; Cosimo never got back to New Jersey.

"I came back in 1927. Mussolini clamped down on Italian emigration and I couldn't leave," he said. "Il Duce finally realized that too many young men were leaving, especially here in the South. So once I came back, I couldn't leave again."

"It was common for the men to come back to marry," I said. "I know my grandfather did; he married a girl from his village here, in Miglionico, and came back at least once again before bringing my grandmother and two children over to the States."

"Yes, of course," said Signore Di Pede. "You needed to marry someone you could *trust*."

There it was again, the circle of trust, ever so tight in Southern circles. Italian society, especially in the South, began at the level of family. Most of the marriages in my grandparents' day were arranged—families negotiating with other families within the ring of expanding circles, never getting too far away from the center. It had been going on here for centuries. It was an issue of trust, of survival.

"And you never wanted to go back to America, not even after the war?" I asked.

"Well, you know, by that time there were children. And I'd been in the Italian army and through the war."

"How did you survive?" I asked.

"Oh, I was quite well off, actually," he said. "I was an officer in the Italian army and they kept me here in Basilicata throughout the war. After the Americans got here, I worked for both armies. I was an English translator by day for the Italians, and an Italian translator in the evening up in Altamura for the Americans." The old man's voice was weakening. He was visibly tiring.

"You know," he continued, softer now, "after the war I made my life here. I started this business and raised my children. It was all right, you know."

He handed me his business card.

> Comm.
> **Cosimo Damiano Di Pede**
> Maestro Del Commercio

The "Master of Business" was clearly well respected, if not revered. Each day I spent in Matera, I'd stop by the appliance store. If I went by in the mornings, Cosimo was always there, and always surrounded by a small group of middle-aged men sitting near him in the shade in the back of the shop. They chatted about nothing in particular while keeping him company. Cosimo enjoyed their companionship, and Michele was plainly delighted by the attention shown his father. He'd pepper his father's stories with anecdotes and clarifications and, when his father would sit silently for long periods, Michele chattered on with all the town's latest gossip.

When his father wasn't there, Michele talked often about his brother Franco, an internationally renowned artist whose sculptures and paintings on the Sassi have been exhibited throughout Europe and Japan. He would also brag about his several very clever nieces and nephews, all of whom had attended major universities in the North and were professionals. I suspected Michele placed little stock in Levi's notion that only those without talent had remained in Basilicata.

Michele began greeting me as "*caro Paolo.*" He chattered away each time I'd visit, telling me stories about the townspeople or upcoming events, all in the rapid dialect of his hometown. Occasionally he'd ask me if I understood, but more often he'd plow ahead, answering questions I'd only partly formed in my school-taught Italian. He didn't seem to mind my lack of quickness in his language. We became close friends. Perhaps because his father had been to America, Michele didn't feel the reticence I'd sensed toward me from others in Matera. "After all," he said, "we're from the same people."

And even though my grandfather had been one of Levi's "young men of promise" who had left this place for good, I knew that, had circumstances been just slightly different, this town could have been my birthplace as well. I was happy my grandfather had gotten out, yet felt strangely defensive about how the people who had remained behind had been treated in both literature and politics since his departure.

3

Amantea, Calabria

ROCCO'S PENSIONE

Crossing the mountains that cut through the western corner of Basilicata and into Calabria shows instantly why the Southern people were so isolated from the rest of the country in language, tradition and mores. People who live here are widely separated by sheer cliffs and deep ravines. In the summer, oceans of green swaying trees cover the steep hills; in the winter, cold, cruel winds rush through the valleys and canyons.

These Calabrians, part of the original "Italian" tribes, had to overcome daily not only the forces of nature, but the challenges imposed by geography as well. Despite the vast tracts of empty land, only a small percentage of it, less than thirty percent, is arable. People who lived here in antiquity had to learn land management techniques that required sophisticated and difficult farming. They wrenched their living from the hillsides, tended herds in the random and rare pastureland, cultivated every inch of usable soil. Their lives were constantly at nature's mercy, a danger compounded by foreign armies that periodically crossed through these passes, usually on their way to other locations to fight for other prizes, while putting the population at risk in the flow of invaders that date back to before the rise of Rome.

I was driving through, an army of one, to invade Amantea, a village just south of Paola on the western coast of Italy's "toe." I crossed the dizzying and heavily wooded mountains on a parallel road to the one George Gissing had taken by coach during his "ramble" in this area slightly more than a century before. The road now includes modern tunnels that barrel through the hillsides and ends with a precipitous descent down to the shore.

The view coming down the hillside overlooking the Tyrrhenian coast is like a living Byron poem. The vast and beautiful sea flows gently onto the horizon. The sun, no matter what time of day, paints vivid colors on the water and surrounding shore. Vegetation along the coast is lush and appears tropical. The descent down that mountain leads to a magical place, once fishing villages and lookout points, now mostly inexpensive vacation destinations for Italians and a few other Europeans.

I'd been guided there by Sam Patti, an Italian scholar from Pittsburgh. Sam's late father was from the Calabrian region. Sam was spending the summer in the area with his family, including his octogenarian mother, with whom he planned to return to her family's original home in northern Sicily. I was hoping to tag along if Sam made the trip. Sam recommended that I stay at a local inn, Pensione Margherita. It was to prove the most interesting and certainly one of the most colorful of all my many stops during my adventures in the South.

I arrived in Amantea late on a Sunday afternoon in the middle of vacation season. Rocco Musi, the proprietor of the *pensione*, greeted me warmly. Rocco was born in Amantea, but he had lived in South America, Canada and Pittsburgh before returning for good to his native town. The moment I shook his hand I knew I had found a friend.

Rocco is a short, thin, well-dressed man—I never saw him without a clean and neatly pressed shirt and long pants, despite the awful heat of the Calabrian summer, and he moves about with the Napoleonic confidence that only short men can pull off. Rocco's gray, slightly thinning hair was always neatly combed straight back past his broad, tanned forehead. His bright smile was always at the ready. But most of all his eyes dominated his features, large, brown, observant and friendly eyes.

Incredibly, Rocco had a room available at the height of vacation season and on short notice. He literally trotted up the two enormous flights of stairs leading to my room, carrying half of my baggage, and never breaking a bead of sweat. I struggled noisily and fitfully behind, bathed in perspiration and short of breath.

"No elevator," I panted.

"No, this is an old-fashioned place." He laughed. "This isn't Amalfi, this is just Amantea."

The room was small and clean, with a balcony overlooking the Via Margherita, which led to the beach a few hundred yards to the west. There was also a television set, the only one in the entire place, as I was to learn later. Rocco assumed that since I was American, I had to have a TV.

"I'm sorry I can't give you an air-conditioned room, but they have been booked for a long time now," he said, as we dropped my load of books and baggage.

"You have air-conditioning?" I panted. I was amazed. This had been completely unheard of in the South just a decade before. A tourist asking for it would have demonstrated a complete lack of knowledge of the area.

"Yes, I had to have them installed just to compete with all of the other places here now. But I couldn't do all of the rooms, only on the top floor. People today want everything in their rooms, like the American motels. This is a small *pensione*, but many people still expect what used to be luxuries. It's costing me a lot of money I'll never make back."

The world was certainly getting smaller.

"I never expected air-conditioning; I brought my own." I pointed to the fan I'd been carrying with me.

"I see you're old-fashioned, too." He laughed. "Do you want to eat here tonight?"

"You have a kitchen?" Most European pensions offered breakfast with the room, but in the South it was sometimes possible to take all meals at an additional cost.

"My mother and wife do all the cooking."

I didn't need to hear anything more. "Absolutely," I said. This was an old-fashioned amenity I would truly enjoy. It was one of the best decisions I'd ever made.

"Good," he said, "we eat once it is dark. Eight, maybe eight-thirty. I'll see you then." He tossed me the huge key as he left the room. I could hear him greeting other guests as he went back down the marble stairs.

I unpacked, showered, and cooled down with the small portable fan that had been my first purchase on this trip, remembering well my lessons from Rome a decade before, before there was any notion of air-conditioning in the South.

I called home on the cell phone a friend had provided for me. Another luxury not available just a few years before. I could punch in a few numbers and talk directly with the United States for less money and complications than what once involved going to a post office, arranging for the call, paying in advance for a certain amount of minutes and hoping the connection could be made. Now, all of the world was available for a few lire and a gadget I could carry in my pocket.

I stood on my little balcony and studied my new environment. A constant noisy flow of people went by below, mostly on foot and mostly in family groups consisting of grandparents, parents and children. The vacationers strolled by in beachwear, shorts and flip-flops, sunglasses. All of them, including the children, sported the deep tans the Italians seem to favor so much. I wondered if there were any Italian dermatologists issuing the same warnings about overexposure to the sun as the American doctors had.

On the near mountaintop, a few hundred yards inland and straight up, the ruins of a castle loomed dramatically above the town. Its partial walls faded from gold to gray in the deepening evening shadows. The remnants stood on the high ground, where the town had been for centuries; down by the sea would, after the Greco-Roman era, have been far too dangerous and open to invasion, especially during the Saracen raids that took place all along this same coast for a couple of centuries. The people lived close to the castle and the town was probably walled in during most of its more than twenty centuries of existence. The beach community where I was staying hadn't been built until the late 1950s.

I watched the warm, long evening overtake the Via Margherita. Headlights now flashed from the cars along SS 18, the main north-south route down to Reggio di Calabria or up to Paola. The pedestrian crowds began to thin. It was dinnertime; the hallowed hour in Italy had finally arrived.

As I entered the large dining room on the ground floor of the building, I was surprised to feel cool air. This room was also air-conditioned, something I'd never expected. Rocco pointed me to my private table, a sort of wooden picnic bench with a bright red-and-white-checkered tablecloth. Several other tables were also filled with guests, mostly families and, from what I could tell, all Italians except for me.

"I'm going to bring you something from here," he said as I sat down. "Something Calabrian." It wasn't a question but a statement. I didn't object.

A few moments later, Rocco served me a plate of *antipasti* of *salumi di Calabria*, or what Americans would call a pepperonilike sausage (*peperoni* in Italy are peppers), very spicy; along with some local goat cheese and bread less airy than the Roman variety of *casareccio*, or homemade. He followed this with a basic spaghetti *al pomodoro* and offered a roasted chicken, which I declined, then a plate of fresh sliced tomatoes with olive oil and a little oregano sprinkled on top. They were the freshest and tastiest tomatoes I had eaten in some time. I was back to eating macaroni—I knew there would be no "pasta" at Rocco's. It was a meal I might have had any Sunday as a child in Pittsburgh.

And it was wonderful.

"This is the sort of food I like best," I said.

Rocco smiled. "Now that I know that, it will be easy to feed you. My wife and mother make everything here, this isn't a fancy restaurant, but if you like simple food, you'll like our food."

"Like eating at my mother's table," I said.

"Your family," he asked, "they are Calabrian?"

"No," I said, "Abruzzese and Basilicatan."

"Ah," he replied, *Lucani.*" He used the word for the ancient tribes in Basilicata. The same name the Romans used to describe them. The name that was used *before* the Roman era.

"Then we are neighbors," he said, smiling.

Rocco moved quickly about the dining room, gathering plates, serving second and third courses, bringing bread and wine to the other guests. He was a blur, an innkeeper with obvious pride in his work. His mother and wife stayed hidden in the kitchen. Only Rocco served the guests.

"Your castle," I said on one of his stops by my table, "what can you tell me about that castle?"

"You should go up there," he said. "You can walk there from the old town. Go see. My brother, Roberto, he can tell you some stories about the castle. You will have no trouble hearing stories in this town. All you need are ears."

I wanted to hear Rocco's story as well, but decided to wait until he could slow down and relax. This conversation on the run was slightly dizzying.

The evening was still hot, but without the sun's intensity. I decided it was time for a walk along the boardwalk. I ambled to the end of the

Via Margherita and strolled beside the bench-high seawall separating the street and adjoining sidewalk from the broad beach. I found a spot to sit atop the wall and watched the parade. The entire walk was filled with vacationers of all age groups, of course, and the most amazing, all-surrounding din.

It was like suddenly finding myself in the middle of a huge flock of birds; the constant chattering from every angle was incredible. The Italian verb *chiacchierare* is aptly onomatopoeic. There were human voices coming from every direction and they overrode the other constant sounds from the *motorini*—cars, passing trains and the general and incessant beeping and buzzing of motorized things in Italian gathering places.

It was a remarkable experience to hear that many human beings passionately exchange that many ideas, apparently at the same time, while moving about the boardwalk, sitting in the little cafés throughout the town, riding on scooters, or sitting on balconies and shouting an exchange with friends on the street below. And, if that wasn't enough of a decibel level, about every half hour or so a small truck drove by with a loudspeaker fixed atop blaring hip-hop music and advertising a souvenir shop with gifts at half price.

I watched the noisy parade pass by from my perch. These were not Europeans at a resort, nor were they Italians so much as they were mostly Calabrians with a mixture of Campanians thrown in and some *americani* there for the summer.

They were different from the Romans; certainly less sophisticated in big-city ways. Their clothing was less fashionable, the colors more intense. The women seemed to have thicker legs, more evident and brighter hair coloring. I saw many more babies than I'd seen in Rome. Three young women passed by riding bicycles, their profiles silhouetted by the lights from a small amusement park. The images were marvelous—they were the very picture of Greek perfection, their faces like the faces of statuary from the Greek colonies here and just down the shore. Their noses, hairlines and lips formed perfect contours against the background of the garish neon light cast off the spinning rides filled with squealing children on the opposite side of the street.

There were no ruins at the beach, only refreshment stands, souvenir shops, pensions and apartments, gas stations, tobacco shops, *gelaterie* and all of the other beach town businesses that represent seasonal prosperity.

I returned to the Pensione Margherita. It was clear that Rocco's place was a gathering point for the beach end of the little town. There were several white plastic chairs and small tables set out in front of the building and each was filled with guests or locals playing cards or talking, adding to the great noise of the place.

As I approached the gathering, Rocco spotted me. He made a series of introductions to his brother Roberto and several of the other men from the town, who all sat or stood in little groups, talking away. Roberto, I quickly learned, had been a high school teacher and was now semi-retired. He was anxious to hear about my interests.

"Your castle," I asked. "Is it Norman?"

"No, the original stones on that mountain are much older than Norman times. We think even older than Greek. Amantea has been here for a very long time and the place where the castle sits has always been some sort of lookout point."

Roberto told me he had taught history and had written a book about some of the local history. He promised to bring me a copy. He gave me a pamphlet he'd helped write for the local Chamber of Commerce outlining the history of the town and selling it as an attractive vacation spot or place to start a business.

During all of the introductions and conversations at Rocco's, not a single sentence was completed uninterrupted. As Rocco and Roberto talked, they would return, in mid-sentence, constant greetings from passersby. A normal conversation went something like this.

"I used to teach at the—

"*Oh, ciao, Domenico, come stai?*—

"local high school here, then a few years ago—

"*Buona sera, Signora Bruno. Va tutto bene?*—

"I decided—

"*Ciao, Enrico, hai mangiato bene?*—

"to take things a little easier."

It was a rhythm, a tempo of speaking I soon became used to, a staccato fragmentation of ideas that somehow made sense. If nothing else, it was very entertaining.

The next morning, before the sun became too hot, I ventured up the mountainside. I drove as far as possible, then abandoned the car and took off on foot. I climbed up a winding series of paths until the walkway ended, then followed a weed-ridden dirt track up to the peak of the hill where the shattered walls of the castle still clung to the bedrock. There was not another soul near the crest of the hill, I'd only seen one person in the old housing at the foot of the castle's hill. There were no signs, no plaques indicating anything about the place. It sat in solitude and bright sunlight, filled with a strange sense of mystery.

From the top of the hill, the outline of the beach resort below was quite clear. It was easy to see how over the years the town had grown and expanded downward until the construction on the lower ground, which was clearly post-World War II. There were no fishermen on the water, only suntanned vacationers splashing and playing in the morning sun. I noted a huge rock just offshore which must have been used by ancient sailors as a key landmark for the town.

I was alone with the castle and the vista and somewhat saddened that this spectacular view had been abandoned for the development below. But it was characteristic of Italians in Italy, a place so old, for its people to want the new. A castle in ruins was nothing unique here. That modern civilization began with people from here and nearby was simply matter-of-fact. Apparently now the important things were deep suntans and air-conditioning.

I could understand that, especially after the poverty that had existed in this region for centuries as one foreign power after another controlled its commerce and wealth. People could get tired of their history if they had been worn down by it.

Yet the castle seemed so evocative. There must have been a time when its thick walls and high vestibule gave these people a sense of strength. There must have been a time when countless others stood where I did on a bright summer morning and looked at the shoreline, and like me, thought of how eternally beautiful this place was. And of how insignificant and fleeting our time here to see it is.

Notes on Rocco's Place

At Rocco's *pensione*, each guest or family sits at a separate table. Singles sit singly, families are grouped together. The family behind me is teaching an infant, a beautiful young girl with a head of curly blond hair, to speak correctly, an interesting Italian lesson for me as well.

The middle-aged woman at the table facing mine dines alone and has an air of solitary sadness about her. A single woman in middle age is very unusual in Italy. Italian women are a very bonded society and seldom venture solo into the marketplace, let alone go on an unaccompanied vacation.

The woman appears somewhat distracted. She speaks politely to the other guests in a general way. The other day she came in after I had already begun demolishing my *spaghetti al' Amatriciana.*

"*Buon appetito,*" she said in passing. The Italians adhere strictly to this formality of wishing one another a good appetite. I assume it's from earlier times when dining was not a regular occurrence, nor was good health an assumption. She seems terribly lonely to me in a culture where anyone alone is rare.

Two young men were here until last night. They are workers in

France but are both from Sala Consilina. They are going to New Jersey in December, to Hoboken, to take a statue of the local saint from their town there and to participate in a procession. It will be their first visit to the United States and they are excited about seeing Hoboken, which Rocco quickly pointed out was Frank Sinatra's hometown, as if they and the entire world didn't already know.

The aroma of tomato sauce cuts through the semi-air-conditioning, reminding me of my mother's and grandmother's kitchens so many years ago. Today for lunch it is *rigatoni al pomodoro*, followed by *polpette* in light tomato sauce with a side of *melanzane ai funghetti*, a marinated eggplant with tomatoes and mushrooms.

An elderly vacationer, la Signora across the way, has complained, again, about the air-conditioning. Her generation hates fans or conditioned air of any type, believing that moving air causes stiff joints and liver trouble. (Italians have a thing about the *fegato*, or liver. All health seems to derive from the well-being of this particular organ. So much so, I assume, that even chilly air can affect it negatively.)

Rocco patiently and politely explained that he was trying to find a happy medium between the guests like la Signora, who disapproved of the chilled air, and the guests like me who are constantly bathed in sweat and find the still air suffocating. He added that he was concerned for her comfort and suggested that maybe a light shawl or sweater would help.

This went by in dialect so fast that I could only concentrate on the nouns, and was amazed by the many new sounds and words I had never heard. The Calabrese pronunciation is very different from that of the Romans, not to mention entirely different words thrown in as well.

But I could understand enough. At one point the older woman's son-in-law tried to inject a comment into the air-conditioning discussion. The older woman cut him off with a curt and very chilly "I'm talking to him, not to you." I had to stifle a laugh.

Rocco later confirmed the obvious. "They don't get along too well." He smiled.

I watched an elderly man at lunch who had arrived just the day before. He peeled and cut a peach, then put the slices into a glass of red wine.

My Uncle Dom was now with me, my quiet, gentle Calabrese uncle who died so many years ago. It was as if he had joined me at my solitary table. I hadn't seen anyone do that with a peach in so long, I'd almost forgotten the custom.

Uncle Dom peeled peaches and soaked them in his wine. It was the first taste of wine we'd ever had as children. Uncle Dom handed us the wine-soaked slices as a special treat, always reassuring my father that it was "good" for us. They had been such a simple little pleasure. I was so grateful for the reminder. I wanted to speak with the man and tell him that my uncle was from near Reggio, just down the road, but I finished my lunch surrounded in silent memories of a man who went to America as a simple gardener and enriched our lives in many ways, not the least of which was wine-flavored fruit.

NORMAN ROCKWELL'S PAINTINGS

I finally caught up with Sam Patti, my American friend spending the summer in Amantea. Sam is a solid, intense man who owns several espresso shops in Pittsburgh. His main shop is in that city's Strip District—a warehouse, dining and shopping area filled with Italian specialty stores in the shadow of the main downtown skyscrapers. Sam's business is cafés, but his passion is Italian-American studies.

"We travel slow," he warned me over the telephone. "My mother is eighty-five years old and this heat is hard on her." We arranged to meet that evening in an air-conditioned *gelateria,* a double treat for all concerned—gelato *and* cooled air.

The elder Mrs. Patti carried a cane, but other than her stiffness in walking caused by hip-replacement surgery, she appeared and sounded much younger than her years. Sam's wife, Debra, daughter Italia and cousin Anita completed the group. We settled into chairs at a Formica-covered table in the upscale shop in the middle of the town's main shopping district.

"This heat is something," the elder Mrs. Patti said to me. She spoke in Pittsburgh-accented English, my native tongue. We ordered from a dazzling array of gelato flavors. I liked the ones with a fruit base, my friends preferred the cream-base flavors ranging from butterscotch/rum (*zuppa inglese*—or "English soup") to vanilla with chocolate chips (*stracciatella* means "shredded chocolate"). Italian gelato contains fewer calories and less butterfat than American ice cream, yet packs a dangerous wallop of flavor. It's an easy addiction to succumb to in Italy, especially in summer, when it seems that every other little sidewalk shop has an alluring gelato display.

The Patti family had rented an apartment on the outskirts of Amantea. Sam had hoped to take his mother back to her Sicilian family's hometown of Gualtieri Sicaminò on the northern coast of the island not far from Messina, but the weather and her discomfort conspired against the trip. I was disappointed we wouldn't be able to get her insights, but Sam confided that she had returned to her family's town only once, several years before, and didn't seem all that concerned about going there again.

"What do you think of Amantea?" the elder Mrs. Patti asked.

"I find it fascinating," I replied.

"It's far too hot in the summer," she replied. "They need to put in more air-conditioning." Mrs. Patti was clearly an American.

Sam, on the other hand, had an entirely different outlook. A former U.S. Army officer, he had been stationed in Germany before being sent to Vietnam. "I was only in Germany a few months," he said, "but I could feel Italy, could feel its pull. I never got there during my military service, but I knew one day I would."

Sam became a high school teacher after completing his military duty.

"This was the mid-seventies," he explained, "and the TV series *Roots* came out. I was fascinated by the story and realized that I didn't know much at all about my own roots, and my family had come to America under much better circumstances than Alex Haley's. I should have known more. I started taking a class here and there on the language and literature, and the next thing you know I wound up with an advanced degree in Italian literature and was teaching at the University of Virginia for a couple of years."

After our gelato the ladies departed for a slow, shuffling shopping trip along the Via Margherita, the main drag running from the beach all the way to the foot of the mountain and the old town. The strip is filled with recently built novelty shops, jewelers, bookstores, cosmetic and clothing stores. Sam and I strolled about in the busy street and ducked into a nearby pizzeria for a drink and more conversation.

"Why did you come here to Amantea?" I asked.

"You know, it's funny," he replied, "my father was born in the States, but his father was from here. My grandfather even brought my father back here to live for a time when he was a boy. I didn't know any of this until I started digging into the family's history. In fact, I didn't realize that my name is my father's *adopted* name until I was in my mid-twenties."

The pizzeria where we sat was a mostly outdoor affair with a large garden enclosed by a high golden-gray stucco wall comprising the main dining area. At the center of the patio was a table filled with children, little girls in party dresses celebrating a birthday party—*una festa di compleanno*. Multicolored balloons floated over the table. The youngsters squealed with delight as their pizza was served and presents were opened. It was a typical evening out in a Southern Italian eatery. Children's laughter filled the air as people of all ages sat at the tables in the garden, eating, drinking and engaged in animated conversations.

"My grandparents had been divorced," Sam continued. "That was a very rare circumstance for Italian Catholics in that generation. Nobody in the family ever talked about it, especially my father. I never knew he had actually lived in Italy until I started probing. That's when I found out about Amantea and made a trip here. That was in the late seventies, and I've been coming back ever since."

Sam has large, intense brown eyes and speaks in an energetic, staccato-like tempo. "I can tell you this sense of heritage became very important to me, it became my life's passion."

"Why do you think that is?" I asked.

"Remember when we were kids and you'd see those Norman Rockwell paintings all over the place? Magazine covers, framed pictures hanging in the school and in homes? They were wonderful portraits of people—of Americans who didn't look anything like me. I never saw my family in those paintings, yet we were just as American as the kids in the pictures. I guess I thought it was important for me to recognize not just the Italian part of my culture but to make sure the Italian-American part got properly represented for my kids. It's been my real life's work since then."

I asked about his mother's seeming indifference to her family's birthplace.

"That's a typical first-American-born-generation reaction," he said. "You know, that first group over to the States was taught to be ashamed of their origins in many ways. They passed that on to their kids. Also, she only learned dialect from her parents, and that inhibits her."

I could identify easily with Sam's words. Born in New York, my father—like so many immigrant Southern Italian children—also spoke only dialect. Somewhere along the line they had been told that their dialect was inferior, illiterate, ignorant. They felt a sense of shame when speaking to Northern Italians or other Italians with formal educations. They didn't want to speak the language unless absolutely necessary.

"I know what you mean," I said. "I could never understand why my father felt so embarrassed by being able to communicate in another language."

"It was part of the inherent prejudice the Southern Italians suffered," Sam explained. "The dialects were just one way the Northerners reinforced the notion of Southern inferiority. Even the words to describe their geographical positions in Italy prove this: *alti*—higher or better, *bassi*—lowly, inferior. We were from the lower reaches; Southerners were never considered to be on an equal level with Northerners. When they came to America, they lived in two cultures, they kept the Italian culture to themselves and lived in the American one."

The "inside-outside" world again. The small tight circle of the Southern family. Even their language had been rejected by others and they used it only with their own, who would understand.

It seemed that every discussion in the South led back to the same basic points, even discussions between two Americans from Pittsburgh.

A woman was now leading the children in a song. I watched as the adults in the garden smiled, bobbed their heads and mouthed the words as the children sang in that child's way of singing with voices just at the edge of shouting, yet somehow maintaining musical pitch. The girls were putting on a little show, which seemed to be appreciated by everyone there.

Sam smiled as he listened to the song, then continued his observations.

"The story of these people when they leave places like Amantea *is* American history," he said, "just as much as it is Italian history. It's important that our generation knows both stories, takes note of who they were—how tough they were—how difficult their lives had been. If we don't tell the story, pay homage, it will be lost to time. I've tried to get involved as best I can with the History Center in Pittsburgh, I'm active in the discussions on Italian-American literature, I've taught courses on the subject, I work with youngsters whenever possible."

A dessert was served to the birthday party. The little girls shouted their delight over their gelato and cake. The birthday girl sat proudly in the middle of the group, a small glittering tiara on her head, a young, glowing princess of Amantea on this balmy summer night.

"Think of this," Sam said. "Pittsburgh was originally settled by the Scots and Scots-Irish. Tell me one thing about those people, about their tragedies or triumphs. They stopped telling their story and now we don't know it. We can't let the same thing happen to our own people."

I thought of the Scots-Irish when I returned to Rocco's that evening, as I sat on my small balcony surrounded by my neighbors hanging laundry of bathing suits and towels, as the crowds moved noisily about on the street below. Sam was right, of course. Every people's story was important, if for no other reason than that the children must know about those who came before them—how they had done things that directly affected them, related to them, had contributed to the quality and value of their lives. Sam and I were like the little girl at the pizzeria wearing the tiara and surrounded by presents and friends; a loving parent had made this happen for us. We had the gifts of language and education. I believed Sam was right: it was our responsibility now to recognize and honor those gifts.

RUMOR OF WAR

A few evenings later I sat at the front of the *pensione* with Rocco and Roberto and, as was the custom, we talked deep into the night. Rocco seemed the more pragmatic of the brothers, his conversation was generally about the comings and goings of his friends and his own experiences in the States. Roberto was more whimsical, talking often about the Greeks and their influence on the place.

"So the Greeks were here first?" I asked.

"No," Roberto replied, apparently happy to have a student again. "This was always an Italian village, but during the Greek times the Calabrians dealt with the Greeks and worked with them very closely. But there are indications that it wasn't a part of Greece proper."

"What indications?"

"Well, we can't be sure since we don't know exactly where the original town was, but there are no ruins to indicate the sorts of buildings that would have had to have been here if the Greeks claimed it as one of their own towns."

Roberto explained the development carefully. Amantea was settled first by Calabrian tribes trading with Greeks, then Romans, and went through continual turmoil through the ages up to modern times. Most scholars believe its ancient name was Clampetia, an important commercial port up to and through Grecian times. The town declined under the Romans and was destroyed in 365 C.E. by an earthquake and tidal wave that washed away all life in the village. A new town was built on the ruins, Nepetia, which became an important port again under the Saracen domination and eventually the seat for a local emir. During this Arab period, the town finally became known as Almantiah—in Arabic, "the rock," which then became Amantea in the Calabrese dialect. The rock they referred to was probably the huge boulder off the coast I'd seen so clearly from the castle.

"One thing is certain," Roberto said. He had the same eyes and gestures as his brother. "We have been here, in one way or another, since before the start of any modern civilization. And we have been civilized way before anyone else in almost all of Italy. Here, Naples, in your home province of Basilicata and in Puglia, that's where Western civilization first began."

I asked if it bothered him that the Northerners thought of the South as backward.

"Why should it?" he asked. "We know the truth here. Our economy was hurt by the unification of Italy, not helped by it. But we don't really think about it all that much."

"Hasn't anyone researched your castle?" I couldn't let go of the lonely, ancient pile of stones looming over the town.

"We don't know, but something's been up there in one form or another since before anyone could write or keep the history. This whole area is a constant history lesson. Did you know that just over the mountains there was a concentration camp during the Second World War?"

"What sort of concentration camp?"

"Exactly the sort they had in Germany. Only this one was run by Italians. They were more civilized. The man who ran the place, a Calabrian, said his job was to protect his wards, not to kill them."

"Where is this camp?" I asked.

"Ferramonti. Near Cosenza, you can see it from the autostrada. But there's not much there now, just some old buildings." Roberto was in a hurry to get home. He promised to tell me more another time.

A concentration camp in Italy. The entire notion seemed out of place, no matter how misdirected Mussolini's Fascists might have been. There was never any organized anti-Semitism I was aware of. I promised myself to learn more about a place I'd never heard of before this casual conversation with Roberto.

AMANTEA EVENINGS

I took advantage of Rocco's plastic chairs and tables at every opportunity during my stay in Amantea. I loved sitting in the balmy evening air and greatly enjoyed the spectacle. Rocco's guests and the gentry of Amantea provided a constant chatter, discussion, motion and fashion show. As we sat in the evening in front of Rocco's, virtually the entire population of Amantea promenaded past on their way to and from the boardwalk for their evening stroll. It was like watching a movie.

Constant *ciao*s were exchanged, jibes and comments passed back and forth, children cried out, men laughed, motor scooters buzzed by, the elderly teetered on the arms of younger family members, teenagers held hands and exchanged glances; in short, all of Amantea's life flowed down the Via Margherita as we sat and watched.

Occasionally I would stroll down to the boardwalk, stand by the seawall and watch the gentle surf as the population passed by. I especially liked it when the beach was empty and darkness about to fall. I could sense Sicily to the southwest. Its presence had dominated these waters for over three thousand years. The Normans began their conquest there in 1061, five years before they bothered with what is now England. That also gives us an idea of ancient priorities and sense of values. Sicily was the key to all the Mediterranean trade. England was a cold island not far from France, with large hunting estates for kings and dukes to fight over.

It would seem that Amantea was small potatoes compared with Reggio and Messina to the south, and Paola, Paestum and Naples to the north. Still, those castle ruins which sat almost directly above my *pensione* were mute evidence of some ancient power. Every town in this area has a wall, a crumbling tower, symbols of ancient worry and vigilance. The Greeks who first came to this place from other shores couldn't sail out of sight of land. It is said the towns are all more or less spaced a day's sail from each other; places for the Greeks to put in at night or trade with the local tribes. This could be an apocryphal story, but each of these towns grew in some ancient way along similar lines and each became a target for subsequent raids by adventuring and marauding outsiders.

Now they're generally beach towns drawing European tourists, mostly from Italy and Germany, and a few Swiss and Belgians. They've gone from a defensive culture to a diversionary one. Now, instead of watchtowers, each town has its beach kiosks featuring plastic blow-up chairs, rubber sandals and colorful towels. Now the invading hordes wear shorts and sunglasses and coat themselves with oil and go into the sea instead of come from it.

It has taken at least four thousand years for this change from defense to diversion to have occurred.

This is the forgotten coast of Italy, the place only Europeans, Italians and, more important, Calabrians seem to know much about. Rocco says the people and culture here are separate from the rest of Italy. The mountains to the east are a major cause of that isolation. The Grand Sila, the highest peak in the Calabrian Range, is almost in view.

When I was a kid people would joke about how the Italians, my family included, talked with their hands. The standing joke was that we couldn't speak if we couldn't gesture. There's something to that. As I attempted a conversation with a woman behind the huge window in the Amantea post office earlier that week, the idea came to me that it's no wonder Italians, especially Southern Italians, talk with their hands. It's because of the overwhelming number of incomprehensible dialects that necessitated pantomime as an essential aid to and sometimes only form of communication.

Looking at this land while driving about explains it all.

These people developed in tiny communities separated by nature, walls and, one presumes, a certain amount of politics at any given time in history. These little towns pop up every ten kilometers or so, and most of them have some ruin on a nearby hilltop. Often a village held only a couple dozen families, all interrelated, and developing a dialect different from hundreds of others scattered throughout the mountains. There are dozens of such dialects. It's a wonder they can communicate with one another at all.

I imagine only the daring went beyond those walls very often and, once the Byzantines, Arabs, then the Normans started to raid these coasts, that vigilance became constant and suspicion ruled the day.

It also explains why I believe these people are so intuitive. They can express more with a raised eyelid or thumb and finger than others can in volumes of syntax. And they seem to sense gestures, concern, determination. As I stood at the post office window explaining my urgent need to get a document to the United States, I watched the woman's eyes behind the counter. She wasn't really listening to me, she was studying me, my movements, the way I spoke. We all do this to a certain extent, but I believe the Italians are the experts in body language and intuitive sensibility.

Most of the guide and tourist books written in English about this section of Italy were written in another age. George Gissing and Norman Douglas wrote from a Victorian point of view; civilized men trying to understand the savage ways. Gissing in particular describes the natives here as nearly incapable of communication, and only the educated are given words and complete thoughts in his writings on Calabria. The peasants are picturesque, but speak in platitudes or mutter darkly. Aside from Gay Talese, there are few other contemporary writers of English who have put serious pen to paper about this region.

Amantea used to be a fishing village; there is a monument, erected after World War II, to the men who went to the sea on the boardwalk near the beach. But there are no longer any boats or fishermen, only marble plaques. Rocco says the men used to go out six at a time in boats they rowed. They must have been strong men, spending their days rowing on this sea. The waters, Rocco said, were filled with sardines, the main industry for the town. But that was more than fifty years ago. Now, he says, the kids want to ride their *motorini* and listen to their CDs.

"They got *reech*," says Rocco's friend, born in Amantea but now visiting from Long Island. The older gentleman explains he is on an extended vacation. He looks dapper with his monogrammed polo shirt, deep tan and combed-back gray hair. Carlo worked for the city of New York and was forced into retirement seven years ago. He's bored but he says the union won't let him both work and collect his pension, so he spends his time between Long Island, where he lives, and Calabria, where he was born.

"All the men from here left for work when I was young," Rocco said. "They went to Argentina or Canada or America and they worked like dogs. Like *dogs*!" He spat the word. "And they weren't treated much better than animals."

"How do you mean?" I asked.

"Well, they weren't well-educated, so they took whatever work they could get. I'm sure you know what I mean. Like your own grandfathers, they went into the mills, the mines, dug tunnels, worked on construction crews, hired out as day laborers on farms and plantations. And they came from the South..."

Rocco looked directly into my eyes.

"You know what the heat is like here in the middle of the day. You've spent time here. This is the Southern sun. We don't work in the middle of the day, we stay out of the sun. Well, they took those work habits with them to the New World. When their bosses saw them sitting in the shade, they called them lazy, thought they didn't know how to work. Ridiculed them as ignorant."

Rocco sat straight up, his chest fully expanded. His gaze was direct, his brown eyes bright. He was about to make a point.

"Now let me ask you something," he said with a shaking pointed finger. "Who's more clever? The men who work like dogs in the morning and evening, but who stay away from the heat of the day?" He paused for effect. "Or the men who work through the afternoon sun and quit early so they can go get drunk? The Italians were ridiculed for having more intelligent work habits than the people they worked for...like dogs in the sun."

Rocco's hands flew up as a flourish to punctuate his story.

"Today, these *keeds* don't want to work like we had to when we were young," Rocco's friend said, in his heavily accented English. He tells of how he went from here to Venezuela, then got a visa to the U.S., where he met his wife and settled down, spending his life like the generation before him with work as his priority. He says he doesn't understand this current generation, they have too much.

"All the men from this village were fishermen since forever, even the ones from my father's generation who didn't go to America," Rocco added. "The commercial fleets do the job now. Maybe that's better." He sighed. It seemed a poignant question.

We were sitting on Rocco's plastic chairs on the sidewalk in front of the Pensione Margherita. There were over a dozen chairs, filled mostly with middle-aged men talking late into the night. Surprisingly to me, they drank and ate nothing, only sat and talked. Occasionally, a few female guests come and sit at the little tables, but mostly it is the older men who spend the evening there.

One evening, Roberto brought me a gift, a copy of his book, a history—*Casanova in Calabria*. He explained that the Venetian visited his mother here when he was eighteen; the mother was an actress traveling with a troupe. The visit lasted three days, but the tract Roberto has written is over seventy pages of thoroughly annotated and researched material, along with photographs and maps. He says he got interested in the subject after attending the bicentennial memorial of Casanova's death in Prague in 1998. The thick pamphlet has a brilliant red cover. Roberto seems justifiably proud of his work. I promised to read it as an excellent Italian lesson and another insight into the characters of Calabria.

THE LETTER

I sat with a group of men who were discussing the virtues of the Italian president du jour, Silvio Berlusconi. The consensus was that, since he was so very rich, he was probably incorruptible, but then, who could really tell when it came to politicians. Another gentleman from the village was bemoaning the lowering of the pension benefits and the accompanying tax increase. It seems that Italy is running out of pension money, not a great surprise in a county that, until just a few years ago, would allow full retirement benefits to people as early as age forty.

While involved in our weighty considerations, Rocco—who was sitting a few feet away with another group of men—shouted over to ask if I knew of the town Toms River.

"Joe McGinniss wrote a book about it," I replied.

Rocco was holding up a letter and pointing out something to one of his companions. I didn't think anything more about it until the next morning when, at coffee, Rocco related its contents.

It seems that a certain Antonio Paolo Politano of Toms River, New Jersey, had learned that there was a man by the same name living in Amantea, Provincia di Cosenza, Calabria, Italy, and had written to say that his parents were from that town and, since both men had the same name, could they possibly be related.

This had created quite a stir, which I had evidently missed by being involved in the political discussion.

The man had taken the letter to Rocco to interpret. The Politano of Amantea explained that he didn't think the letter was for him. Since he didn't know anyone in the United States, it had to be a mistake. His sister insisted that he open it, and when he finally got around to it months later (this is *so* typical of the Italian mind-set—if one does not know the contents of a letter or is not sure of the sender, the letter may sit for weeks or months before any action is taken) learned that it was in English, a language he didn't know. So, naturally, Rocco, the *americano*, was consulted.

"What are you going to do?" I asked Rocco, when he showed me the letter.

"I'm going to go down to the *municipio* and check the records and see what I can find."

"Why are you going to do that?" I asked, thinking I probably knew the answer.

"Because it's important," he said, as if I'd lost my mind.

"Why is it important?"

"Because this man's family is from here. From our town. He could be a relative of Antonio."

"But why is that important?" I continued, trying to act the bemused interrogator.

"Because this could be his family. They are from here." I could tell he was getting a little exasperated with my line of questioning. Rocco spoke as if the word *family* needed no further explanation. Why would I question someone trying to find family? "You should know how important this is," he said, "you looked for your family."

"But I wonder what this is, why I think it's important, why you think it's important, why the Politanos in Toms River, New Jersey, and the ones in Amantea, Calabria, think it's important. Will it prove anything? Or are we just people of sentiment?"

"This could be family," said Rocco, "that is important. That is what we have here."

I smiled at Rocco's intensity. Antonio Politano of Amantea, a workingman who spoke mostly in dialect, seemed dazed by the sequence of events. He kept repeating how he didn't think the letter was for him. He was a thin man, immaculately dressed in a starched blue short-sleeve dress shirt, his waist flat and small, his gray pants creased. He sported the deep tan of everyone in the beach community; it complemented his brilliant white hair. He launched into a story I needed a lot of interpreting to understand.

It seems that recently he had been quite ill, his hair had been falling out, he was losing weight and strength, the doctors didn't know what to make of it, but everyone had been very concerned. He had gone to the hospital, thinking the end was near. Then he heard the voices of three young women, in a sort of vision—only, he said, it couldn't have been a vision since he only *heard* them, he didn't actually *see* the young women. They told him not to worry, that it wasn't his time to go yet.

He immediately regained his strength and his health.

I'm not sure just what this had to do with the letter from Toms River, but it was a fascinating story which I greatly enjoyed, especially since much of it was done in pantomime, since he knew I had no idea of what he was saying in dialect. The hair-falling-out part was easy, he plucked dramatically at his head, but the voices part of the story got a little complicated. He seemed very pleased about the letter and it was somehow tied into the voices he'd heard.

Communications from abroad caused powerful reactions in Amantea.

4

North Versus South

DUE SICILIE

Professor Carmine Colacino is a man of strong beliefs and sentiment. His writings on the Internet are known to anyone interested in the current discussion of Italian affairs. A biology professor at the University of Basilicata in Potenza, Dr. Colacino's real passion seems to lie in the discussion of politics and history. He was born in Naples in 1956, the son of a Neapolitan mother and great-grandson on his father's side of an Albanian refugee and career army officer, a profession his father also practiced.

We met on the Internet and begun a vigorous discussion. I was anxious to continue our exchange in person. Even before settling into my Matera apartment, I made the hour's jaunt over the Basentana, the four-lane highway connecting Potenza with Metaponto and Matera.

We met in person for the first time at his university, in a huge new wing of the school on the eastern side of Potenza. The university was only fifteen or sixteen years old, yet was in the process of constructing a completely new science facility adjacent to the region's new and largest hospital and trauma center.

A short, stocky man, Colacino's bright blue eyes and shy grin revealed a warm personality not evident in his strong and aggressive writings on the subject of Southern Italy. He is part of a group, the Associazione Culturale Due Sicilie, that claims it would separate Italy by North and South and make the Southern region an independent nation.

Colacino and I shook hands in the parking lot. We'd spent the previous hour on the cell phone as I drove about Potenza looking for the right road. He finally came to retrieve me with his car, a bright red Japanese-made station wagon, and led me over a country back road into the university complex.

I found Potenza more confusing than any other city I'd driven about in Italy. My only other visit to Potenza some years earlier had been unsettling. I'd thought the city was strangely inhospitable and very difficult to navigate, and I was having the same experience on this second trip nearly a decade later. There was no clearly marked city center as in almost every other Italian city I'd seen. Mostly the result, I assumed, of two terrible earthquakes in this region in the twentieth century. The most recent and devastating quake occurred in 1980. The town had been almost completely reconstructed in the recent past.

The new university complex on the outskirts of the town had an Orwellian feel.

"It looks as if everything here is very new," I said, as Dr. Colacino and I walked across the parking lot. Heat waves wafted skyward as it baked in the hot sun. This was the kind of day that defined il Mezzogiorno. "There's obviously a lot of money being spent around here."

"Don't let that fool you," the professor replied. "It looks like we're being brought up-to-date, but they're about a century late in figuring out what's going on." We walked into the shade of a huge, seemingly abandoned new school building. It was midsummer and the students were on a break.

Two flights of stairs later, we walked down a long, empty, hot and airless corridor. Finally, Colacino stopped at an unmarked door and fumbled with his keys. He showed me into his office and I settled into the only chair opposite the desk, wiping the sweat from my brow and neck with a soggy handkerchief. It was stifling hot in the room. The professor served coffee in little espresso cups and, as he played with the controls on a small electric fan, he broke with the usual Italian social custom of small talk and launched directly into the subject I had come to discuss, even before finishing his coffee.

"You know, one of the worst things to ever happen to the South was the so-called unification of Italy. When they held the first referendum in Sicily, Garibaldi rigged the election. There's no way ninety-nine percent of Sicily wanted to unite with Rome. Most Sicilians hadn't even heard of Garibaldi, or if they did, backed him only because they thought he was trying to oppose the pope."

I felt the slight breeze from the fan, it was a welcome relief to the still, oppressive air. I sipped my espresso, but I could not get used to hot coffee in the heat of the day. I felt a strong American desire for a Diet Coke with ice.

The professor spoke with slightly accented American English. I assumed his ease in the language was the result of his work at the University of California at Berkeley. He appeared highly organized; his desk was immaculate, every paper seemed perfectly arranged. His laptop occupied the center of his work area.

"I'm told," I said, "that the election after the Second World War to form a republic was also rigged. I've heard some say the monarchy was really preferred by the majority of Italians."

" 'What ye sow, so shall ye reap.' They got what they deserved. The Savoy monarchy was a disaster for the South. They didn't know anything about us. When the new government was formed—and only a very few could vote for it at the time, mostly landowners—one of the first things they did was build rail lines to run north and south down both coasts. Those rails weren't for us here in the South, they were to transport troops to control the Southerners."

He talked nonstop, his blue eyes looking directly into mine. I felt, in a way, as if I were being proselytized into some sort of antimonarchial cult.

"We were considered a bunch of bandits, illiterates and ignoramuses. They felt they had to control us militarily. That was what the new state of Italy meant for us. The new king couldn't even speak Italian, let alone understand our economy. They were aligned with the North, they wanted to be part of Northern Europe."

Colacino steamed on with an endless stream of facts and events. He spoke with great fervor and without any attempts at humor. However, his serious talk, and any attempts at my conversion, was constantly interrupted by his cell phone, or *telefonino*. The phone chimed a faintly reminiscent melody as it rang. Each time he answered it, the professor's personality changed; he smiled and joked with his callers. I could see he was a man of high humor as well as zeal.

"That song," I asked, "the one on your cell phone. What is it?"

He laughed for the first time with me, then said something in Italian I couldn't understand.

"That's in Neapolitan dialect." He laughed again. "My phone plays a Neapolitan folk song by Aurelio Ferro. In formal Italian it's called, '*Carmela è una bambola*,' or 'Carmela is a doll.' Do you recognize it?"

"It sounds familiar. My father loved Neapolitan songs."

"Your father was Neapolitan?"

"No, his family was from the Matera area, but he grew up speaking that dialect because his uncle ran a boardinghouse and men from Naples stayed there. He told me that almost every single boarder played a musical instrument. His uncle made wine. In the evenings, after working long days at the local steel mill, my father said they'd drink their wine and sing and play Neapolitan songs. I've often thought that was a beautiful way to spend a childhood."

"But you don't speak the dialect?" he asked. It was more of a statement than a question; he seemed to know my answer.

"No, my father spoke it, and the Basilicatan dialect, which I guess is similar, but never in front of me or any of the other children. He loved Neapolitan songs, but played his records when we weren't home. He knew only dialects and said he always felt bad that he didn't know proper Italian. Both he and my mother only spoke English with us at home."

"Ah, this is very sad," the professor said. "Our Southern dialects are so very rich with metaphor and humor, yet your parents and their parents were told over and over that they spoke an inferior language, were ignorant, uneducated. It was another way for the North to control us."

"What is it about the Southern dialects that make them so inferior to proper Italian?"

"The prejudice of the North," he said softly. He offered another coffee, but the room was finally cooling, another hot drink wasn't the least appealing; I declined his offer.

"I tell you," Colacino continued, "there is not a difference between a Genovese dialect or a Calabrian dialect; they are both variations of the common root language. Even today, when I go to the North, I often hear other college professors joke in their Northern dialects. Everyone laughs, they love the old way of speaking. But if I were to say something in Neapolitan, it would be considered distasteful, crude, crass. It's the arrogance of the Northerners and the hangover from the reunification when they created myths about the South to explain something they didn't understand and didn't care to learn."

"I've never understood that, Professor." It was a very confusing subject to most Americans, whose only concept of dialect was regional accents.

"Please." He smiled again. "Call me Carmine. It's not an easy subject. Everyone thinks that the Bourbons were such a disaster for Southern

Italy, but when you look at the facts, we were better off under a separate foreign kingdom than we were under an Italian one." He sighed.

"Your grandparents spoke a dialect that had very ancient roots," he explained. "The original tribes in this area, the Lucanians, were a very resilient people who lived mostly in the mountains, but ranged as far west as Paestum, and south of the Abruzzi through what is now Basilicata and Puglia. The ancient language they spoke was Oscan, the roots of many of the modern Southern dialects. We Southerners have always had the sense, since we were a civilization before the Greeks arrived, that we were the older civilization on this peninsula. But now that works against us."

"How do you mean?" I wondered.

"By the fact that our older language is considered so unsophisticated by those speaking newer dialects, the dialects more closely aligned with Northern Europe and the newer languages of Northern Europe. Remember, the Germans were nomads and didn't start settling into cities until around 900 C.E., thousands of years after our ancestors had accomplished the same thing. England was a forest filled with roving hunters until Julius Ceasar showed them how to build a city. Yet our language was considered barbaric."

His *telefonino* rang again, the Neapolitan melody filling the room with a disconcerting sense of urgency. Colacino laughed during his short cell conversation, then changed back into a serious mood when he returned to our discussion.

"You know," he said sadly, "if they hadn't forced so many Southerners to emigrate, we might be speaking to each other in the same dialect today. Instead we have to speak English. It's a shame you don't have your father's dialect, it is wonderful to speak and hear."

I felt truly sorry I didn't know any dialect and was happy that at least I could barely function in my school-taught formal Italian.

Carmine returned to his favorite topic.

"The Bourbons or Spanish kings respected the differences between us. The Piedmontese, the Savoys—our kings after unification—didn't. Why did we have to kick the Bourbons out? No one thought they had to liberate England from their German king. The Bourbon period was the only period of actual Southern independence in modern times."

"And huge estates owned by foreigners exploited the local workers," I added. "And many tell me that they badly mistreated the villagers."

"That exploitation is overstated," Colacino replied. "At least our people were allowed to speak their own language, determine their own farming methods and products. Under *latifundia*—large foreign-owned estates—farmers had some rights the Bourbons respected. Under the Piedmontese, all land rights were taken away, public land became private and in the hands of wealthy Northern industrialists, and church land also became closed and owned by the state. And we were starting to develop industry. Did you know the first immigrant ship carrying Southern Italians to arrive in the U.S. was built in Naples?"

I didn't.

"But were those immigrants free to leave under the Bourbons?" This was an interpretation of the Bourbons I'd never heard before.

"That's a discussion for another time. But we did build the ship, and Naples was then the second-largest city in all of Europe."

"If the South was so advanced," I wondered, "why was there so much poverty when the country was unified and why was it concentrated in the South?"

"Because the North did not understand agricultural markets in the same way. In the 1880s they declared a trade war with France, mostly because they couldn't export the materials from the heavy industries of the North—steel, rails, construction materials and the like. Sicily and Southern Italy supplied almost all of Northern Europe with its fruits and vegetables, especially France and England. When the government barred trade, they destroyed the Southern economy without a second thought. And that's when everybody started leaving for America and other places. After 1880."

"The Bourbons had also been terrible economists," I argued. "According to several of the histories I've read, they needed money so badly they sold titles to anyone who could afford to pay for them. I'm told that meant many Northerners buying titles and estates and moving South, where they mismanaged or essentially looted the land and its workers. Is this not true?"

Carmine sighed heavily. "It's true that land reform was very late in coming," he said. "And it's true that many came here hoping to exploit the land and its workers. Unfortunately for us, that started with the Roman Empire and has continued ever since. But the world has an image of a unified Italy that doesn't exist and probably never will."

We talked for the next few hours as I filled the pages of my journal with Carmine's observations and statistics. It was getting late and I wanted to return to Matera before dark. The Basentana was a fine highway, but the last twenty miles or so to Matera was a two-lane road over hilly terrain. It seemed that no matter what time of day I'd driven the road, there was always someone behind me trying to pass at breakneck speed around blind and dangerous curves. It was not a road I was comfortable on at night.

Carmine escorted me out of the building, almost apologetic for his ardor. In all the time I'd spent in Italy, I'd never before heard anyone clearly define the Southern side of the argument. I'd had Northerners tell me openly and quickly what a problem the South had been and continued to be, but never the reverse. It had been an eye-opening afternoon.

"Have you heard of the brigands?" Carmine asked, as we reached the parking lot.

I had.

"The Northerners believed that the young men who lived here were all bandits and rogues. There were large bands of roving gangs who thought of themselves as a sort of Italian Robin Hood, young men who could find no work. There was no market for the farm products. The

North sent their armies instead of their economists. It's a stereotype they still hold." He shrugged and smiled.

"Do you know what they used to say about the young men from that time?"

I lifted my eyebrows.

"*Briganti o immigranti,*" he replied. "Do you understand?"

I nodded.

"In other words," I ventured, "there was very little choice and no regular employment. 'Steal or leave.'"

"Exactly," he said with a big smile. "You can't speak the dialect, but maybe we can still reclaim you as a son of the South."

I said good-bye to Carmine and got into the car, opening all the windows to release the trapped hot air. I was grateful for the air-conditioner and would enjoy the cool drive back over the mountains between Potenza and Matera, following, in much greater comfort, the same route the Roman legions had traveled more than twenty centuries before. Carmine had given me a lot to think over.

That hot day in Potenza, Carmine and I began a friendship; I continued to rely on him and his insights throughout my stay in Southern Italy.

Lucani nel Mondo

A few days after my initial visit to Potenza I ran into a group of young people while having a morning coffee in Matera. One young man was from New Jersey. He explained that he and all the others were children of Italian-born immigrants, that all their families had some Basilicatan roots. All spoke their parents' native language and were in Southern Italy on a state-sponsored cultural exchange program. One of the youngsters gave me the phone number for the program administrator in Potenza.

I called the administrator's office to learn more. The woman who answered my questions told me she would talk with the head of the program, *il presidente*, and pass along my request for an interview in Potenza. She gave me directions to what I thought was their office. This was all said in Italian on a *telefonino* and over a cellular connection that obliterated every other syllable.

Later that day, I received a call from *il presidente* himself. He asked a series of questions in clear and slow Italian, interrupted only by occasional cellular static. He seemed delighted to learn that my grandparents were from the Basilicata region, and invited me to meet with him the next day.

The following morning I found myself lost in Potenza once again, driving about the quarter of the town where the older section of the university was supposed to be. I hadn't much hope of actually finding the place as I was stuck in a gigantic traffic jam going up a hill toward the city's center. A very attractive female police officer came over to the car, leaned toward my window and asked if I needed any help. My foreign plates and my undoubtedly lost expression had not escaped her alert eyes.

"Are you Swedish?" she asked.

I am always surprised by the questions I receive in Italy. This one was truly stunning. I had never before been mistaken for a Swede.

"No," I said, "just a lost *americano*." I explained I was looking for the university.

In basic Italian, the tall, thin, blond policewoman with blue eyes, who was far more Swedish-looking than I, gave me a complicated set of instructions. They involved a U-turn, a left turn and a warning not to make a right turn or go down a hill at some point, somewhere. Potenza continued to confuse me.

I turned the car around and headed down the hill, hoping at least to follow the outline of what I just heard. Halfway down the hill, the policewoman miraculously reappeared in front of me, driving a tiny police car with a yellow light rotating on its roof. She indicated for me to follow her. I thanked the heavens for her insight into my complete geographical dysfunction, but couldn't for the life of me figure out how she'd gotten ahead of me. She led me to a gate for the university on the side of a hill—a location I probably would have missed without her arm-waving and finger-pointing.

"*Skoal!*" I shouted. It was the only pseudo-Swedish word I knew.

I entered the small lot, got out of the car and was prepared to show the guard my identification, but he waved me inside the complex without a word. I asked a passing student for the president's office, and was directed to the last building on the right. I found a parking spot I hoped was legal; there were cars all over the place—on the sidewalks, in the street and in the little alleys next to the buildings. I entered the main administration building. A guard sent me to the second floor, where I was met by a young male secretary in the president's spacious wood-paneled suite.

I got the wrinkled nose. The young secretary was clearly uncomfortable with my accent.

"*Un appuntamento?*" he asked me. "You are certain you have an appointment?"

"*Si*," I replied. "I made it by telephone yesterday. For ten o'clock this morning. It is now ten."

"*Con il presidente?*"

"*Si*, I spoke with a woman, someone in the press office. And I spoke with the president himself."

He got on the phone and called the president's office. He read my name from my card.

"What was this about?" he asked, holding the receiver between his shoulder and ear.

"The young people from Basilicata who are back here on the cultural exchange program."

He repeated my words to his boss.

"Cultural exchange program?"

There was something very strange going on.

"Yes," I said a little more emphatically than I intended, "they were in

Matera yesterday and they have a program here in Potenza today with the president."

He repeated my statement.

"With *which* president?" the young man asked, the phone still cradled.

"You mean there's more than one?"

"My president knows of no such group."

I was beginning to think I was under some sort of Potenza curse, doomed to be forever lost, confused, or in the wrong place at the wrong time.

Finally I noticed I had scribbled the name of what I thought was a professor on my notepad. I repeated it with my American accent, watched the nose of the young clerk wrinkle again, then his eyes widen in recognition.

"Professsore Lerra, Aula Magna?"

"Ah, you mean the lecture hall. That's a program run by the government, it's not a part of the school. They're using the room. Professor Lerra is taking part." He explained this to his president, clicked off the line, called another number and had a short conversation in rapid dialect. A few seconds later, an older man with a huge potbelly and a cigarette dangling from his mouth entered the paneled room.

"This man will take you to where you need to be," the secretary said. He shook my hand and wished me luck, pleased that he had protected his boss from a lunatic intrusion.

The potbellied concierge smiled through a cloud of smoke, then led me out of the building and halfway up the hill toward the guard's stand. He pointed out the lecture hall and told me I'd find what I was looking for directly inside.

I entered a huge theaterlike room, the seats declining steeply toward the large stage. In the center of the stage sat two middle-aged men, both wearing neckties and suit jackets in the semi-air-conditioning, talking quietly to a group of about fifty or so younger people spread about the room in various groupings. I recognized some of the young people as from the group I'd seen in Matera the day before. They occupied about a quarter of the available seating.

I tried to slip silently into a last-row seat and observe the proceedings. As I reached a chair and was about to arrange the movable desktop, I heard my name called by one of the men on stage.

"Signor Paolicelli?"

"*Sì*," I said, hating the loss of anonymity. I had the nightmarelike feeling of being back in school, late and unprepared.

"Ah," he sighed. "*É arrivato il Signore Paolicelli, un giornalista americano. Prego, signore, venga qui.*" He was motioning for me to come to the stage.

What was this all about?

"I'd much rather just listen, if I may," I said, stumbling over my pronunciation.

"No, no," the man repeated. "*Prego, venga qua.*"

I self-consciously walked down the aisle and up onto the stage, where the man greeted me with a handshake.

"I am Rocco Curcio," he said. "We spoke yesterday by phone." He handed me his card. Nearly fifty students sat in the hall and quietly watched this exchange. The card identified Dr. Curcio as the correct *il presidente*. He was the head of the Regional Commission of Lucanians Abroad, a department of the Basilicatan government.

"Sit here, please," he said, pointing to an empty chair between him and the man I was now introduced to, Professor Antonio Lerra. "We've been waiting for you."

I had thought this was going to be a private interview. I had clearly misinterpreted or lost some rather key words in the erratic cellular conversations from the day before, and I was beginning to recant my admiration of modern communication.

Dr. Curcio turned to the audience. In a very clear and slow Italian, he explained that I was the American journalist they'd awaited, that my grandfather had immigrated to the States from "Lucania"—the word Basilicata seemed to have disappeared—and I was there *to talk to the group*.

Apparently, *I was the day's speaker.*

First mistaken for a Swede, now this. It was turning into a truly bizarre day and it was only ten in the morning.

"But Signor Presidente," I ventured, "I am not prepared to—"

I was interrupted by a disruption at the back of the hall. A local television crew from RAI—the state-owned TV network—had arrived, apparently to tape my presentation. I had truly fallen down the hole chasing the white rabbit.

"I know you speak Italian well enough, because we spoke it yesterday," Dr. Curcio said. "Not all of these young people can speak English, nor can I."

I took stock of my situation; I had come to Potenza to talk with the professor about his program. Now I was suddenly and unexpectedly in the middle of a stage with fifty or so young people sitting in front of me, expecting me to do or say something relevant concerning their reconnection with their parents' birthplace. And do so in the Italian language in which I consistently butchered verbs and their tenses. And my alleged presentation was going to be taped and broadcast to the people of Italy.

On that first trip to Potenza some years ago, I'd been accompanied by my sister, Marie, and her husband, Bill Ireland. Over the years I've come to rely on my sister's intuition in certain situations. That day she decided she really didn't like Potenza and wanted to leave as soon as possible. We spent that evening in Miglionico, the village where my grandparents had been raised. When I told a cousin about my sister's reaction to Potenza, he said he wasn't surprised. In ancient times, Matera and Potenza were rivals and fought each other on several occasions. I joked at the time that my sister had a biological memory of an ancient enemy, thus her negative reaction to the place.

Now, on a stage in front of a group of international youngsters, and with a local TV crew setting up their camera, I was beginning to think I just might be under some ancient familial or tribal curse of the Potenzans.

I spotted the young man from New Jersey and asked him to come up and sit next to me, dubbing him my official translator. I then did the only thing I knew how to do; I asked questions of the group about their experiences, both in Italy and in their homeland.

Dr. Curcio and Professor Lerra had slipped out a side door into an adjoining patio and were smoking cigarettes. The RAI crew snapped on lights and moved about the room taking shots from several angles. The youngsters were slow to reply, but I was persistent and eventually they opened up to my desperate questioning.

One young woman from Argentina said she felt completely at home in both places. Many Italians had emigrated to Argentina throughout the past century; Evita Perón was of Italian descent, as was her husband, Juan. In addition, Italians had originally worked in the coffee plantations, and now many Argentineans of Italian origin were major plantation and factory owners. The assimilation of Italians into mainstream society had been very quick in Argentina, in part because of the similarity between Italian and Spanish, in part because of the similarity of cultures. The Italians weren't looked down upon. Third- and fourth-generation Italian-Argentineans also had legally maintained Italian citizenship. There was a stronger linkage between the two countries than between their North American counterparts. The young lady explained that most Italians in Argentina knew their geographical origins in Italy and had maintained some contact with the Old Country.

Another young woman from Canada said that she didn't "feel Canadian," but rather she believed herself to be "an Italian living in Canada." Her observations struck me as unusual and I probed to find out why she "felt" outside the community in which she lived. "It's not that I don't like Canada," she explained. "It's just that we have Italian traditions in our home and we speak Italian at home and that's what I'm most comfortable with. I don't want to change that."

The RAI crew was taping away. I was glad they were focusing on the audience and not on me.

These young people were all the children of immigrants to other lands who had left Italy after the 1950s and 1960s. The largest group of immigrants to North America during that period went to Canada, with others sprinkled throughout the globe. It was a completely different time and a completely different mind-set that applied to their generation. Linkage with Italy was a natural result of this migration; by the time their parents left Italy, literacy was the norm, jet travel and telephonic communications were not only available but in common usage, and the level of wealth among both the immigrants and the native Italians had grown considerably over the years since the end of the great immigration wave of 1880-1920. The stories of their integration into their new countries were nothing like the stories I'd been told about my grandparents' generation.

Did they feel like a part of Italy, as well?

A great deal of head-nodding.

"I'm very proud of my heritage," said one young man from Peru. "I don't feel I have to give it up to be part of another culture, but that we can live in both cultures." These were ideas I don't think could have occurred to my grandparents.

The president and the professor had finished their smoke and were now back in the hall.

"We need to maintain this contact on both sides," Dr. Curcio added. "It's extremely important in modern Italy, especially here in Lucania, that we reach the younger generation so that they will keep the contacts alive and pass them on to their children. We've lost so many of our people in previous generations."

Fortunately for me, the session broke up early, with the youngsters heading off to prepare for an afternoon field trip. I was introduced to the RAI reporter, Renato Cantore, and we talked about his interest in this sort of program.

"I have done a documentary on this subject," Cantore said. "I will be showing it to this class in a couple of weeks; you must come and see it." I agreed to return to Potenza on the day he indicated.

Later that morning, Dr. Curcio and I shared an espresso at a nearby coffee bar. I asked about his organization's ties with the United States.

"Our largest group is in Denver," he said.

I was surprised. Denver was not a place I'd have guessed to have a high concentration of Italian immigrants.

"These are people who emigrated recently?" I asked.

"Yes, within the past thirty or forty years," he said. "Unfortunately, no one thought to keep accurate records a hundred years ago, when the greatest number of our people left. We know, for example, that there were a great many Lucani who, like your own grandparents, went to Pittsburgh and other towns in Pennsylvania. But we don't know how many. There is no organization of Lucani there."

"The Italian government didn't keep records?" I asked.

"Not to the extent we need. We do know this: There are currently six hundred thousand people living in Basilicata. The best estimate is that over two million of our people left during the great emigration of the last century. Assuming they had the normal reproductive rates, there's millions of our people scattered about the world, mostly in America, whom we can't claim and who might not even know where their family originated. Our best hope now is with the children of the recent immigrants. We can keep contact, maintain the ties. It is extremely important for us to do so."

LANGUAGE LESSONS

A few weeks later I drove to the university again, this time without the help of any Swedish police. And this time I did slip anonymously into the back of the room as Renato Cantore showed his documentary on *Lucani nel mondo,* or "The Lucanians in the World." Cantore had tracked down successful sons from Basilicata now living in Argentina, the United States and Canada, as well as Northern Italy. He conducted lengthy interviews with them, all men, and detailed their businesses and their lives in their adopted lands.

One Lucani was a New York State senator from New York City, another a successful factory owner in Canada, a third a restaurateur in Argentina, still another American operated a car and limousine service in the New York area. The last profile was of the heir to a popular worldwide liqueur maker originally located in the Taranto area, but now headquartered in Milan.

The New York senator's comments were interrupted by peals of laughter. He was using a combination of dialect and the Italian he had probably learned in the States. His pronunciation and grammar were both antiquated and, judging from the audience's reaction, quite amusing. I clearly heard his American accent, but marveled at the continuing ridicule of improper usage.

My generation of Italian-Americans couldn't understand this at all. When we, my cousins and extended family, spoke with foreigners, no matter their origin, we were generally quite pleased that they were attempting to speak English. We never corrected grammar or pronunciation unless we were asked to. I would venture to generalize that most Americans tried to communicate without judgment. It was the way the melting pot of America had always operated; there was no other choice for a multicultural society but to try and understand one another.

But in Italy, even to this day, an educated Italian looks down on someone who cannot speak the educated form of the language. Strangers feel obligated to correct the mistakes of other strangers, or interrupt to correct pronunciation, or to find humor in another's mistakes.

"You have to remember," an Italian-American friend in Abruzzo once told me, "your grandfather left here speaking a language from a hundred years ago. Now, when the few who come back and know that language speak it, we hear something very old. It would be like driving into town in a Model T Ford. It's quaint. And very funny."

One thing was certain: Language played a role in Italian society that was difficult for an American to grasp. Italians judged other Italians on the basis of verbs.

FRENCH CLASSES

Nicola Zitara laughed when he remembered his childhood in Calabria.

"You know," he said, his bright eyes twinkling as he sipped his coffee and then settled his large frame into a lawn chair, "the Calabrians have always been excellent farmers. We have known this land better and longer than anyone and have known how to work it since before the Romans and even the Greeks. We supply most of the citrus and vegetables to Northern Europe and have been doing the same thing for a very long time. After the so-called unification of Italy, what we needed from the new government in Rome were markets, not regulations. They weren't interested in trading oranges, they wanted to build their Northern heavy industries and pretend they were part of Northern Europe."

We sat on a patio at the back of a large private house, still rare in Italy, on the outskirts of Gerace in southern Calabria. It was the home of one of Zitara's childhood friends. The terrace overlooked the sprawling valley below leading to the Ionian Sea. It was in this area where the Greeks settled first around 700 B.C.E. Gerace was the fortified hill town above the Locri original settlement and ancient seaport destroyed by Saracens in the eighth century. Gerace has been rebuilt to look mostly as it does today from the tenth century on.

"We were civilized in this area when Rome was still a mosquito-infested swamp," Zitara continued. "We were going to the theater, voting in elections and discussing philosophy before the Romans discovered togas. When the Romans spoke of the 'Italian people,' they were speaking about *us*, about all of us in this region who lived either with the Greeks or near the Greeks and who had absorbed their culture."

I had met the author through Carmine Colacino. Carmine admired Zitara's books on Southern Italian history and had become a champion of the Kingdom of the Two Sicilies. He and others like him argued that the South of Italy had been better off under foreign rule than it has fared under the unification of Italy. While technically they seek separation from Northern Italy and a return to the divisions prior to the Risorgimento, in fact they are trying to educate both the government and the general public on how badly they believe the South has been treated; how the economy of the region has been all but destroyed by the combination of bad politics, bad policy and bad press.

"The Northerners thought of us as only farmers," Zitara continued, "and therefore as peasants, as *terroni*, or people close to the land but far away from sophistication. They've never understood that we have intuitive civilization. That all the bad government in the world—and we've had many bad governments—couldn't eliminate that knowledge."

It was a theme I would hear repeated often throughout my journeys in the South; this concept of intuitive self-awareness.

"Think back for a moment of what it must have been like over two thousand years ago," Zitara said, his eyebrows dancing. "Greece and Rome were vying with each other. Southern Italy was the melting point of both cultures. The Romans were always envious of the Greeks; they thought them more sophisticated, older and wiser. Educated Romans spoke Greek.

"Now, think about who lived here. The natives, the Italians, had been dealing with the Greeks and Carthaginians and anyone else who stopped by and didn't declare war. They absorbed the knowledge that Romans or Carthaginians or Greeks brought with them.

"While the Romans were planning roads or war and the Greeks were fighting among themselves, the Italians sat on the hillsides and studied the stars. They knew the great stories of the stars, the myths that the Greeks and Romans shared. A father would tell his son all of the stories as they studied the sky. Those stories were pure metaphor; the struggle, victories and losses of men and gods became symbolic.

"And that continued for ages. I'll bet your grandfather sat with his father and heard the same stories from thousands of years ago.

"That was the education of the South. It wasn't in books or classrooms. It was handed down. It was the same knowledge and lore the Romans studied to consider themselves educated. The Southerners knew the eternal qualities of mankind, the basic questions of life. They lived here while new ideas were being developed. They listened well."

Like Carmine, I was falling under Zitara's spell. I had met him earlier in the summer, but after a series of rescheduled meetings had succeeded in spending only a short time with him and his wife in their garden in Siderno, just a few miles up the coast from Locri and Gerace. I had arranged for a translator to accompany me, a very bright young woman from the local YMCA in Siderno, but it turned out the Naples native had only a single hour to spare.

The instant I met the Zitaras I knew I would need much more time. We sat in their garden under orange trees and enjoyed a cool glass of fresh juice. When I asked the professor a question about modern Southern sensibility, he answered by talking about pre-Grecian times. A single hour didn't begin to cut it.

Carmine had helped me set up the Gerace appointment and came along on the interview. When I had met up with Carmine earlier that day in Gerace, he was with two dark and intense young men whom he introduced as journalists from a local paper, *L'Indipendènza*.

During the time between our two meetings, I had read over Zitara's books and discussed his ideas with Carmine. I was much better prepared with time and ideas for this second interview.

The climb up to Gerace was especially breathtaking that day of our second meeting. The usual summer haze was gone and the air was crisp, the sea below shimmered brightly, the beach was a brilliant white-gold. We met that afternoon at the only hotel in Gerace, also owned by Zitara's boyhood friend.

Zitara was in the company of his friend, the proprietor, a large, heavyset man with thinning gray hair and a pleasant smile. Over the course of the afternoon, it became apparent that the friend was a businessman and not an academic like Zitara. They had been boyhood friends, but the hotel owner spoke a more regional and accented Italian and didn't participate in any of the substantive conversation.

We quickly learned from Professor Zitara's friend that he had built the hotel with the equivalent of one million dollars of his own money and another half million from the state. He was obviously pleased with the result. It was a beautiful hotel, small, but four stars all the way. A marble entry with an antique staircase from the original palazzo led up to a well-furnished anteroom. The elegant dining room had a very high ceiling with tall French windows on the opposing wall, which lent both elegance and light to the beautifully decorated, columned room.

We were treated to lunch. The waiters wore white jackets and gloves and each course came covered with silver-plated domes which were uncovered in unison.

The meal consisted of several dramatically presented courses: smoked salmon, turkey and *bresaola* with shredded lettuce; a risotto with mushrooms and wild vegetables; veal in a light wine sauce with spinach, and a Macedonia fruit salad for dessert.

Our group of professors and journalists chatted about generalities over lunch, which our generous host did not join. Across the table the two Italian journalists sat gabbing away. One, a very dark young man of about thirty, dominated the conversation. The younger man apparently was his assistant; he said little and took notes throughout the day. He had filled a notebook with scrawl by the end of the afternoon. The dark man spoke nonstop to the point where Professor Zitara had to interrupt him in order to get heard. I was never quite sure of just why they were there.

Carmine's Neapolitan folk songs played during lunch. I overheard him tell a friend on his *telefonino* that I had *un sacco di domande*, or a bag of questions, for Zitara, and that Zitara seemed to find my questions interesting.

After lunch we got into two cars and went partway down the mountain to the beautiful new home of our host. It was built into the cliff next to an old olive orchard and ancient farm. Zitara's friend showed us to the patio and offered drinks before we sat down and began our discussion in earnest. Our host disappeared after the drinks.

"When the lowly peasants would go off to America, they would go to New York and feel comfortable there," Zitara said without prompting. His passion for the subject was equaled by the speed at which he spoke. "You see, they carried with them the knowledge of civilization, the knowledge of how people work, so New York didn't intimidate them. On the contrary, they would leave here, poor farmhands from Calabria, with only the clothes on their backs and no education, and succeed in New York. When they would come home, they would laugh at how easy it was."

"Laugh?" I asked.

"Yes, they considered the Americans to be an innocent lot, not like the plotters and Machiavellians they'd known here. It was easy to deal with the Americans and with America—they offered honest pay for honest work.

"And for the *paesani* here, that was all they ever needed to get ahead. You wonder why so many successful Americans have Southern Italian roots—that's your answer. They went to America without formal education, without any wealth or influence, but they carried with them over two thousand years of knowledge of culture and of people. And they thrived. They knew the stories of mankind.

"They or their children became governors of New York and motion picture directors, famous athletes, physicists, actors, professors and bankers. They were Southerners, mostly, carrying with them the *Southern* sense."

At this point, the professor decided that he needed a nap.

I didn't oppose the suggestion, I'd been all but overwhelmed with his stream-of-consciousness way of talking. Besides, this was Southern Italy, and one didn't dine as we had without a proper afternoon rest.

The professor found a couch inside his friend's house. Carmine and I chatted while the two younger journalists huddled and talked rapidly and nonstop for the entire respite.

When Zitara awoke again, we spent a frustrating fifteen minutes or so, all five of us, trying to figure out how the coffee machine worked. We were saved by our host, who reappeared as mysteriously as he had disappeared and made coffee for us all. He joined us on the patio and sat in a large chair behind his friend Zitara. We began again, with coffee and sweets to renew our energy.

"Don't forget that many small things also made Southern Italian history," Zitara said, his eyes slightly puffy from his nap.

"Small things?" I asked.

"The mosquito; don't forget the *zanzara.*"

"You mean malaria?"

"Exactly. Southerners have fought that disease since man arrived here. The Greeks write of their battles with the fevers in Sicily and Magna Graecia. It's always been a key factor in life in Southern Italy, and sometimes a destructive one. Have you been to Paestum?"

I had.

"Then you'll remember that the entire community was abandoned because of the malady. Every Southern town has fought the effects of this tiny insect; fever was common and it was one of the original negative stereotypes about the South."

Our journalist friends from *L'Indipendènza* had buzzed like a pair of mosquitoes throughout the afternoon. They seemed to be dissecting every sentence the professor spoke. Zitara seemed a little irritated with the buzzing and would cast a glance in their direction from time to time, but the asides never dampened his apparent enthusiasm.

"You know," Zitara continued, "the nobility here were great admirers of Napoleon and of the French traditions. For nearly two centuries, the upper classes thought that true society was transacted in the French language. It was a European custom at that time; French was considered the language of the educated and the aristocracy." Zitara laughed.

"That all evaporated in 1943," added the professor.

"The War?" I surmised.

"That's the year the Allies got here." Zitara laughed again. "When the Allies came through here on their way to the North, they met with the town leaders, the mayor and his key people. But the American officers didn't speak Italian or French. The townspeople, the ones who had been in power here for so very long, couldn't speak English, only Italian and French. And that's when we knew the future."

"The future?"

"Well, guess who had to do the translating? It wasn't the hoi polloi or the educated class. It was the peasants who had been to America and had returned and, for whatever reasons, had been forced to remain here during the war. The *paesani* who in this village were only qualified for shit work, they were the only ones who could communicate with the greatest military power on earth. They were the only ones prepared for the changes that were about to come. The same people no one had taken seriously, the refuse who had gone off to America because there was nothing here for them.

"When the Allies landed it was very clear: The French-speakers, the educated, those who thought they would hold power and influence forever, became instantly irrelevant. The rough little farmhands and service workers were the only ones who could communicate with the New World.

"It was really funny and, for me, it showed what the people here were really all about—they've always known what was going on in the world and how to deal with it. They did this instinctively. They learned English because they knew that the American world was where they had to go to survive, while those who thought they knew what was going on stayed behind, kept their French lessons up, and played up to the government in Rome. It was the very nature of the peasants here to be on top of world development, absorbing culture, without even being able to articulate the thought or spell it out on paper."

The sun was setting in a brilliant orange ball. Long shadows drew themselves over our patio. A definite chill was in the air. It was time to end the thousand thoughts Zitara had tossed my way like so many dandelion spores floating on the wind. It was almost too much to process.

Our mysterious host took me by the arm and led me to an edge of the patio overlooking an animal pen. Three large pigs moved about below.

"Do you know what you're looking at?" He smiled broadly.

"Pigs?" I ventured.

"*La festa di capo d'anno*. Our New Year's feast." He laughed. "But don't tell the pigs. They've only a few months left."

Carmine was spending a brief vacation in Castrovillari, the mountain home of his Albanian ancestors, and still a village with Albanian dress and customs. He was anxious to join his wife there, and the dark was coming on.

We drove back up to Gerace, said our good-byes in a little square where we had parked, and got into our various vehicles to return to our various homes.

I descended the steep road to the highway, found the main drag and drove across the toe of Calabria. I reached the *autostrada* in Rosarno and followed it north for several hours. My mind was filled that night with a jumble of thoughts without an apparent connection. Notions of Romans and Greeks and English-speaking peasants and doomed pigs all tumbled about as I navigated the dark highway and returned to my temporary and ancient city.

5

The Concentration Camp
at Ferramonti

IN SEARCH OF THE PAST

About thirty-five kilometers north of the Calabrian capital of Cosenza, hidden among the mountain ranges to the east, west and north, lies a barely distinguishable spot called Ferramonti. The little village is a section of nearby Tarsia. Like every Norman hill town, Tarsia stands at the very top of one of the several steep peaks throughout the region.

The place is not easy to find; road signage is poor to nonexistent. You have to know where you are going before you can get there. The only indication from the autostrada that Ferramonti even exists is a big sign in yellow letters on a nearby gray block building indicating the hotel of the same name, not the village.

Roberto Musi's stories of a concentration camp in Calabria fascinated me. Until he told me the story in Amantea, I'd never heard of the place. All of the Italians I'd asked about the camp were also unaware of its existence.

The name Ferramonti does not ring bells.

Small wonder. There's very little to draw attention to the place in local lore, literature, or in physical markings in the area.

The highway that leads to the village is the Calabrian State Road SS 19, which is a narrow strand of asphalt paralleling the autostrada and barely wide enough for two modern-sized cars to pass each other safely. The road winds along hillside farms, occasional vineyards, several decrepit and decaying old buildings, scoots back and forth over a small winding stream, and shoots through occasional small crossroads not clearly marked. SS 19 is definitely a byway. Only locals use this path now.

What was once a train station sits next to the road, an abandoned building long past its prime. The railroad is not used; the section of tracks crossing the highway shine silver, the rest of the rails are now dark-red rust.

Just past the rail station sits a modern factory; Ultimo Jeans, or "The final word in blue jeans." There seem to be no other businesses in the area and thus no need for modern rail transportation.

In 1940, the station was used for the shipment of human beings, Jews and political enemies of the Fascist regime, shipped to what became the only concentration camp in Italy during the Second World War.

Campo di Concentramento

Just down the road from the dilapidated station and before arriving at the hotel, I finally found an old yellow and rusting sign indicating the Campo di Concentramento. Another sign, partially covered by vegetation, was a half block away, at the small intersection in the road by the town's general store. The sign pointed to the left. If the casual traveler wasn't looking for this place, he would never find it. There are no large or clear signs, no appropriate markers, nothing to indicate that a piece of Italian and world history lies in these now bucolic farm fields. And the lack of signs clearly indicates that people don't want to remember what happened here.

I drove down the road a little past the autostrada underpass. A few abandoned buildings stood in a partially cultivated farm. I got out of the car and walked through the fields. I looked through empty window frames into one of the buildings, a barnlike structure. It had evidently been built for some public purpose, but had not been used in a very long time.

Several other buildings dotted the field, none with intact roofs. Lizards scampered over the crumbling heat-baked walls in the bright afternoon sun. In between the buildings lay haphazardly placed vineyards and gardens.

The buzz of the highway adjacent to the field was constant. Some of the material used for the highway maintenance and the constant road rebuilding in this part of Italy lay at the bottom of the section of the field closest to the elevated highway.

I went back to the little general store and asked if the field I had been in was part of the camp. A young man behind the counter answered, surprisingly, in English.

"Yes," he said, "that was a part of the camp. The rest is on this side of the highway."

"This side?" I repeated. I had passed what looked like a marble wall and a gate leading to a private estate.

"That's the main part of the camp, the part that's left," he said.

I asked if there was any printed information available on the place, any pamphlets or tourist books.

"Maybe in Tarsia," he said; "there is nothing here."

The young man accompanied me along the thirty or so paces to the iron gate. I realized that what I had thought was a wall was, in fact, a white marble tablet. The inscription had been invisible to me from the car. The plaque marked the fiftieth anniversary of the dissolution of the camp in 1944 and had been placed there by the Ferramonti Foundation.

"This is what is left of the camp," the clerk said, waving toward a group of buildings all but hidden behind a tall iron fence.

The young man returned to his store. I walked to the big iron gates, held shut by nothing more than a piece of wire or heavy string. I untwined it and let myself in.

The place was a mess.

It was obvious that no maintenance had been done here for some time. On the contrary, there was a great deal of evidence of petty vandalism. The largest of the buildings stood in a state of decay, its main room—the contents of which I could see through a broken window—filled with abandoned household goods: overturned tables, a bicycle frame, what looked to be an old stove.

In the building that, judging by the sight of the two moldering brick ovens, had been a kitchen, an old wooden paddle for placing and retrieving bread lay next to the oven. The floor was littered with rotting leaves and pieces of trash.

Faded Italian and European Union flags waved in the slight breeze above what must have been the administrative building for the foundation. This building had obviously been updated since the end of the Second World War; a modern tile floor had been added and an oil-burning stove was placed along one wall. However, most of the windows in the building had been broken out, shards of glass littered the tile floor, and there was evidence of recent squatters; impromptu shades made from what looked like old tablecloths still draped across the windows of the two rearmost rooms.

If there was a foundation taking care of this place, they didn't meet very often and they certainly didn't visit here more than every couple of years.

Aside from the lizards and flies, I seemed to be the only other living thing interested in this place on this day.

And yet a long human drama had been played out here in real time less than two generations ago. These shabby and forgotten buildings, dilapadated and filled with a strong sense of inattention and shame, had served for four years as housing for almost four thousand inmates and seventy-five soldiers and guards. It stands today as an evocative epitaph to both the Italian Fascist past and, ironically, the nature of the Southern Italian character.

It seemed fitting that the place was empty and deserted. By the end of the Second World War, the forty million good Italian citizens who had been considered Fascists virtually vanished in Italy. Forty million republicans had miraculously taken their place. The Italians proceeded with their lives, seemingly making every attempt to erase the memory and history of things not fondly remembered and best not recalled.

It came as no surprise that a monument to anti-Semitism—which the Italian people have never really believed in or practiced—would not be something they would publicly mark. Nor would they be anxious to be reminded of Mussolini—whom the Italian people did embrace as an answer to the economic and political problems. Whoever made decisions around there apparently thought the place was best left to the weeds and hot summer winds.

Piecing together the story of Ferramonti was difficult. I could find no English-language texts published on the subject. The Italian texts—mainly three books written by Francesco Folino—are not readily available.

I called a friend, Lina Filice, a college professor in Cosenza, for help. I'd met Lina and her husband, Pino, at Rocco's place. Her family is originally from Calabria, where Lina was born, but her parents had immigrated to Canada, where they and Lina's three sisters now live. Lina wound up returning to Italy and marrying there. Her sisters and parents visit regularly and stay at Rocco's when they vacation at the beach.

"We really love the food there," said Lina. "There are certainly more luxurious places to stay in Amantea, but there's something very basic about Rocco's *pensione*."

I agreed.

Lina made a few calls on my behalf and we made arrangements to meet one morning at the hotel in Ferramonti. From there we planned to go up to the town hall in Tarsia. I had asked Lina to come along to help with translations and the local bureaucracy.

Lina was accompanied by her husband, Pino, and another fellow, Livio Volpintesta. We had coffee at the hotel and Pino explained that Livio knew someone in the Tarsia city hall. He would tell them I was an American "cousin" visiting from the States. That little subterfuge was designed to vouch for my character and would help get me the information I needed.

My "cousin" Livio Volpintesta was a pleasant middle-aged man dressed neatly in a gray business suit, and he seemed pleased to help with my quest. It is the way business is done in the South: know someone who can recommend you. Calling on a local city hall without help could wind up in a hopeless bureaucratic runaround. People are polite to strangers, but with a "cousin" from the area, a lot more would happen, and much more quickly. I was grateful that the Filices had been so thoughtful.

I asked about Calabria's role in the Fascist party during the Mussolini era.

"We were never as keen on Fascism in this area as they were in the North," Pino said.

Pino worked as an administrator for the city hall in Cosenza and had grown up in the Calabria area.

"In the South, it has always been a question of trying to satisfy Rome on one hand, while keeping them at a distance on the other. Mussolini did help some with the problem of unemployment during his early years in office, but his designs for foreign empires and military might were pipe dreams to the average Calabrian. We still needed railroads, highways, adequate medical care. We supported Fascism only to the extent that it could help us here with our problems—problems Rome had always had trouble understanding."

"We weren't so much Fascists as we were and still are pragmatists," Livio added. "This camp here meant some employment, so I'm sure some of the locals thought it a good idea. But we never backed the Nazi government and never believed in anti-Semitism."

We left the hotel and arrived at the hilltop city hall at the exact time of the appointment—which in Southern Italy meant we were early. We were escorted into Livio's friend's office, exchanged pleasantries, had the inevitable coffee. After a few minutes of small talk, my "cousin" said that I was interested in finding out more about the camp at Ferramonti. His friend said he had arranged for a bright young student from the area, Barbara Spina, to spend some time with me and accompany me to the camp. He explained that Ms. Spina was a graduate student at the University of Cosenza and was writing her thesis on the very subject, and assured me she could answer any questions I might have. She would be happy, he said, to share her information with an American writer. Especially the "cousin" of a local family.

Within a few minutes we were introduced to Ms. Spina, my "cousin" Livio returned to his work, and the Filices and I drove down the mountain with the young woman to the Ferramonti campsite.

Over the following months, based on Barbara Spina's wonderfully detailed account of the site; the Filices' translations and Pino's knowledge of the area as a native Calabrian; the memories of Cristina Marrari, the daughter of former camp marshal Gaetano Marrari; the Simon Weisenthal Center in Los Angeles; and Walter Wolff, a survivor of not only Ferramonti, but Dachau as well, I was able to gather the following story of Il Campo di Concentramento di Ferramonti....

"Enemies" of the State

The story of Ferramonti begins in the 1930s with the Mussolini government's imitation of Hitler's anti-Semitic laws. At first Mussolini opposed such legislation, smirking at the notion of racism, the myth of the "Aryan" superiority. But over time and with serious military failures in Albania and Greece, il Duce had to conform with his German Axis partner, whose assistance he now desperately needed for any further military actions. Under pressure from Hitler, anti-Semitic laws similar to those in Nazi Germany were enacted in Italy in late 1938.

While Italian Jews were not at first deprived of their property or deported under the Mussolini government, foreign Jews—mostly refugees from the northern parts of Europe where the Nazis had taken over—were detained. It was decided that they and other foreign "enemies of the state" should be rounded up and imprisoned together. Some political enemies, most notably Carlo Levi, as he clearly documented in his *Christ Stopped at Eboli*, were sent to the "backward" provinces in the South under house arrest.

The rolling mountain ranges of Calabria, Abruzzo and Basilicata were perfect for the physical, social and political isolation of troublemakers. The regions are remote, and communication with the rest of Italy and the world was extremely difficult during a period when the telephone was still not a common utility.

In June of 1940, the community of Tarsia was granted the concession by the state to erect a camp for the rest of the so-called enemies of the state. The property-owning Ferramonti family of Calabria gave up a substantial portion of its land in the hills north of Cosenza for construction of the camp, which began on June 4, just six days before Italy's official entry into World War II. By late June, enough work had been done to begin taking in prisoners. At that point only foreign Jewish men who had been arrested in the large cities of Northern Italy were being detained. By September, however, the camp included women and children as well. Ultimately, the entire inmate population came from France, England, China, Greece, Yugoslavia, Bulgaria, Poland and Hungary.

It was apparent early on that the Italians took a different approach to a concentration camp from their German allies. One original prisoner, a Pole named Chaim Pajes, asked Mussolini's permission to finish his studies at the university before being incarcerated. The police discussed his request with his professors and the university officials, who agreed to hear his dissertation prior to his arrest. It was arranged for him to meet with his faculty at 9 P.M. on the evening before his detainment so that he could leave for prison with his education completed. While the government was willing to strip him of his civil rights (a concept that really didn't exist in the Europe of the Axis), it didn't want to deprive him of his degree.

Not all inmates in Ferramonti were Jews; later on, political enemies from the Yugoslavian States of Slovenia and Croatia were included in the inmate population. The Chinese prisoners also fell into the political category, since no one in Mussolini's administration seems to have known just what to do with Chinese nationals in Italy.

The overwhelming majority of the inmates were highly educated professionals in various fields, such as the law, philosophy, medicine, dentistry and the rabbinical clergy.

It didn't take long for the inmates to organize themselves. Ninety-two drab barracks buildings were erected on the site for housing, each originally designed to house thirty-two prisoners. Each barrack elected a leader and, in turn, each barrack leader voted for an inmate "capo." A German Jew named Dr. Landau became the leader of the prisoners under this system and represented the inmate concerns to the camp commandant.

Inmate lawyers became trustees and helped mediate internal problems among the prisoners. They quickly created a school for the children, had a program for pregnant women, who were supplied with the necessities for their infants, created a library, formed a theater group (one inmate was a former famous Viennese actress), made up sports teams and did whatever possible to maintain a positive morale.

THE GUARDIANS; SOUTHERNERS IN CHARGE

Two Southern Italians ran the place. The original camp director was a Puglian officer, Paolo Salvatore, of Bari; while Gaetano Marrari, a sergeant major from Reggio di Calabria, was the "marshal," or head security officer, of the camp for its entire existence.

It seems that Marrari saw his principal responsibility as keeping the small contingent of Fascist militia stationed nearby out of the camp and its business.

"I'll tell you about Marrari," Roberto had said one evening in Amantea. "He saw his duty very clearly. He said his job was to see to it that those people survived the war. And by God, he was very successful. He certainly wasn't a murderer."

Marrari died in 1987. His daughter, who now lives in Reggio di Calabria, says her father remained in touch with many of the camp internees for his entire life. She added that he received innumerable letters, pictures of families and many presents over a span of forty-three years from grateful former prisoners. According to Signora Marrari, her father interpreted Fascism in his own way.

And it's in the philosophy of the camp officials where the story of Ferramonti becomes unique, and uniquely Italian.

Unlike their German counterparts, the Italians—both Northern and Southern—involved in the "legal" depravation of civil rights of the Jews and political enemies of the state had no anti-Semitic beliefs, no taste or liking for the situation and, in fact, took steps to make the camp as tolerable as possible for all involved. There were no mass deaths at Ferramonti. Four prisoners did lose their lives, but not as a result of Italian actions.

The Crati River flows through the area of the campgrounds. It runs to the south, where it joins the Busento in Cosenza, the town at the confluence of the two rivers. From there the Crati flows south to the end of the Italian peninsula and into the Ionian Sea at what was once the extraordinarily wealthy and luxurious Greek settlement of Sibari.

Legend claims that not far from the confluence of the two rivers, a little way up the Busento, the Visigoth Alaric was buried in the fifth century C.E.—the same Alaric who sacked Rome and ended the western Roman Empire. As he traveled south from Rome after the sack, his ships were destroyed in a storm at what is now Reggio di Calabria. The army returned to the north—some think to sack Naples, which he had failed to take on his initial run to the south—when he took sick and died in Cosenza. According to the legend, the course of the Busento River, upstream from the Crati, was diverted to bury the conqueror in what had been the riverbed, along with much of the loot of Rome. The river was then redirected to its natural path, but the actual location, if this tale is true, has never been found. There are currently archaeological efforts underway using infrared technology to study the terrain for any factual evidence of the story.

It is the same Crati making its way south through what was the camp at Ferramonti during the Second World War. And the river was a major focal point for camp activity. This was not a work camp; the inmates were imprisoned, not enslaved. The river served as a source of water, as laundry and bathing facilities, and a meeting point with the townspeople, where a very active barter began to take place. The inmates were given a stipend each month by the Italian government and regularly received Red Cross parcels, as well as letters and cash from their families. In one of the poorest areas of Europe, these stipends, parcels and money gave them a fair degree of wealth for that period and place.

Townspeople began a vigorous barter in eggs, clothing, fruits and vegetables, for items from Red Cross parcels and, of course, any form of currency.

It also seems there was a brisk trade for professional services.

"My grandmother had a toothache," Barbara Spina recounted. "She didn't trust the local dentist in Tarsia, so she would sneak past the guards, through the barbed wire and into the camp at night, to have her tooth fixed. She traded things from the family garden for the work."

Barbara's grandmother, Maria Carmela Greco, was nearly forty years old when her tooth acted up. Dentistry was not a common commodity in wartime Southern Italy, so the dentists at the camp were prized for their services.

Signora Greco had a cousin who had a problem with her leg. The cousin also preferred one of the internee doctors to whomever was available locally.

It also seems that sneaking into the camp at night was a great diversion from the grinding poverty and dullness of wartime Calabria. It was her grandmother's stories about her adventures in the camp that captured Barbara Spina's imagination and curiosity and led to her formal study of the place.

The original director of the camp, Paolo Salvatore, was aware of the barter, but, without giving official approval to the system, apparently looked the other way as it took place.

Looking the other way at some of the camp goings-on apparently cost Salvatore his job. In January of 1943, he was relieved of command for not fulfilling his orders and having an "attitude" that was too "benevolent." He was replaced by Mario Fraticelli, who announced that he was going to instill discipline in the place. He immediately instituted thrice-daily roll calls. The inmates readily complied, then went back to carrying on exactly as they had before, only now with Fraticelli calling the roll and *then* looking the other way.

The prisoners built a still in which they made a liquor from walnuts and figs, which helped "keep them warm" in winter and which was approved by the new commandant. They took over the camp ovens and baked unleavened bread in order for the Orthodox to be able to follow dietary rules. Three synagogues had been set up in the camp, along with a Greek Orthodox chapel, and places of worship for at least two other minor Eastern European religious denominations.

Since the prisoners were from so many differing countries, a great deal of sign language was used to communicate. There was much laughter at roll call over the Italians' pronunciation of the various foreign names. Only the Greek prisoners seemed to have taken umbrage with the roll-call mandate. All inmates were ordered to make the Fascist salute during the roll call. One Greek prisoner refused. He was eventually arrested by the Fascist militia that Marrari had worked so hard to keep away from the place. He seems to have been the only prisoner disciplined in this manner.

The fact that Southerners ran the camp is important.

"You have to remember," Pino Filice said, "the South has never followed the national law to the letter anyway, and especially during the Fascist period they did whatever had to be done to make the Rome government happy and go away.

"After all," he continued, "everyone here knew everyone else. They knew they would have to live with one another after the war. Ferramonti was hidden because it was something shameful for all of Italy and for the people here. But the Calabrians gave solidarity and food to the inmates. It wasn't much, but it was all we could offer in those times."

WALTER WOLFF

Walter Wolff, a German Jew, was born in Aachen, Germany, in 1917 and grew up in Frankfurt am Main. Imprisoned by the Nazis early on in the Third Reich, he was granted an unlikely and highly unusual release from Dachau. He and his family fled to Italy in the late 1930s, thanks to an entry visa granted by the Italian consulate in Germany (such a visa had been denied by the United States and several other countries). For a while, the Wolffs—Walter, his mother and brother—lived in relative peace in Salerno. But then Mussolini enacted anti-Semitic laws and the family wound up detained at Ferramonti.

Wolff, who is now retired on Long Island, New York, has written a memoir about his war years in Italy, *Bad Times Good People,* in which he tells the story of his family's survival during the Holocaust, their incarceration and escape and his years as "Valter Monti" in Casale Monferrato and Milano living with and protected by the Italians.

"Oh, I remember Ferramonti well," he says. "You know, the Italians were never really very serious about anti-Semitism. When we were first arrested, we were rounded up into a large group and guarded by five *carabinieri.* Only they didn't have any guns. They asked us to promise not to run away, and we didn't." He laughed at the memory. "You know, the Italians could be disorganized and that could be bad, but it's also very good. I like the Italian people. They were very kind to me. Many strangers took risks to save me during those years."

I pressed him for his recollections of the Calabrian camp.

Wolff had an ailment that was either beyond the scope of the inmate doctors or occurred prior to their arrival; he's unsure of the chronology.

"I went to the camp director and told him I needed to see a doctor. He told me to come back the next morning and he'd arrange for a police escort into the city. The next day there were three others waiting with me when a policeman showed up and took the four of us over to the train station and on into Cosenza. When we got to the city he asked us if we knew where we were going. We did. He told us to go off on our own and to meet him back at the train station at four-thirty that afternoon. He left us to wander off unaccompanied.

"Well, at four-thirty we were all back in the station, but no policeman. We were very concerned; we had to go back to the camp. After all, there could have been trouble, paperwork, unnecessary attention. We split up and each went in a separate direction to check the local bars. Sure enough, we found the fellow before too long, dragged him back to the train station, and made it back in time for dinner."

Wolff and his family were allowed to leave the camp for "house arrest" in the community of Casale Monferrato. There was another fellow named Wolff in the camp, who said he wanted to go along, so they told the director the man, who was in fact no relation, was a cousin. The nonrelated Wolff was allowed to leave with the family.

"It's funny," Wolff said more than a half century after his experience in Ferramonti, "at the time we thought we'd be better off away from the camp. But, in truth, we'd have been much better off if we'd stayed in the South. In the North we had to hide, forge documents and adopt new identities to avoid being sent away by the Germans. But in the South, at Ferramonti, the Germans never came."

THE ROUNDUP

One summer evening, Commandant Fraticelli and his wife backed a truck into the camp and began rounding up the internee children. In all, there were about a hundred youngsters held captive at Ferramonti. Twenty-one had been born in the camp. The inmates were puzzled when Fraticelli showed up with the lorry and demanded that the children be placed on board.

A rumor spread that the children were being sent to the northeast and would never be seen again. Mothers bordered on panic, fathers brooded with concern, a general pall was cast over the place.

One of the reasons for their fear was the knowledge of what was going on in other parts of the world. In early 1943, two young men who had escaped from the death camps in the north came through Ferramonti and told the prisoners of the horrors they had witnessed in Poland and Czechoslovakia. They had heard rumors of the gas chambers. They knew of mass executions starting to occur with more and more regularity as the Nazi regime became more and more barbarous.

However, a few hours after the children's departure on that summer evening in 1943, they were driven back into the camp and returned to their parents.

The Fraticellis had taken them into town for a *gelato*.

If there was ever a symbol for the extraordinary differences between the German and Italian camps, the night of the gelato run stands out as the most profound example.

There had also been cause for fear in the camp because everyone there realized how remote they were from civilization, how easy it would have been to commit atrocities such as were then occurring in the north without anyone's really knowing what was going on. It was a world gone mad. The inmates in Ferramonti had no guarantees of sanity on the part of their Italian captors.

In 1943, prior to the Allied landings at Salerno, the camp was bombed by the Americans, who had mistaken it for an Italian military installation. Four inmates were killed in the raid, another eleven wounded. The dead were buried in a religious ceremony at the public cemetery at Tarsia. They still lie there in graves marked with headstones paid for by the local government. The wounded were treated by both camp doctors and Italian doctors from the area.

MUSSOLINI FALLS. WHO'S IN CHARGE?

In the summer of 1943, a shadow of great uncertainty fell over the camp, as it had fallen over all of Italy. The Mussolini government had been "dismissed" by Vittorio Emanuele III in an almost comic opera series of circumstances.

The aging king had never fully understood his legal prerogatives and only turned on his dictator when the will of the Italian people turned clearly and overwhelmingly against the war. Only the Fascist fanatics continued to support what most other Italians believed to be a losing cause. Vittorio Emanuele became finally aware of his constitutional responsibilities, timidly removed Mussolini from office, and ordered him imprisoned at the Grand Sasso in Abruzzo.

"It was like a scene from a silly comedy movie," Carmine Colacino said during one of our many conversations at the University of Basilicata in Potenza. "The king finally got the *palle*–the balls–to fire Mussolini, then fearful of being bombed, or captured by Germans, ran around the country looking for a safe place to conduct a government, terrified by what he'd done. It was the final and most pathetic example of the complete failure of the House of Savoy to deal with the difficult and pressing problems affecting the country, and especially the South."

Leaving Rome was a catastrophic mistake by the king and his advisers. By absenting himself from the nation's capital, he created a vacuum of power which the Germans quickly moved to fill. Hitler ran a daring raid to Mussolini's mountaintop prison, rescued il Duce from his Italian captors and reestablished a puppet government at Salò in the North. This ultimately resulted in the breakout of civil war, the Nazi occupation of the northern half of the country, and bloody and costly battles for the Allies as they were now forced to advance north from Salerno and Anzio.

There were forty-five incredible days in between the fall of Mussolini and the formal surrender of Italy to the Allies while the king and the new government established themselves in Bari. Anything could have happened, and no one knew for sure what was happening. The king could have quickly surrendered the entire country to General Eisenhower, had he been able to secure the airport at Rome and a few other key military positions. Had he done so, the entire Allied Italian campaign might never have taken place. The king's run around the country made communication with the Allies virtually impossible.

The English played a role in the confusion. Anthony Eden, England's wartime foreign secretary, insisted that Italy unconditionally surrender. Prime Minister Winston Churchill wanted the Italians to join the Allied cause. The two leaders' dispute destroyed any meaningful negotiations during the critical month and a half.

The Germans moved into the Northern part of the country and Rome. They then began a war of retribution against their former allies. Their subsequent treatment of both Italian soldiers and citizens was as barbarous as their treatment of other "captured" enemy nations, fueled by their sense of betrayal by a former ally.

Had the king been able to convey the nature of his new government quickly and effectively to the Italian people, Mussolini's control in the North and the German occupation might never have occurred. But instead, there was continuing contradiction and confusion. No one knew who was in charge or what to do. The king's choice for his new prime minister was seventy-two-year-old Field Marshal Pietro Badoglio. The aged general, a pro-monarchist and anti-Fascist well past his prime, was seemingly befuddled and painfully unfamiliar with effective and complicated foreign relations.

In fact, Badoglio's dithering and complete lack of advance planning led to the wholesale slaughter of Italian troops in the Aegean, once the Italians did negotiate an armistice. As Richard Lamb so clearly documents in his seminal work, *War in Italy 1943-1945, A Brutal Story*, there were absolutely no plans made for the disposition of the Italian troops. Commanders in the field had no idea of just what was expected of them. Some fought with their former German allies, others surrendered, still others tried unsuccessfully to join Allied forces. Italian officers were shot by the hundreds, thousands of troops were either executed or sent into slave labor and still others died fighting the Germans with no hope of reinforcements or supplies. Churchill had been pushing to use the Italian troops to help with the war effort in the Aegean theater. Eden, of course, opposed that position, but no one imagined that the end result would be ruthless massacre.

Despite Anthony Eden's anti-Italian stance during the Second World War, Italians have always admired the English. During the war, the English monarchy stayed with their people. Photos of the king and queen were seen worldwide as they defiantly walked through the wreckage of London in the aftermath of the blitz bombings, offering solace and showing solidarity with their people. The English king and queen stood stoically in London, and their eldest, his daughter (the future queen), volunteered as an ambulance driver.

The Italian king ran to Bari with a group of ineffective ministers.

After the war the Italians voted against the monarchy and forbade the king and any male heir from ever again entering Italy. In early 2002, the Italian senate, under the leadership of Prime Minister Silvio Berlusconi, voted to rescind that ban. Press reports at the time said that the king had been ousted as a result of his pro-Fascist stance. But the Italians I spoke with recalled that his flight and his having signed the anti-Jewish legislation were the real reasons for both his shame and his banishment.

FERRAMONTI'S FINAL DAYS

The collapse of the Italian government in late 1943 meant no one at Ferramonti knew to whom to report or what to do about the concentration camp. A unique solution was reached: the leader of the inmates, Dr. Landau, and the commandant, Mario Fraticelli, would go to Rome together and get clear instructions. Since Dr. Landau would be considered an enemy of the state by the Germans and the Germans were moving south, the journey would have to be a secretive one. The two would have to travel by foot and by night.

It took three months for the two men to make their way from Ferramonti to Rome and back again. Three months of staying hidden and away from the Germans, who were now occupiers of an enemy country. And when they reached Rome, Fraticelli learned from the now German-controlled Fascist government that a letter had gone out to the camp ordering that the prisoners be sent to Bologna, a staging camp for Jews being transported to Poland and Auschwitz. The letter had never reached Ferramonti. The postal service in Cosenza had managed to "lose" it.

Meanwhile, as Landau and Fraticelli were wandering the countryside, most of the male inmates slipped out of the camp and moved toward the Allied lines or into the hills to join the resistance. The women and children remained, but the threat of deportation still hadn't ended.

One day shortly before the Allies arrived, a German general on his way to the North came through the area by rail. He decided to stop and inspect the camp. Word went out in the community that a Nazi officer was about to pay a surprise visit.

The inmates thought quickly and ran up a quarantine flag in place of the Italian one. The local priest came hurrying over and met the general at the main gate. He made up a story about cholera being rampant and that the general was welcome to enter, but only at his own risk. The German declined the priest's offer, and once again the inmates of Ferramonti were spared the fate of the other captives of the Third Reich.

Finally, on September 14, 1943, the British liberated the camp, the first of any concentration camp to be liberated. The site continued in operation for another two years as housing for displaced persons. Many of the original Ferramonti inmates stayed in the area after the hostilities and married local Italians.

Jews in the North of Italy did not fare as well. As soon as the Germans had taken over Rome, they immediately went to the largest Roman synagogue next to the ancient Forum and collected the records for the congregation. They then began a systematic rounding up of all of the Roman Jews they could find. Those who could not find a hiding place or didn't have the health or wherewithal to leave the city were captured, taken to the large prison on the Lungotevere at the foot of the Vatican Hill and then shipped north, first to a staging camp in Northern Italy and finally to Auschwitz. Of over twenty-one hundred Jews caught and deported from Rome, only five came home. Of the 44,500 Jews living in Italy at the start of the war, including its then-territory of Rhodes, 7,680 were deported, almost all *after* the German takeover. Only a small percentage of those deported survived. Others in the North, like Walter Wolff, spent nearly two years on the run, in hiding, living with false identities and spending every waking moment trying to avoid the Germans and remain alive.

The fate of the inmates in Ferramonti speaks of the nature of the Calabrians who ran the place, their instincts and essential humanity. They were not the brutes their Northern neighbors had become, they were not anti-Semites. Yet they were technically Fascists, had endorsed Mussolini and backed many of his programs. The Fascist government had built Ferramonti and had written laws that denied civil rights to several minority groups in Italy during the war.

That these "enemies of the state" were sent to Ferramonti was ironically their ultimate salvation; their basic human freedoms had been stripped away, they were incarcerated and forced to live in cramped and public housing, they were denied the right of citizenship and deposed of their property—not by the Germans, but by the allied Italians.

And it was Italians, the Calabrians in particular, who built and managed the camp, and who kept them alive.

Had the inmates not been sent so far south, had the camp been built in what became a German-occupied area, they would have assuredly been transported to the death camps and most would have perished in the Holocaust. It was the South and Southerners who kept them alive, while still going along with the system that denied the nearly four thousand Jews and political detainees their freedoms.

It is not a subject that sits comfortably with people in Calabria, even to this day. The location of the camp, the extremely poor signage leading to the area, the autostrada running through the middle of the site, construction equipment being stored on what had been campgrounds; all of these are strong indications that people don't want to be reminded of a bitter past, of their relationship with Mussolini and his Fascist and Nazi friends. After all, this is a country with very well-preserved Greek and Roman ruins, some outdating Ferramonti by more than two millennia. A memorial from the relatively recent past wouldn't be that hard to maintain if there were a desire to do so.

MEMORIES OF DACHAU

Standing in the heat of the baking fields of Ferramonti, I thought about the first concentration camp I'd ever seen: Dachau. That camp, near Munich, is a place almost diametrically opposite the one where I now stood. While stationed in Germany with the army, I'd been to Dachau as

part of my work. We had a unit there attached to our Bamberg headquarters, which I'd visit infrequently.

While in Dachau on temporary duty, I was housed in a section of an
old German casern that had been the headquarters building for the
Nazi SS during the Second World War. I stayed in a room that had been
used by one of the top-ranking SS officers. It was a large room with a
private shower—very rare for both the army and Germany in those days.
The room had a small balcony that looked out over the camp. I'd stand
at the window and stare at the massive yard of gray pebbles and
couldn't even begin to imagine what the officer who occupied that
room during the war must have seen, or, even worse, what he must have
been thinking.

It had to have been a ghastly, sickening sight. Tens of thousands of
Jews and political prisoners died at Dachau, most from abuse or star-
vation. Some were the victims of medical experiments. All were terror-
ized and brutalized by the Nazi state. Only the healthiest and
strongest survived this horror. All but impossible to imagine in a time
far away.

My sister, Marie, had visited me one summer after her graduation
from high school back in Pennsylvania. She had been staying in Bamberg
with some married friends who lived off the base. I took a leave and traveled with Marie south by train through Bavaria and Austria, visiting
Salzburg and Vienna, and on returning stopping in Munich. While there
on a Saturday evening, Marie suggested we find a church and go to
Mass the following morning. I countered with the suggestion that we
visit Dachau. I'd never seen it as a tourist and wanted to go through the
campgrounds. She agreed.

The next morning we took the short seven-mile train ride to the
camp. Following the markers pointing the way, we entered through the
original gates. The words "*Arbeit Macht Frei*," scrolled in wrought iron
above the entrance, still announced its ironic, deceptive, evil message.
The original curved cement posts built to hold barbed wire outlined the

boundaries of the camp, and the original watchtowers still sat menacingly at its corners.

A large exhibit hall was at one end of the grounds and an interdenominational chapel at the other. In between, cement curblike structures outlined the spaces where barracks once stood. Only a few original buildings still exist. The entire camp area, which was officially opened as a memorial park in 1968, was then covered with gray gravel. Small signs along the way give the ghastly statistics and facts of the place. In the main hall there are several photographs with accompanying text.

I'd never anticipated the effect the place would have on my sister. She knew of concentration camps, she'd read *The Diary of Anne Frank* when she was ten or eleven years old and had been deeply affected by the story. She had kept a scrapbook of articles on the Jewish girl from Amsterdam who died at the hands of the Nazis at the end of the Second World War. I was sure she knew of the shameful and sickening events that took place in Germany and at Dachau from 1933 to 1945. But one look at her face told me that if she'd ever heard of this place, she'd never truly understood its meaning until this summer Sunday morning near Munich. She became physically ill. We had to leave.

"I can't believe the way they keep the place," she said later that afternoon as our train sped north toward Nuremberg. "These people seem so normal, so human. Yet, they act as if this camp were a normal part of history. How could anyone do such things to other people?" It was a trauma that would last for a long time and I felt guilty for having inadvertently inflicted it. "What's most awful to me," she said, "was how calmly everyone went about their business. It's like some sort of sanitized amusement park."

Hers was not an uncommon reaction.

It certainly wasn't an uncommon reaction in Calabria, even during the Second World War. If there is any redemption for those who supported the Fascists in Italy, it is that they didn't behave like the Germans. Eighty-five percent of all the Jews living in Italy at the start of the war survived, many with the help of the Italians—and especially the Calabrians, who built and ran the only large Italian concentration camp.

There were so many contrasts. In Dachau there are vendors along the way to the camp selling everything from souvenirs to food. In Calabria, it is hard to find anyone who even knows about the place.

In Dachau there is a large building filled with photographs of the most awful and painful human degradation, an empty camp starkly outlining the many buildings that once housed starving and dying prisoners.

In Ferramonti there are no photographs or exhibits. Buildings have been completely neglected, vines and weeds have taken over the barracks outlines.

In Dachau, guards sat in watchtowers and murdered anyone trying to escape. Prisoners were forced to stand for hours wearing thin rags in frigid temperatures during interminable roll calls. Guards routinely beat or summarily executed prisoners.

At Ferramonti, Cristina Marrari recalls her father, the top guard at the camp, smiling as he walked arm in arm with the inmates. There is no record of a single inmate having been physically abused or harmed. When Marrari died, his daughter received dozens of condolence letters from his former prisoners.

Yet, while Dachau has been turned into a place for remembering, Ferramonti appears to be a place forgotten.

They had to stack the bodies on truck and train beds to take the dead away from Dachau.

All but four prisoners were living and walked away from Ferramonti. Many—no one seems to know the exact number—remained in the community and married locals.

A professor at the University of Cosenza has staged a protest in the Calabria media regarding the Ferramonti camp's condition. He has charged the politicians of Tarsia with neglecting the decrepit facility, and is especially concerned that the highway department is continuing to store construction materials on the site. The mayor of Tarsia has replied on the defensive. All involved in the debate claim to support the memory of the camp and the inmates.

Yet the heat, flies and lizards seem to be the only permanent guardians of this decaying artifact from the past, a unique and ironic monument to Fascist evil and, ultimately, Southern Italian humanity.

6

"U Figlio di Giovanni"

NEW YORKERS

While staying at Rocco's, I struck up a conversation with the two young men who came from the Campania town of Sala Consilina. I had smiled when I heard the name of their *paese* and told them I had been there. They seemed surprised.

"Do you have family there?" one of them asked.

"No," I said, "but a friend in the army did and we visited his family there many years ago."

They were happy to hear that I knew their town and had visited the place. I was happy to be reminded of one of my first important experiences in traveling about Italy. That initial venture into family searches would stay in my memory for a very long time and serve as my only experience of finding an Italian family until my own search many years later for my own family.

Tommy Durante was a New Yorker who had been drafted and, like the rest of us in Germany at the time, somehow wound up in Europe during the height of the action in Vietnam. We all counted our blessings.

The New Yorkers I met in the army were always special. They had a way of carrying themselves and of dealing with the military the rest of us could only admire. In a word, they were *gutsy*. There was an air about them, an aura that said they would take just so much guff and no more. I always believed the rest of us were more easily cowed.

The New Yorkers even wore their uniforms a little differently, talked with their brash and broad short *a* accents and, most of all, compared absolutely *everything* on the face of the earth with its counterpart in New York, even if it had no counterpart in New York. For them, New York was the fundamental, absolute seminal start and definitive end to, and for, all things.

Tommy was no different, except that he was not a classic tough guy, but an amiable young man who enjoyed laughter and, while being fully convinced that nothing could ever equal anything that New York could offer, was at least willing to try some of the food in Germany while waiting his time to get back home.

Tommy did bring one thing with him that even most other New Yorkers couldn't pull off: he showed up with his cousin, Mike LaGrega. The rest of us were in complete awe of that particular coup over military planning and logic. None of us had been able to stay with friends or relatives, but these two New Yorkers had managed to come into the service through the same draft board and wind up at the same duty station together. It was an astounding feat.

Mike and I became roommates of a sort; we shared a small squad room with a few other soldiers. I made a study of Mike. He became the colonel's driver, seemingly without effort. It was a plum job that, until Mike showed up, at least, had required political connections and the finesse of a ballerina. But Mike heard the job was open, decided he wanted it and went in and asked for it.

I never saw Mike in anything other than a perfectly pressed uniform, his fatigues stiffly starched, his boots so highly shined they reflected the light in bright radiating beams. He was always immaculate, his hair was always perfectly cut, even his mustache was trimmed to an exact measurement.

Tommy, on the other hand, wasn't quite as gung ho as his cousin. He tended to be a little more casual in dress and manner, his uniform a little more baggy and less starched than his cousin's, his boots a little duller. Tommy's father's family, the Durantes, were related to the famous American singer and entertainer Jimmy Durante. Mike LaGrega was related to Tommy on his mother's side.

All of the New Yorkers whom I recall from the army had one goal: to get back to New York. While most of us tried to save up money and leave-time for exotic runs to Paris or hurried train trips to Amsterdam or short hops to London, the New Yorkers insisted on spending their leaves and money in New York. Especially if there was a young woman in the picture and, given our ages and hormones at the time, there almost always was.

I remember asking Tommy why he didn't bring his girlfriend to Europe. Wouldn't they see something new they couldn't see at home?

As I recall, this struck him as a rather novel, though doubtful, idea.

While the rest of us would charge about the local towns and villages on the weekends and travel to the larger cities over holidays and leaves, the New Yorkers, Tommy and Mike included, seemed perfectly happy hanging around the barracks, shooting pool and killing time.

And so I was completely flabbergasted one day when Tommy and Mike suggested a trip to Italy. I think Tommy's young lady might have disappeared from the picture by that time, but whatever the reason, it was a really bold move for my New York buddies.

And, while I'd like to flatter myself that my two friends wanted to enjoy my companionship, I was also the only one of their acquaintances in our unit who had his own car—an old VW Beetle—and some connections in the supply room to help with camping gear and food. Of course, it didn't hurt that we all shared vowels at the end of our names so that, even though I wasn't from New York, I was at least semi-acceptable in their social circle.

Tommy had a family friend who would be visiting relatives in Naples; he wanted to visit with her family; then we would all make a pilgrimage to the Durante family homestead, which Tommy described as "somewhere near Naples."

I, too, had wanted to go off searching for my roots, but without a word of Italian and absolutely no idea of where my family came from, I didn't want to venture that far on my own. (My father had written that he thought my grandmother had "a brother who was a farmer near Potenza." Some years later I would learn that the only almost-correct part of that statement was that my grandmother had two brothers who had remained in Italy. Everything else was completely wrong, but that wouldn't be cleared up for decades to come.) Searching for Durantes seemed a fine project for me to tag along on, so, on a clear July day, we loaded the roof rack on the VW with a case of C rations my supply-room friend had provided, sleeping bags, tents, a few personal items, and took off for the South.

THE SUMMER OF '68

We crossed over from Germany into Italy via Austria and the Brenner Pass. The little blue Beetle groaned up the mountains with its load of soldiers and their belongings.

A group of young Germans passed us—as nearly everyone did—as we struggled up a long grade. As they drove by, they made pantomime signals which we couldn't interpret. They seemed concerned about something; it didn't seem they were playing a prank on us. Finally, the car overtook us and slowed down. One of the young men kneeled on the backseat, reached into the back window ledge and struck a match.

"A match," I mulled. "What could that mean?"

"My God, *we're on fire!*" Mike shouted. "That's what they've been try-ing to tell us."

I pulled over to the narrow shoulder as quickly as I could, and we popped out of the car like circus clowns, running about in circles in search of smoke. We finally determined that we had been flagged down for violating German road propriety, the car was fine. I had the habit of driving with the lights on, a radical departure from the European norm at the time. In Germany or Austria, one did not put headlights on in the daytime. The fellow striking the match had meant "light," not "fire."

I turned the lights off and we proceeded undisturbed. (I'd forgotten the incident until my most recent tour through Italy driving a new Euro-pean car made to American specifications. This car came with lights that automatically came on when the car was started. I was subjected to a constant barrage of flashing headlights and inventive hand signals from my road companions for the entire journey. Europeans don't give up their traditions and customs lightly.)

We drove south, camping out along the way to save what little money we had. One night, at a camping site next to Lake Bolzano, we had a meal of tomatoes, fresh bread and sausages we'd bought at a nearby market. We arranged our shelter halves into a sort of tent arrangement attached to the side of the little car and climbed into our sleeping bags just as it became dark. Before long, we heard a strange scratching sound. Sleep was impossible. Tommy got out a flashlight and told us we were surrounded by "huge" lizards wildly thrashing about in the dark. I don't know if they were searching for the crumbs from our meal or what, and I never really got a close look at one; all of us were in the car in a matter of seconds and spent the night jammed and sleeping as best we could in our little por-tions of the VW, soldiers utterly defeated in our battle with nature.

We were the typical first-time tourists in Italy. Stopping in Florence, we did a mad dash through il Duomo and the area surrounding it, waited in a long line at the Galleria to see Michelangelo's *David,* battled tourists and heat to have lunch at a nearby sidewalk café for our first taste of genuine Italian pizza. We decided it would be too expensive to eat in restaurants, we spent our evenings in campgrounds, amply provided throughout Italy for budget-minded travelers. It was then I vowed I would one day return to Italy when I could afford to eat anywhere I liked—that would become my standard for success in life. At first light the next morning we took off for Rome, thinking we'd learned something about Florence and the Renaissance.

In Rome we drove directly to the Vatican. In those days it was still possible to find on-street parking, a modern-day fantasy. We hurried through the great basilica, saw the *Pietà* for about fifteen seconds, and headed on to the museum. Like all first-timers, we were amazed at how long it took to get to the Sistine Chapel. Once there, we strained to see the darkened Michelangelo ceiling as we were pressed by the throngs of sweaty sightseers and hushed and rushed through by the urging of the guards.

It wasn't what any of us had expected.

The Sistine Chapel is all but impossible to comprehend under normal circumstances, let alone while jostled and hurried. (Years later I would return with an artist friend on a cold, rainy morning in February to avoid other tourists and take the time to really look at the place. By then, too, thanks to the Japanese, who had donated the funds, the restoration of the ceiling had just been completed. The colors were sharp and bright and the composition is simply awesome and demands much more than a casual run-through.)

All of us good Catholic Italian boys bought rosary beads for our grandmothers and other religious mementos for our families. The small replica of Michelangelo's *Pietà* remained on my uncle's mantel until his death more than twenty-five years later. I'm still finding souvenirs from that trip in the homes of my relatives.

The following day we ran through the Forum and Colosseum area accompanied by a borrowed guidebook. I took another oath: One day I would return and revisit these places without a timetable. That first experience wasn't even a taste, more of a tease. It was not a satisfying or illuminating visit, though I would see hundreds of tourists doing exactly the same thing while I was living in Rome many years later.

The evening we spent at the camping grounds near Rome stands out vividly in my mind. The camp was filled with young travelers, mostly Europeans who, like us, were making do on a limited budget. The area included a cantina where we purchased fresh-baked bread, salami and vegetables—this was Italy, after all—and we sat at nearby communal tables and shared food and drink with our camp mates. We met a group of young Australians and naturally gravitated toward them, happy to communicate without need of translation.

I had bought a copy of the English-language *Herald Tribune* in Rome. The headlines that day were about the 1968 Democratic Convention in Chicago, where police had moved in against antiwar demonstrators and, from the looks of the pictures we saw in the paper, all hell had broken loose.

It seemed so odd to be sitting in Rome in the cool evening of a perfect summer day and read about riots and bloodshed at home. The disturbances in Chicago that summer followed the Tet offensive in South Vietnam that January, and a spring of assassinations and riots throughout the United States. Robert Kennedy and Martin Luther King had been murdered. It was an election year. Lyndon Johnson was leaving the presidency, choosing not to run again, but mostly forced to leave office by his failure in Southeast Asia. Opposition to the Vietnam War was reaching a fevered pitch. In many ways, it was the strangest year I can remember. (And it would get even stranger and far more personal just a month later, when the Russians would march, heavily armed, into Czechoslovakia to quell that country's drift toward democracy. We were stationed thirty-five miles from the Czech border. We would spend several weeks in the field that cold fall on official alert, thinking we could be going to war at any moment.)

Many of our fellow campers that July evening in Rome stopped by to commiserate with us, to ask us our impressions of what was happening in America. It was a question for which we didn't have an answer. In those days, very few had any answers. To have spent 1968 abroad, as we did, was like looking at America through the skewed lens of another language and culture. The times seemed all but incomprehensible. It was that year, and the events of that year which, more than any other factor in my life, led me to journalism as my profession. I had to get back and start asking questions. That night on the outskirts of Rome was a troubling turning point for me; I experienced a feeling of isolation and confusion I've never forgotten, just as that summer was a pivotal one for our entire American generation.

And though we had no way of evaluating conditions in Italy during our first visit there, 1968 was also the pivotal year for Italy and the Italian economy. Still referred to as "*the* year" by older Italians, it marked the first year in the post-World War Two era that Italy finally reentered the world market as a strong and viable competitor, its people now fully evolved from poverty and need into middle-class wealth and comfort.

REUNION IN SALA CONSILINA

Despite the backdrop of international turmoil, our little self-appointed patrol was happy to continue its hurried discovery of what had once been home to all of our ancestors. While disturbed by the news from home, it was not going to interfere with our journey into our heritage and history.

We reached Naples and spent a night on the floor of an apartment belonging to the relatives of Tommy's family friend, who was fluent in Italian or, more appropriately, the Neapolitan dialect, and had visited often. She encouraged us to learn the language and evidently had a great love for Naples and Italy.

It was a link my family had long lost. I felt a stranger in this mini family reunion from both sides of the Atlantic, but a welcomed stranger, nonetheless.

The next afternoon we headed off through the incredible jumble of crowded streets in Naples, found the main north-south highway (the autostrada was still being built at that time) and headed southeast.

On a beautiful summer's evening, we reached Sala Consilina.

It was my first immersion into a virtual live Italian grand opera.

Tommy had no idea of where his aunt lived. He knew the name of the town, had an address, but none of us knew where we were, or where we needed to go. Our lack of information was further hampered by the fact that, between the three of us, we spoke maybe six or seven Italian words at best, and they were questionable words at that. I pulled over to the side of the road after passing through the city gates. Almost immediately we were surrounded by youngsters on bicycles, attracted by the bright green USA plate on my Beetle.

"Americani!" We could hear the word fluttering through the growing crowd of youngsters. Of course we knew at least that much Italian; they were referring to us.

"Dove è la casa Beatrice Cairo?" Tommy asked a nearby youngster in the over-pronounced poor Italian that only Americans seem able to speak.

The boy asked a question in return that none of us understood.

"Famiglia Durante," Tommy said, pointing to his chest.

"Durante?" The group now completely encircled the small car. I felt like Captain Cook on some exotic South Pacific isle being closely scrutinized by the natives.

"Sì," said Tommy, now gaining confidence in the language he couldn't speak.

"Giovanni Durante?" asked one of the youngsters.

"My father," said Tommy, smiling. *"Mio padre,* John Durante."

"Giovanni?" the lad repeated. There was something apparently very special about this name that none of us was aware of.

"*Sì, mio padre,* John Durante," Tommy said. It was clear they understood the word *padre.*

The cry went out through the youngsters and from them to anyone within earshot. "*U figlio di Giovanni,*" they shouted. "*U figlio di Giovanni.*"

Passersby stopped and asked questions of the kids. They in turn called out to others in the houses along the street.

"*U figlio di Giovanni, u figlio di Giovanni.*"

"Who the hell is Giovanni?" I asked, completely puzzled, as the chant grew louder on the street. "I thought we were looking for someone named Beatrice?"

"My father, John, I guess," said Tommy.

"But how do they know him?" I wondered.

"He stopped by here during the war," Tommy said.

"*La casa Beatrice…*" Tommy started again.

"*Sì, sì, Signora Beatrice. Venga, venga.*" They waved, motioning for me to follow their bicycles.

What happened next can only be described as an impromptu parade. Suddenly we were at the center of a huge group of youngsters on bicycles. Passersby walked alongside our crawling blue Beetle, children ran ahead and behind calling out to neighbors, townsfolk came out onto the street and called to the marchers, all of whom shouted back the same Italian phrase, "*U figlio di Giovanni.*"

"If this Giovanni is your dad, he must have made some impression here," Mike said.

"Must have," agreed Tommy.

The parade led up a hill on the outskirts of town and into a small *vicolo,* a lane just wide enough for our Volkswagen. We stopped midway up the cobblestoned street in front of an ancient facade. Several of the youngsters were already knocking on the huge double-paneled wooden doors. An old woman finally poked her head out to ask what was going on. A great deal of rapid Italian got exchanged, with "*U figlio di Giovanni,*" repeated often as she asked questions. The kids pointed excitedly to our car.

Tommy smiled brightly.

The old woman came over to the passenger's door where Tommy sat. Tommy began speaking some strange language, English pronounced like Italian and as many Italian words as he knew, all rapidly jumbled together. He pointed to his chest while using a variety of near Italian nouns to describe himself as Tommaso, son of Giovanni, and every other family name and relationship he could put into his semi-language.

It was clear by her reactions that the old woman recognized something in Tommy.

Beatrice opened the door and pulled Tommy from the car with a great amount of hugging and sighing. Then she greeted Mike and me, mostly through gestures. She called out to one of the youngsters, sending him flying off on some sort of errand. Beatrice smiled shyly as the crowd of bicyclists and pedestrians cheered and celebrated Giovanni's son's arrival. She motioned for us to follow her into the ancient home.

We passed through a small courtyard and entered the surprisingly well-furnished and comfortable house. Beatrice called out to someone on the upper floor as we clustered about the center of what was apparently the family room.

A middle-aged woman descended the stairs and greeted us. From the few words we could follow, we learned that she, too, was named Beatrice, apparently the daughter of the older Beatrice.

The older woman showed Tommy a wall of photographs, undoubtedly every picture that had ever been sent from America. She and Tommy pointed out Tommy's father and family and they spoke in an excited and rapid jumble of English and Italian as the pictures explained their relationship. This was clearly an event for the family in Sala Consilina.

The second Beatrice, in turn, called out to still someone else on the second floor. This time a beautiful young woman about our age came down the stairs and was introduced as the daughter and granddaughter—still another Beatrice—now three in all. Dante would have loved this house.

There was a great deal of hand motions going on. I stood off silently to the side and took it all in. It was quite a show. Eventually we were seated about the room on chairs that had been fetched by the youngest Beatrice as the middle Beatrice poured wine into small water glasses the eldest Beatrice had distributed.

"I know this wine," said Tommy, "my dad makes this at home." The wine had an aroma that reminded me of so many family gatherings in Pittsburgh. It was becoming clear to me that so many things about the Italian-American experience were fairly universal and not always what they seemed. Wine was a beverage, but this wine was a symbol of hospitality and unity, the same way the church used it.

I was starting to understand the layers.

SAM AND GIOVANNI

A knock at the door interrupted the festivities. An older man was admitted into the house by the youngest Beatrice. He entered the living room, nodded perfunctorily in our direction and spoke rapidly with the eldest Beatrice for several minutes as we all sat silently and wondered about the exchange. He was asking a series of questions of the older woman and looked our way several times. Beatrice replied calmly to each of his queries and pointed to the photographs she had taken down from her wall and arranged neatly on the coffee table in front of her. We heard the phrase *"U figlio di Giovanni"* again a couple of times during the conversation.

Finally the older man turned to us.

"Hi, guys," he said in New York-accented English. "I'm Sam. I'm from Brooklyn."

We all laughed.

"I just wanted to make sure you were who you said you were. Beatrice sent a messenger to ask me to come over and translate for her. I didn't want anyone trying to take advantage of this woman."

We were all delighted to add Sam to the party, and Tommy seemed especially relieved that our communication problems were apparently over. Within moments, the middle Beatrice had provided Sam with wine.

"Salute!" or "Cheers!" we all shouted in unison.

It was like being home on a Sunday afternoon with the neighbors stopping by.

The next several hours flew by in a rush of sensations. Before we knew what was happening, we sat at a large table filled with food. Neighbors brought over additional courses at what seemed like five-minute intervals for at least an hour.

Beatrice apologized several times for "not being prepared" for our visit and proceeded to feed us a meal the likes of which none of us had eaten in a very long time, while changing the tablecloth three or four times in between courses, as if serving visiting royalty. We had *macaroni* with tomato sauce, olives and sausages native to the area, cold meats, a variety of breads and cheeses, several bottles of wine both homemade and branded, condiments of every sort, roasted peppers in oil with garlic, marinated eggplant, fresh tomatoes and cucumbers—more food than we could eat, all the while accompanied by smiles and toasts from the ladies Beatrice.

It was a fascinating and moving experience for all of us, though this was clearly Tommy's evening. Mike, the youngest Beatrice and I sat mostly silent and smiling in the shadows while watching the performance.

Sam told us his story; he had retired from a government job in New York and had returned to the village of his birth to live on his pension. It was a common thing for many Italian retirees of his generation to return to Italy during that period; their American pension checks went much further there than in the States. Sam was plainly enjoying himself and undoubtedly had served as interpreter before, a role he seemed to take quite seriously, given his screening of our credentials. I'm sure he enjoyed the food as well.

The elder Beatrice, through Sam, asked about my family; where were we from in the States and where had the families originated from in

Italy? She brightened when I told her we thought my father's family was from Potenza.

"We have many relatives there," she said; "our families are neighbors."

Sam told us about the village—a story that I was to hear many, many times over the next several years—how all the men his age had left there in the early part of the twentieth century. Most had settled in the New York and New Jersey areas. All had gone to find work.

"There was nothing here for a young man when we left," he said. "The only work in this area was farming, and if you didn't have land, you were out of luck. This was no place to live as a young man." He sighed, then smiled as he looked about the table at the many curious faces. "But it ain't bad for an old man, I can tell you that." He laughed.

Tommy, Sam and Beatrice the eldest went over the exact identities of the people in the photos that adorned the signora's wall. Then the Beatrices three retrieved a family album which they showed Tommy and pored over with much oohing and aahing as they went along. There was always special reference made to Giovanni, Tommy's father, who had been the only other member of the family to have returned to this homestead from the extended family in the States.

Oddly, Jimmy Durante, the man I would have thought to have been the most famous name from this village, was never mentioned by anyone that entire evening. Instead, the talk was always of John Durante, "Giovanni."

THE WINTER OF '43

"When did Giovanni get here?" I asked. "At the end of the war?"

"No, it was during the war," Sam told us. "It was the winter of 1943. Do you boys have any idea of what was going on in Italy that year?"

We shook our heads. I had seen the movie *Two Women*, and that film had provided me with almost my entire frame of reference for wartime Southern Italy. We had some sense that there had been fighting here. We knew, of course, about the Allied invasions at Anzio and Salerno, and also knew the Italians had changed sides and ended the war with the Allies, a move that had made them the butt of hundreds of jokes about military ineptitude we'd all heard growing up in the States. But it was clear none of us knew many details about the war in Italy.

"That was a terrible year for us," Beatrice said as Sam translated. "All of the men were gone, either to the war or they were in America. Only the old, the sick, the women and the babies stayed behind. It was a very cold winter and there was not enough to eat."

Sam smiled and said something to Beatrice, then turned to us. "I told her you boys are much too young to know anything about those times. But let me tell you, these people really had it rough during the war. If they didn't grow it, they didn't eat. And with the men gone, there was always something going wrong and no one to fix it."

The middle Beatrice seemed to be able to follow Sam's English. She interjected a comment and Sam translated.

"She wants to know what your father told you about this town. You know, he played a big role here during that winter."

"No," said Tommy, fascinated by the story. "He never said much about his visit here. He didn't say it was winter; we just knew he'd come to see the family. He was a sergeant, an infantryman in the U.S. Third Army as they fought their way to the North against the Germans."

"Well, it was winter," said Sam. "The winter of '43. And it was rough. And your father kept these people alive."

"Kept these people alive..." Tommy was hearing this for the first time.

Sam translated his comment for the ladies, who nodded in agreement, and the two older Beatrices spoke excitedly together in a confusing duet for Sam.

"You see, your dad stopped by here to see how the family was. He had heard there wasn't enough to eat, that these people were facing winter with nothing in the stores. He showed up with an entire truckfull of food which he distributed to everyone he could."

"I'd never heard about that," said Tommy.

The second Beatrice continued the story. "He came back at least three or four times, each time with a truck loaded with food. It was army food, not fresh, but it was food and it kept us fed until things would turn around."

Sam smiled as he translated.

"And everyone around here was damn glad to have it, I can tell you that," he added. "Your dad wasn't even from here, his parents were. He was an American, born in the States, but he was very concerned about these people and did so much to help."

"Was he a mess sergeant?" I asked Tommy.

"No, he was in the infantry."

"Where did he get the food?" I wondered aloud.

Sam laughed. "They never asked on this end," he said. "Who knows? Maybe there's some mess sergeant still wondering what happened to his supplies."

"But why would the kids who greeted us know anything about that?" Mike asked. "They weren't even born when that happened."

"No," agreed Sam. "But that story is a famous one from this place and they have all heard of the *americano* soldier, John—Giovanni—Durante, who helped their families before they were born. This is a small town and our stories are well-known."

Beatrice nodded in agreement. "Your father, Giovanni, was one of our sons," she said. "My brother's boy. One of the many who had left this place to find a new life in America. And when America came here to fight, to fix things, our brother's and sister's sons came back and helped us. For us, America was our own boys making things better."

It was my first look at the other side of the Italian World War Two story. We were stationed in Germany and I had a good feel for the effect of the war there, its causes and devastation, the complete upheaval and reformation of an entire society. There were no more Nazis in Germany and the people who had favored that war were either dead or silenced forever.

But Italy had technically ended the war on our side, yet still suffered the destruction, humiliation and degradation of the losers. And strangely, many Italians, unlike the Germans, felt that the Allied armies—their enemies for the first three years of the war—were comprised of their own relatives, Italian-American sons, nephews and cousins from these villages and towns, especially in the South, like Sala Consilina. After all, over eighty percent of all Southern men had left these villages and gone off, most to America, at one time or another. During the Second World War, while the Fascists called them the enemy, they were still held in loving memory as children from the Southern villages, still thought of and missed.

Virtually every home in the South had, and still has, a wall of photos filled with well-dressed couples looking darkly into the past. The first American photographs sent back from the first generation to arrive showed stiff collars and long dark dresses bearing sepia-toned testimony to the wisdom of the couple's departure, the success of their new lives in their new country. Their identities are fading now, but in their time they still stirred sighs, broke hearts, brought tears. The soldiers during the Second World War were the children of those determined-looking couples.

John Durante's mother and father had left. Their fading picture occupied a place of honor on Signora Beatrice's wall. Their son John was born in their new life in their new country. John Durante, a New Yorker, an American, could have easily ignored his ancestral roots. Yet, when he came back as an American soldier, he still felt an allegiance to the town where his parents had been born. He obviously felt a pull, a connection, along with a need to help.

It was this draw, this sense of connection and relationship that began to fascinate me that evening in Sala Consilina, and it has remained a point of fascination ever since.

When I contacted Tommy many years later to reminisce over our adventure that summer, he was surprised at my memory of detail. His father

John had died in 1994 at age seventy-nine. He always downplayed his role as Sala Consilina's savior, Tommy said, and, like most combat veterans, said very little about the war. Tommy had returned once to Sala Consilina and said that the family still owned some acreage in the area. He intended to return to Italy in the near future. The linkage between the New Yorkers and the Campanians remained.

"That trip must have made quite an impression on you," he joked.

As usual, I admired his New York flair for understatement.

TO AN UNKNOWN SOLDIER

The stories are fading from memory now, but there were literally hundreds, if not thousands, of tales told in Italy of World War II American GIs of Italian descent who came to the aid or rescue of distant relatives during the last years of the war. The Durante family's story was the first of those I'd heard, but certainly not the last.

On a bright and hot summer day during my most recent journey in Italy, I met up with Anna Clara Ionta. Anna Clara is a language instructor in the Chicago area who was visiting her family in Scauri, a small town just north of Naples. We met in the seaport of Gaeta, a strikingly beautiful bay, once the site of the Emperor Titus's summer villa, and now the home of the U.S. Naval Fleet in the Mediterranean.

Over the years Anna Clara has shared many stories and insights with me about her experiences as a first-generation Italian-American. We lunched at a lovely outdoor café in Gaeta's central district. Anna Clara ordered the meal, which consisted of a wonderful fresh marinated anchovy appetizer and a spaghetti *vongole,* or clam sauce, that made me rethink my normal dislike of seafood. The anchovies were from local waters and were nothing like the very salty canned version of the fish I'd experienced before.

Anna Clara tells wonderful anecdotes with great humor and infectious laughter. On this day she told a tale of her family and the effect of the war on her grandparents in the area surrounding Gaeta. It was a rare gem about another American GI helping an Italian family—only this time the soldier didn't know the family and was not related to them.

It seems that Anna Clara's grandfather, like most of his generation, had gone off to the United States to earn a living. He brought his family—his wife and three children—to New York, where he ran a successful shoe store. In 1938, his wife and children returned to Italy.

"She had to take care of the old folks they'd left behind," Anna Clara said. "It was a duty and responsibility to take care of the parents, who were getting old and were alone. It meant a big sacrifice for my grandmother, but she had no doubt about what she had to do. My grandfather went back and forth to visit many times during this period."

It was not a good period to be separated. In fact, it was probably the worst period in the entire history of Europe for families to be separated. Time and events took over, World War II broke out, and Anna Clara's grandfather found himself an ocean away from his loved ones. He couldn't return to Italy, his wife couldn't leave. They were separated by politics, war and an ocean.

The grandmother and her three children had returned to a village in the shadow of Monte Cassino, just outside the town of Cassino; a place that would prove both dangerous and crucial as the Allies advanced to the North. The elderly parents she had gone to care for had died by this time, but the war had already begun. There was nowhere else to go.

One day an American soldier came into the grandfather's New York shop to buy shoes. After a brief conversation with the young man, the grandfather learned that the GI was a Sicilian-American about to be shipped to the European battlefield. He told the soldier of his family's dilemma, and gave the young man a wad of American bills, along with the address of his wife and family. He asked only that the soldier get the money to them, if possible.

In other words, he gave a complete stranger money that represented survival for his family in Italy. And the stranger was on his way to battle, his own survival was in serious question, not to mention his honesty. The man could have been killed in combat, or just simply disappeared around the corner, gone off on a toot, and the grandfather would have never known the difference.

But that was not the case.

The soldier, whose name has been lost to Anna Clara's generation, fought his way up the Italian peninsula. The Germans had made Monte Cassino their main defensive line in stalling the Allied advance. The battle continued for over eight bloody months, raging throughout the area in every little town, village and hamlet. Every Italian living in the area had been uprooted; people had seen their property and homes badly damaged or destroyed; many starved to death while still others died in artillery crossfire and aerial bombings.

It was the worst possible scenario for finding anyone.

Anna Clara's grandmother and her children—one of whom would become Anna's mother—spent those terrible eight months foraging in the hills outside the city and living in earthen huts which they shared with farm animals. Yet somehow, this Italian-American soldier found them and gave them the money he'd gotten in New York from the anxious husband and father. Needless to say, those dollars were of great help to the family in a terrible time of need.

"I have no idea how that man found my family," Anna Clara said, "especially in all that confusion during the war. No one was where they had been when the war started, the entire Cassino area was a battlefield. Yet this man must have been really determined, not to mention honest." She laughed.

"We have a picture of him with my grandmother, my mother, my uncle and aunt taken on the hills near Cassino," Anna Clara added. "It is a very precious heirloom for me. I only wish we knew his name, but those times were so difficult and so many details got lost."

For me, Anna Clara's stories were another example of those very exacting Southern Italian values. A man's job is to protect his family. A mother's job is to care for her family. Anna Clara's grandfather undoubtedly suffered over the separation from his wife and children by an ocean and war. The grandmother and her children lost their home, their safety, almost their lives, all doing what they saw as their duty. The grandfather chose to trust a stranger with his story, and his money.

But not just any stranger, a fellow Italian-American.

While Anna didn't say so specifically, I'm convinced that her grandfather knew that the soldier, from the same origins as his own family, shared his own values. The grandfather could reasonably expect that no Southern Italian in those circumstances would steal money meant for suffering women and children. It was a value both men had learned through their own families. The fact of war, that Italy had declared war on the United States, was irrelevant here.

This was a matter of blood.

It was a question of survival, something both men understood intuitively, for their families for ages upon ages before had faced similar problems. And it was only in drawing the circle closed, in protecting the family, that one survived the madness. The grandfather trusted a stranger from his outer circle of relations. And, as the story shows, that trust had been well founded.

Just as Signora Beatrice had said, "For us, America was our own boys making things better." It was something in the blood. Some ancient memory deeply rooted and plainly communicated that placed family above and beyond any politics. A Southern tradition that had been going on for at least two thousand years.

BACK IN ROME

Since I was in the area to meet with Anna Clara, I couldn't resist. I needed to visit an old love before returning south: *Rome....*

*   *   *

The chaos continued.

It had been several years since I'd lived in Rome. They'd cleaned up the place a bit for the Jubilee and Millennial Year 2000. Still, one could hardly call Rome clean. It had remained dirty and very noisy, yet it was still inspiring, intriguing, invigorating and one of the most fascinating cities in the world.

The weather was hot, but perfectly clear and bright. The Romans themselves seemed to be very busy. It was hard to reach people by phone. It seems that the entire Italian telephone world now relies on voice mail instead of direct conversation. And, even though every single Italian I was to meet throughout my entire stay came equipped with a cellular phone, it was never easy actually reaching anyone on the instrument. I was drowning in message hell. But I was in Rome, so while waiting for return calls I could at least eat well.

It was a good time for the dollar in Italy. The American currency was worth nearly double its value from my previous stay. Gasoline was still expensive, of course, but four dollars per gallon in 2001 money seemed a bargain when compared with five dollars per gallon in 1994.

The city had lost none of its unmistakable wealth. New cars streaked about, there seemed to be even more motor scooters and motorcycles ridden by well-dressed youngsters, if that was possible. A new automobile had become popular, a little two-seater called the Smart Car, designed by Mercedes Benz for moving about the crowded city and parking in tiny spaces. Judging by the numbers of these diminutive cars darting about the streets, the Romans were doing quite well. And, according to an article in a popular magazine, the average Italian was also ten pounds heavier in 2001 than a decade before. While still far from fat, Italian waistlines were starting to gain on the American and German ones.

Surprisingly, I found something a little meaner in Rome this time as well. The graffiti were more angry than the *"Fabio ama Silvia"* type I'd seen so often before. Now I spotted occasional signs telling others what to do or not to do, strong statements using vulgarities. There was a big ugly scrawl over a doorway in Trastevere marring the seventeenth-century feel of the place and demanding that people not use the street as a trash can. I saw, for the first time ever, four-letter English words on the Vatican walls.

The eternal Italian contradictions continued. The year 2000 census counted just about fifty-seven million Italians. When the birthrate was projected out to 2050, and with emigration no longer a factor in population growth, the number is expected to go down an astonishing 12 million to 45 million citizens. Italy keeps its title as the least reproductive of all nations, despite its high numbers of Roman Catholics who, canonically at least, oppose artificial birth control. Italian men are staying home with Mama until they marry, and that age is getting ever older. It is not uncommon for a forty-year-old single man to be living in his parents' home. Italian women, like the women in other Western economies, are entering the professions in ever-increasing numbers and delaying or forgoing childbearing in equally growing numbers. Women now outnumber men in institutions of higher education.

It's an Italy the first-generation Italian-Americans would barely recognize.

Italian television seemed to have been taken over by blond Northerners. All of the female hosts on the few music programs I'd watched had long, thin legs and bodies, flowing yellow hair, and used frequent English expressions.

Once, while I was staying with my Italian family a decade before, an old black-and-white episode of *Perry Mason* was run on one of the state-owned channels.

"Ah," I said, "Perry Mason dubbed in Italian."

La Signora looked at me and said with great surprise, *"Anche in America?"* You have that in America, too? I found her naïveté amusing. It wouldn't happen today in Italy. The youngsters have taken over the airwaves and the standard of beauty seems to be blond.

Italy is also fully into the computer age. Bank machines have replaced many of the cash-exchange businesses that once lined the streets in the city center, but strangely, now those machines seem to be mostly *fuori servizio*, out of service.

On my first full day in town, I'd tried eight separate machines; none worked. In desperation, I finally went into a bank to exchange money. I had a pocketful of wadded-up small denominations of Swiss, Swedish and German bills and no idea of what they were worth.

Entering an Italian bank is no easy chore. You have to wait to be admitted through an initial security door, then go through a second security door into the bank itself. An impatient signora ignored the direction that *only one person enter at a time* and scurried into the security door with me. She could tell I wasn't familiar with the system; she told me to take a ticket and wait for my number to be called.

"It's a bit complicated," I said.

Her reply was typically *Romano*: "Yes, it's complicated for you and me, but the thieves can get in here anytime they want."

I waited nearly a half hour for my number to be called; the computer changing the numbers had malfunctioned. When I finally reached the cage, I learned that my pocketful of bills came to less than twenty dollars, hardly worth the long wait in the semi-air-conditioning. My Roman companion made the wait interesting with a running commentary on the maladies of the Roman banking system. She decried the fact that "the machines are taking over the world but the computers never work. They are like having slaves."

I inferred from her comment that there was a slave revolt.

I'm still amazed by the basic innocence of the place, bank robbers aside. I've never lost my sense of awe in Rome as I watched well-muscled young men, probably single and living with Mama, pull up to an outdoor stand on their motorcycles in the late evening, hop off and order a cold slice of watermelon. They usually join an eclectic group of citizens standing about in the little piazzas or wide spots in the road, simply to enjoy a cool piece of summer fruit. The same behavior can be seen in the bars, where crowds of young people will order varieties of coffee, seldom alcohol, and laugh and converse among themselves. I've never seen rowdiness or drunkenness here among the Italians. Rome is one of the world's most beautiful cities and, aside from the motorists and graffiti, still one of the most polite and innocent on earth.

LOST FORTUNES

I caught up with old friends, the Bonomos. Michael, an American, works for the World Food Program. His charming wife, Aynur, is Turkish by birth and works as a translator and travel adviser. The couple has two young daughters, the oldest just slightly younger than my daughter, who'd sent a present along with me for the children. We'd exchanged photos and the children were excited about forming a transatlantic friendship.

Over a wonderful Middle Eastern meal on the deck of their Portuense apartment, Michael told me an amusing story. Some years ago I'd introduced him to an Italian I'd met with the same last name, Giovanni Bonomo, and joked at the time they might be cousins. They established a friendship and soon called each other *cugino*.

It turns out that Giovanni had done considerable research into the Bonomo name and took the subject very seriously. He really believed that he and Michael were distant cousins, though he could find no genealogical link. Michael's grandfather had sailed from Marsala, Sicily, to the United States in 1914. Giovanni's family was also from Sicily, but not from the same town.

Giovanni told Michael that he'd traced the Bonomo family all the way back to Constantinople during the Byzantine Empire, and eventually from there to Venice, where they were a family of considerable influence and power. But they apparently sided with the wrong faction in a

Venetian war with the Barberinis, lost their properties and were then scattered throughout Europe. Part of the family went to France and they are now known as the Bonhommes. Another part, apparently Giovanni and Michael's ancestors, wound up in Sicily.

Giovanni is a redhead whose mother is Scottish. A lawyer by profession, he's a portly man, and quite demonstrative and dramatic in his actions and movements. I recall him telling stories with a great deal of arm-sweeping and voice inflection. Michael said that when he told the story of the scattering of the tribe, he had tears in his eyes.

"Cugino mio! Il nostro palazzo!" "My cousin, our palace!" he wailed, as he mourned and cried over the family's alleged loss from five hundred or so years before.

Michael chuckled over the family's lost fortunes and agreed with me that five hundred years for an Italian was a very different time frame than five hundred years to an American.

Rome had not lost a whit of her marvelous charm. I loved observing tourists who saw her for the first time; loved overhearing their comments. This is a city that never becomes stale or boring. The Romans see to it that there is never anything such as a routine meal or business transaction; there is always an element of showmanship in the slightest public doings. Few machines actually functioned, but it didn't really matter since it was always the people who made this city so vibrant and fascinating. The weather was hot but beautiful, the colors in the recently cleaned city dramatic, the people eternally charming.

It seemed to be aging, but Rome hadn't changed.

7

It's a Wonderful Life

THE GODFATHER

On my return from one of my recent trips to Italy, I stopped in Geneva to visit close friends, Wayne and Irene Wittig. Wayne and I had been soldiers together in Germany and had remained close friends ever since. After several years at the Pentagon and White House, Wayne was now working with the United Nations helping advise developing African economies. I was invited to accompany the Wittigs to a barbecue in France, just over the border from Switzerland. It was a beautiful early fall day, the sky a clear blue ether, whipped-cream-like clouds circled the tops of the surrounding Alps. I was impressed to be going to a party of career diplomats. I had attended other functions with Wayne over the years and it always fascinated me to see top White House and Pentagon officials close up and away from the press-conference atmosphere. I anticipated a stimulating afternoon.

I met an American couple from the Midwest. They asked what I was doing in Geneva, and I explained that I was just passing through on my way home from Italy. I mentioned that I had recently spent some time in Sicily and was fascinated by the many causes that had led to Italian emigration to the United States.

"That's an easy one," the man said. "You can sum that up in five letters."

I looked at him, uncertain of his meaning. "Just what would those five letters be?" I asked.

"M-A-F-I-A," he spelled out with a smile.

I had expected a far more reasoned response from a career diplomat.

"Actually," I replied, not thinking too diplomatically, "that's a fairly facile interpretation, and it's got nothing to do with anything that I've been working on. In fact, it's got very little to do with the Italian-American experience in general, except in the movies. And some of the best of those films were produced by and starred Italian-Americans in the real life role of artists, not criminals."

The fellow quickly demurred. I could see he thought I was rather radical because of my response.

My father had been a defender of Italian-American honor. I was always amused by his objections to television programs like *The Untouchables,* and movies like *The Godfather.* For me, they were nothing more than entertainment with an Italian theme, actors and music. A sort of Perry Mason with *marinara* sauce. I never felt they reflected on me, or my family.

But lately, as my journey through my heritage continued, I had acquired a newfound respect for my father's side of that issue.

In 2001, the Order of Sons of Italy in America cited some interesting statistics: the U.S. Justice Department placed the number of criminals involved in organized crime in the United States at about 5,000, out of the entire U.S. population. This number includes members of five ethnic groups in addition to Italian-Americans. Even if *all* of them were Italian-American, that would account for only .0025 percent of all Italian-Americans.

Yet a nationwide Zogby opinion poll of American teenagers, commissioned by the National Italian American Foundation that same year, showed that *over forty percent* of our youngsters believed that movie and TV roles for crime bosses and gang members would be best played by Italian-Americans. In other words, America's youngsters thought of Italian-Americans as representing a criminal class.

Professor Ben Lawton of Purdue University says that "there is absolutely no reasonable correlation between the extremely limited involvement of Italian-Americans in organized crime and the pandemic depiction of this alleged involvement in the media." Lawton goes on to say that, on the contrary, there's considerable evidence, and statistics show that Italian-Americans have been some of the most law-abiding ethnic groups in the United States. Yet, "*Mafioso* has become a synonym for Sicilian, for Italian, for, in short, Italian-American...."

I had spent most of my life ignoring statements like the one from the diplomat in France, but now found myself getting irritated when the "criminal class" comments cropped up.

Hollywood, more than anything else, has helped drive the image of the modern Mafia, if not define it. Perhaps no other film in recent times has had as much to do with the image of Italian-Americans as *The Godfather,* based on the book of the same name. And if the Italian-American image was damaged by that story, then Italian-Americans have no one to blame except other Italian-Americans.

Mario Puzo wrote the book. He had written two critically acclaimed but commercially unsuccessful books prior to *The Godfather*, and he decided he wanted to write a best-seller. He'd been fascinated by the televised testimony of Joe Valachi before a U.S. Senate subcommittee investigating organized crime in 1963. Puzo wrote the committee for a printed copy of Valachi's testimony—which has been described by some observers as being of "questionable accuracy and importance" in the first place—and then combined that testimony along with his very accomplished imagination and considerable writing talent to bring the book off. He later confessed that he had based the main character of Don Corleone on his own mother. When he submitted the book for publication, it became the largest paperback sale up to that time.

The film was directed by Francis Ford Coppola. His father, Carmine, had roots in Basilicata and Puglia. Coppola didn't like the project at first, but used all of his artistry and creativity to craft a film of extraordinary visual power and well-developed characters. He collaborated with Puzo to write the screenplay.

Italian-American actors filled major and minor roles in the film, which eventually became a trilogy over the following decade. Robert De Niro won the Academy Award for his portrayal of the young Corleone in the second of these movies, despite the fact that he only spoke a few sentences in English during the entire film. Coppola and Puzo won Academy Awards for writing and directing.

If anything, *The Godfather* is a celebration of Italian-American artistry and craftsmanship. Coppola is the son of a conductor and composer. Puzo was an Italian-American writer who, despite the fact that many thought he had intimate inside knowledge of "organized crime," based his entire story on his research and exceptional instincts and writing skill. He'd never had so much as a traffic violation. De Niro's father was an artist. Al Pacino, another star in the film, grew up in the Bronx and was encouraged early in life to pursue what others saw clearly as an exceptional acting and dramatic talent.

All of these men, and several others involved in the project, *accurately represent the Italian-American experience*; all belong to a generation that had it better than their parents and grandparents, all were able to pursue their careers and dreams, all were highly artistic and the sons of either artists or of parents who encouraged art and creativity. All were the

American dream fulfilled for their Italian immigrant parents and grand-parents.

And all of that skill, artistry, insight, sensitivity and creativity went into a project that created an image of Italian-Americans as thugs, murderers, drug dealers, schemers, adulterers, plotters and, ultimately, complete losers. The exact *opposite* of the Italian Americans involved in the project.

According to statistics compiled by the Italic Studies Institute in 2000, the film spawned hundreds of imitations. The survey points out that before *The Godfather,* there had been 108 films produced in the genre which the institute terms "mob movies." After *The Godfather* in 1972, there were 314.

"Unfortunately for the Italian-American image," Ben Lawton writes, "the film, which is included among the best films ever made by virtually everyone, was so successful, and misunderstood, that it elicited hundreds of imitators…" Italian-Americans dominate the criminal roles in these films and thus take on the same role in the mind of the public.

THE WOES OF SICILIA

Poor Sicily.

If ever a place suffered from the bad and the criminal image, Sicily is it.

According to sworn testimony in the Italian courts, during the Italian national Mafia crackdown of the nineties, and the top experts in the field at that time, anywhere from fifteen hundred to five thousand criminals made up the Sicilian Mafia. That's out of a total population of just over five million people. Yet, such is the Mafia's reach and reputation that the entire island and, for that matter, the entire Italian population in both Italy and the United States seems to be darkened by its shady doings.

The modern-day Mafia is most definitely real and is obsessed with power and money. According to a consistent barrage of Italian newspaper reports, it has been very effective in finding suppliers and customers for its drug trades, money laundering and other illegal businesses, and has, without doubt, insinuated itself into the Italian public works structure. It also has unfortunately been capable of buying politicians to aid it in its nefarious dealings.

But the shame of the Italian Mafia has as much, if not more, to do with Rome's inability to control the criminal organization and its ineffective or wavering resolve to clean up the corruption, as it does with the Sicilians themselves.

The myth of the Mafia is that somehow criminal activity is endemic to Sicilian culture, and that one has led to the other. The Mafia is a group of brutes, thugs and murderers. But they are not the average Sicilian. It's as if the entire population of the United States were considered to be sympathizers with the Ku Klux Klan, since that particular hate group of cultural morons exists and functions in our country, despite the fact that the overwhelming majority of Americans despise its principles and very existence.

In 1992, the Italian state finally moved to clean up the Mafia's criminal reach throughout Italy. The chief judge in the case, Giovanni Falcone, was brutally murdered. Falcone and four of his *carabinieri* guards were blown to bits as they drove along a highway near Palermo.

But the real story in the Falcone case was the speech given by Rosaria Schifani, the young and beautiful widow of one of the slain policemen. She spoke to the congregation at the funeral of her husband, but also spoke to the entire Italian nation as the speech was televised live on RAI-TV. I was one of millions of viewers mesmerized by her poignant and touching message.

"*Mafioso, io vi perdono ma vi dovete mettere in ginocchio.*" "Mafiosi, I forgive you, but you must get down on your knees," she said.

Rosaria Schifani's defiance, courage and dignity defined the modern attitude toward the Mafia thugs that pollute the Sicilian economy, its political and social systems. Her grief and eloquence marked a genuine turning point in both the public's attitude toward the Mafia and the nation's resolve finally to clean things up.

Sicily is the essence of Southern Italian culture; the essence of people who, after nearly two thousand years of domination by various militant occupiers—on an almost generational basis—have developed a mistrust of anyone claiming power, wisdom and governance. *Including* the Mafia. That the Mafia has survived on this island is partly the result of the Sicilians' lack of trust and reluctance to turn to a disinterested and distant government that continues to be ineffective in solving their problems. Many Sicilians, in print and in private, still believe that Rome does not fully understand or care about their problems, and not without cause; as recently as two years ago, the Italian government published a new "official" map of Italy, *omitting* the islands of Sicily and Sardinia. A map undoubtedly drawn by a Northerner.

Omission of Sicily has deep roots. The Italian revolution relied in large part on the liberation of Sicily from Bourbon rule, and achieved that liberation with the cooperation of Sicilians. Yet, after the Italian reunification, or Risorgimento, Sicily was often treated like a foreign country by its new government. Rome's main interests were in developing heavy industry and aligning itself with the other industrial states of Northern Europe.

As John Dickie so clearly illustrates in his comprehensive book *Darkest Italy—The Nation and Stereotypes of the Mezzogiorno, 1860-1900*, the South was regarded as a picturesque but backward, illiterate (its illiteracy rate was as high as seventy-five percent) and sometimes dangerous region. Dickie demonstrates how the South was portrayed in the popular press of the time as picturesque and filled with wandering minstrels and poor but charming waifs, or roving bands of dangerous brigands, but there were few articles written that gave a realistic picture of the

Sicilians and their economic woes. The Southern economy was mainly farming. The needs of the post-unified South—foreign markets, a redistribution of the land to eliminate the remaining large plantations, a massive infusion of capital—were often at odds with the new government in Rome.

The new Italy was in a hurry to enter the Industrial Age fully, after having languished behind the rest of the Western World—in part due to the political and religious influence of the Roman Catholic Church. The new nation needed an army, rails, heavy arms and heavy industry to produce them. Sicily's economy was, as it had been since the dawn of civilization, agricultural. Even after the elimination of the Kingdom of the Two Sicilies, the economy and social structure of small farms and a small middle class that made up the economy could not change very quickly. Rome mostly ignored the problems. Sicilians had developed a mistrust of Rome that began under the emperors and continues to this day. A mistrust which, over the centuries, resulted in the system of *omerta*—keeping silent about opposition to the government, or to criminal activity, which in Sicily, where the government was inevitably a foreign oppressor, was often the same thing.

And, ironically, it's the United States who must share some of the responsibility for the strength of the modern-day Mafia. The criminal organization was moribund, reduced to ashes with only a few determined, glimmering coals left after Mussolini's totalitarian reforms. The Fascists had done their best to destroy the Mafia and all other power structures in Sicily. As part of the invasion and war effort in the early 1940s, the CIA's forerunner, the OSS, recruited anti-Fascist forces that included the remnants of the Mafia. The OSS sent money and supplies, and a few paroled U.S. mobsters, to aid with guerrilla counter-warfare against the Fascists and Nazi troops then holding Sicily. That action helped reestablish the Mafia's influence, fund it, and inadvertently gave it new ability to function beyond its wartime role.

Sicily is a land that has been misused, abused, captured, lost, raped and exploited with great social and political upheaval over the endless centuries of its existence. And despite, or perhaps because of all this constant evolution, the island has produced a people of incredible vitality, wit, humor, instinct and skill. To be Sicilian is to be a clever survivor; only the fittest could have made it this far.

A Most Beautiful Place . . .

I told Anna Ionta that I was going to Sicily.

"Have you been there before?" she asked.

"Yes," I said.

"Isn't it the most beautiful place you've ever seen?"

I agreed. "I didn't know anything about Sicily except for what I'd seen in the movies," I told her, "but I drove over with a friend to look up some records for his family a few years ago. We drove across the island from Messina to Agrigento. It was one of the most spectacular landscapes I've ever seen."

"I know," she said. "I couldn't believe my own eyes, and I'm Italian. It's a garden. No wonder everyone has wanted to own this place over history. Who could blame the Romans for fighting Carthage over Sicily?"

Her comments were typical of both the Italians and Americans I have known after their first visit. Even in Italy, Sicily exists more in myth than reality. The majority of my Roman friends think the only island off the Southern coast is Capri. Most have never ventured to the end of the peninsula and crossed the Messina Strait. In fact, all of my Roman friends worried over my safety because of my determination to spend more time in Sicily.

"We have to get you some sort of boot you can weld to your car," Enrico Borsetti said, "I don't think you'll ever bring that car back from Sicily. I'm worried about you."

I pointed out to Enrico that the only problems I'd ever had with theft had been break-ins to my car in Rome, and every single one of my friends in Rome had their apartments burglarized at one point or another. The Italians hold their regional prejudices closely. If they believe a place unsafe, no amount of anecdotal testimony to the contrary can sway that opinion. I stopped trying, but never stopped singing the praises of Sicily.

Driving through Sicily *can* be quite difficult. The superhighways are mostly elevated and speed along the coasts. Secondary roads wind through farms, orchards and vineyards, over mountains, or snake along the spectacular sea hundreds of feet below the autostrada. There are frequent *deviazioni* around construction sites or repair zones. But it is not the construction or the detours that makes driving difficult.

So many things strike the eyes and imagination at the same time. Driving in Sicily is like driving through a real-life multimedia show. Paying attention to the road takes discipline and effort.

Sunlight plays magically on a small village atop a distant hill, illuminating tan-white walls, as if lighting a faraway set for a surreal film.

Mists envelop a mountaintop the Greeks must have made myth from.

Grand vistas lie sun-struck or shaded by great clouds as the land rolls on into the horizon, undulating forever green and brown, the light dappling and dancing on the well-worked fields.

The sun lies in patches on a still sea, an almost-pond, upon which civilization formed itself, came here from the South. You can all but see the ancient wind-puffed canvas and hear the creaking of the barks.

Olive groves filled with carefully spaced silver-green trees shiver slightly in the September chill.

…And everywhere broods evidence of another time in crumbling bricks or stone facades or nearly collapsed walls that once were tall, once held important land or buildings, had once stood strong and kept watch over often disputed land.

Sicily is not a place to be driven through quickly. One can sense, all too clearly, time that has passed forever and is passing now. Moments become precious and escape too soon, like the constant gentle waves on the island's soft shores.

The ferry service between Calabria and Messina has become competitive. A few years ago, only the state-run service was available, now an independent service competes with the state. The result of this breakup of the state monopoly is more frequent and more efficient service crossing the strait. It is also the perfect way to approach Sicily—from the water, as every invader or visitor came since the Greeks arrived at Naxos in 734 B.C.E. until the invention of the airplane.

A huge bridge, the world's largest suspension bridge, has been designed to span the strait. Like most Italian building projects, the proposal has been widely debated and held up until the proper balance of funding can be found. The Berlusconi government has approved the project, but only if the private sector pays fifty percent or more of the costs.

The two-mile strait is subject to strong winds and earthquakes—Messina and Reggio di Calabria were flattened in 1908, and evidence of that quake can still be seen in both cities—posing challenging engineering problems. Even the legendary Odysseus feared the strong currents and coastal rocks of the strait, which can be a temperamental body of water guarding the Mediterranean basin's largest island of nearly ten thousand square miles. (Imagine Vermont in the Atlantic two miles off the coast of Maine.)

The Romans, the world's most accomplished engineers of antiquity, dreamed of a bridge to the island. It is now planned and designed and, according to recent news accounts, awaiting final funding despite some protests by Italian environmentalists. The current argument in favor of the bridge is that the work will improve the country's infrastructure, increase commerce with the island, and have an economic ripple effect throughout the Mezzogiorno.

"I've heard about their 'ripples,'" my innkeeper, a native of the Messina region, told me my first night on the island. "We'll see. We've been promised such things before. They're still trying to get those 'ripples' to Naples after the last earthquake there nearly twenty years ago now." The innkeeper's attitude might typify the Sicilians and Calabrians who have seen billions of public-work dollars disappear into the Mafia's pockets or into failed industries.

The first people to cross the Messina Strait were native Italian tribes. The first written record of the island is from classical Greece. Even Homer got into the act. Not far from Messina, in Capo di Milazzo, there's a plaque that marks the original mouth of the river Mela, now a mere torrent, and quotes Homer's description of the once powerful and mysterious stream. While Homer wrote about the area, the Greeks didn't actually settle there until another four or five hundred years had passed. The Greeks traded with the local tribes and explored the island long before their need for expansion into what became Magna Graecia.

Of course, once Greece expanded, Sicily was its first priority. Greeks began their settlements along the eastern and southeastern shore at Syracuse around 729 B.C.E. They were followed in quick succession by the ancient Carthaginians, who settled first in what is now Palermo on the northwestern part of the island. There were several centuries of battles between the Carthaginians and the Greeks until the Romans settled all the issues by defeating Carthage and taking control of the island. The cliché goes that Romans gave the people "bread and circuses." Much of that Roman bread was made from Sicilian grain as the island became known as Rome's bread basket. Wheat is still Sicily's principal crop.

Mount Etna dominates the horizon of the northeastern quarter of the island. Pure white smoke streamed from its crater as I drove by. It was erupting in the summer of 2001, and video of the streaming lava led each night's news reports. The volcano towers eleven thousand feet above the seabed and is surrounded by lush groves of oranges, lemons and olives. It is undoubtedly one of the most dramatic and beautiful spots on earth.

I spent a day at Taormina becoming overdosed on seascapes and mountain vistas. From the top of the mountain, where the Greeks founded their settlement, Etna is in clear view to the southwest, the Ionian and Tyrrhenian seas converge in the strait, and the Sicilian coastline snakes below, dotted with the masts of bobbing sailboats moored offshore as thousands of brightly colored bathing suits and towels randomly splash the sand. The end of the Italian boot and the city of Reggio di Calabria sit stately across the strait, clearly visible through the slight haze, as the huge ferries and cargo ships plow their white wakes on deep green water between the island and the mainland or up the coast toward Naples and Rome. The people might have been poor here for a very long time, but the views are certainly some of the richest in the world.

On the northern end of the island, the autostrada parallels the shore and cuts through the mountains on its westerly course. The Tyrrhenian Sea seems rougher in the north than the Ionian in the south. The winds feel stronger here. Lipari, an island to the north of Sicily, is just visible on the northern horizon. The mainland slowly disappears in the east.

The dramatic horseshoe bay that surrounds Palermo is clearly visible from the superhighway for miles before reaching the city. Palermo's westernmost point, Mount Pellegrino, protects the bay. It's easy to see how and why this port is so ancient and valuable. It's no wonder the Carthaginians hopped over the westernmost and more exposed coastline to settle here when they first arrived in the seventh century B.C.E. And, interestingly, the Greeks surveyed and traded with, but never settled, Palermo. They called the place Panormus, or "broad harbor." But it was settled by Carthage, who called it Ziz, or "flower"—until its defeat by Rome in the Punic Wars.

I was glad to be in Palermo; I'd run out of descriptive adjectives. I needed a rest and refill.

I found a hotel with a secure parking lot and full-time guard—so much for Enrico's worry about my car—and set about my solitary and short exploration of Palermo. My actual destination was a very small town in the mountain range to the south of the city, but I couldn't pass through such a remarkable place and not spend some time.

Parts of Palermo struck me more like Paris than any other place I can compare it with. The shopping district off the Piazza Castelnuovo is comprised of broad, tree-lined boulevards which run for several blocks to the west and are filled with expensive and toney famous-name boutiques, clothiers and jewelers, interspersed with outdoor cafés and restaurants. There is nothing in this district to indicate either poverty or crime, the supposed hallmarks of Sicily.

Palermo is an amalgamation of Arab architecture and Norman castles, and is jumbled up with state-built housing and several other architectural styles and varying degrees of wealth. Some buildings are clearly tenements and exist in odd juxtaposition with new glass-and-steel structures, a sort of Paris adjacent to Tijuana. Like Rome, everything is in motion, in constant coming and going. Ships in the harbor sound gigantic horns as they arrive and depart, a constant counterpoint to the city's busy traffic of cars and trucks—hundreds of trucks driving about the city center—people, and, of course, ever-buzzing *motorini*.

I absorbed the sounds of the city as I walked from my hotel along the bay front to an office near the Via della Libertà, where I met with Franco Maresco, a Sicilian film director. Maresco's most famous film, *Lo Zio di Brooklyn*, or "The Uncle from Brooklyn," is described as an apocalyptic view of life in post-modern Palermo.

"Ah," Maresco greeted me warmly, "you are a friend of Enrico Borsetti's from Rome."

My arrival had been well announced. Enrico and I have been friends for several years, having met while we were both playing trumpet in a Rome conservatory jazz big band. Enrico's passion is jazz music. He is a frequent contributor to jazz journals and has been involved in several projects regarding the preservation of early jazz. He was currently working on a documentary project with Maresco, and suggested that I meet with the director.

We chatted amiably in Maresco's editing studio, a few members of his staff joining our conversation. Maresco, a native of Palermo, also a jazz buff, was hoping to produce a documentary on Italian jazz musicians, a work Borsetti described as a "work of love, but no money."

"If you know Enrico," Maresco said, "then I'm sure you know that many of the United States original jazz musicians were Italian and, in fact, Sicilian."

"You can't know Enrico and not know that," I joked. Borsetti was a walking *Who's Who* of Italian and Italian-American jazz musicians.

"I know the Americans have done much on this subject of American jazz in general," Maresco said, "but no one ever seems to know that the first jazz recording ever made was made by an Italian, Nick La Rocca. He was born in New Orleans, his father was from here in Salaparuta, Sicily. And New Orleans was a very Italian city when jazz was born. A major port for Italian emigration."

"And don't forget Tony Scott," I added.

Scott and Buddy De Franco, another Italian-American, were considered to be the two greatest bebop jazz clarinetists. Scott was raised in the States and came to musical prominence there, but now resides in Rome. I'd met him in Rome some years ago while I was playing with a jazz group at an outdoor concert. He introduced himself, as if I didn't know who he was. He'd given me an autographed photo of himself with Billie Holiday and Charlie Parker taken during a concert at Carnegie Hall in New York City in 1952, a photo I've come to treasure. Tony Scott was a living Roman legend among young musicians.

"Ah, yes. Another Sicilian," Maresco said. "And Joe Venuti, Charlie Ventura, Louis Prima, Louis Bellson, the Assunto Brothers, who were known as the 'Dukes of Dixieland,' and twenty-five or thirty others I can't remember just now."

"It's safe to say that music is a part of the Southern culture."

"Not only safe, but certain," Maresco said intently. "The people might have been poor, but they have always been highly cultured."

I heard strains again of Nicola Zitara's and Carmine Colacino's defense of the South.

"Music is, after all, one of the highest statements of a culture."

Maresco spoke in a low raspy voice, smiled and joked as he talked. He seemed to be a man at ease with himself. He asked why I'd come to Palermo.

"Actually, I'm going down to Bisacquino," I said. "I have an interview there with a relative of a friend."

"Bisacquino," Maresco said excitedly. "I have been there. I went there many years ago to see Frank Capra, the famous American director. It is his hometown."

"When was that?" I asked.

"In 1977," Maresco replied. "I was so surprised."

"Surprised?"

"Yes, surprised. I expected to see a big Hollywood movie star, I guess. But Capra was a short man with a little potbelly and Sicilian eyes. He looked exactly like the *contadini* from the mountains. I couldn't get over it."

"He was from here," I said.

"I know," Maresco laughed, "but somehow I expected him to look more *American,* I guess. And then he spoke in that low voice, the almost growl-like tone that they speak with in those mountains, and I couldn't believe it. Here was one of the world's most famous motion picture directors and he was just a little *contadino* from Bisacquino. I will never forget it...."

IT'S A WONDERFUL LIFE

As I scaled the mountains south of Palermo, I found it impossible not to look back over my shoulder. From the heights I could see the entire sprawl of the city, the fantastic horseshoe bay with steep mountains erupting from the dark-blue water and shooting straight into the air. The ancient perimeters of the bay and the town are clearly defined. It is certainly one of the most stunning and beautiful cities I've ever seen. And it's little wonder so many civilizations have claimed it.

The hills to the south, however, are a different issue. They are rugged and beautiful, too, but in a different way. Interspersed with farm and grazing lands, this part of Sicily is less brown and seems less played-out than its middle; there is more green vegetation. The road was an ancient trading route coming overland from Agrigento on the southwestern coast of the island.

Sicily was once filled with trees, lush forests. But over the centuries and successive governments, almost all of Sicily's timber was used for shipbuilding or carted away for fuel or construction material. Now the island is oddly denuded of trees and the resulting soil erosion means that it can never regain its original forested beauty. And, because of the erosion, the once-mighty rivers like the Mela have silted in and are now only seasonal torrents. Passing through the mountains to the south of Palermo, the lack of trees is especially notable and lamentable. One can only imagine how truly lush these now green rolling fields once were.

I was headed to Bisacquino by way of Corleone.

Corleone, despite its cinematic reputation and its actual role in the Sicilian Mafia, is a rather drab place, hot and dusty, sitting on a small plateau. The newer section of the city, or the post-World War II quarter, looks as rundown as the older, pre-war section. There are no tourist signs or markers to indicate historical or religious sites. You get the feeling in Corleone that they're not all that much interested in visitors.

Mario Puzo, of course, made Corleone the hometown for his *Godfather* character. In fact, Corleone did father a real-life Mafia leader, the infamous Salvatore Riina, who was finally captured in the *mani pulite*, or clean-hands movement by the Italian government in the nineties. In 1994, the mayor of Corleone even took to the streets, along with hundreds of citizens and students, to parade against the Mafia's actions and in favor of government reform.

About twenty miles farther down the same highway lies the little town—just slightly larger than a village—of Bisacquino. Aside from its former Mafia connections—the town produced the leading Mafiosi just after the Second World War, until they were unseated by the Corleonesi in the late 1950s—not much has ever happened here. A farming village, the town lies north of and forms a triangle with Agrigento in the southeast and Castelvetrano in the southwest, and is settled snugly into the mountains that separate all the interior towns in this region of Sicily.

A hard-to-find travel brochure of the area, in Italian only, describes the town as a Saracen settlement from just over a thousand years ago. The Arabs farmed the surrounding land with great efficiency. And, as with all of their settlements in the region, built it with an eye on defense; the town sits on a mountain crest overlooking surrounding valleys.

Like all modern Sicilian villages, this one, too, saw most of its men— at least seventy-five percent—go off to other lands, most to America, in the early part of this century.

One of those men was a dreamer who, despite his peasant birth, longed for a life filled with music and without the dreary drudgery, sweat and dirt of farming someone else's land. This Salvatore had, by all accounts, the soul of an artist, but he had been born in the wrong place and time.

One of Salvatore's sons, Benedetto, had gone off to America and, after a few silent years, finally contacted the family and encouraged them to join him in that ethereal and dreamlike place called California—

Los Angeles, to be exact—or "the Italy of America," as it was being advertised at the time.

Salvatore's wife, Rosaria—called Sara or more familiarly, *Saridda*—strongly supported the move. She didn't think her husband could be either successful or happy as a tenant farmer in Sicily. So the couple decided to pack up the rest of the family and make the move to America.

It was 1903.

By this time, however, their oldest daughter, Ignatzia, was already married with a child and another on the way. Some say that she wanted to make the trip to America with her parents, but her husband became terrified when he saw the sea for the first time at Palermo and refused to get onto the ship. But, for whatever the reasons, one small branch of the family remained in Bisacquino as the others all set sail for the New World and "the Italy of America."

It was to be a fateful crossing.

Sailing in steerage on the crossing over, Sarrida and Salvatore's youngest child, Francesco, celebrated his sixth birthday on board the SS *Germania*. The boy was soon to become just plain "Frank," and was destined to become the most American of the entire clan rocking about on their way to a new life.

Before young Frank was thirty, he was helping define America through the art of motion pictures. In fact, he had become a major voice of both his industry and his country and has left a legacy in the art of filmmaking that still must be studied and evaluated by any serious student of the medium.

Frank Capra became and remains one of the few directors of motion pictures whose name itself could draw an audience. There is an entire film genre that takes its name from his style of films: *Capraesque*. And that style is definitively American, uniquely suited to Capra's time and place in America, a clear artistic and social statement that defines a generation.

Capra, like so many other Sicilians from that small island after the turn of the twentieth century, needed an opportunity—the soil in which to grow—and their native talents flowered, grew and enriched their new land. Had he remained in Sicily, the only path available to Frank Capra in 1903 would have been the life of a peasant farmer, grueling and difficult, and he'd have probably never seen a motion picture camera up close. America and the world gained from his escape, gained from the native skills and energy of so many immigrants, so many Sicilians in Capra's generation who, in almost clichélike fashion, found America, made it theirs and gave definition, style and meaning to their new country.

But what about those not living the American dream? What about those who stayed behind?

LA FAMIGLIA TRONCALE

I had learned about the Troncale family from their cousin, Frank's son, Tom Capra, a friend and former colleague from our days together in television news. When I'd first met Tom in the mid-1980s, I didn't even know the name Capra was Italian.

"What did you think it was?" said Tom, laughing.

To me, Frank Capra had been the epitome of America and Hollywood. I'd never even thought of the family origin.

I read Capra's autobiography shortly after Tom and I met, and quickly learned how much Capra's childhood and origins had influenced his thinking. Several years later, when Tom mentioned the family in Sicily, I decided to go there and look them up.

It was the Troncales' life that fascinated me. Frank Capra's life was well documented, the story of the American dream itself. I wanted to know if Frank Capra represented the good citizens of Bisacquino or, like a Mozart or Einstein, was the exception to every rule.

In the course of several phone calls from Matera, I finally reached Tom Capra's first cousin, Antonino Troncale, and asked to make an appointment. He was reluctant to talk with me. He finally agreed, but the dates for our meeting kept changing for a variety of reasons.

We finally settled on September 12, 2001, when I would drive to Bisacquino from Palermo. On September 11, 2001, like every civilized human being, I watched in horror as the events in New York, Washington, D.C., and Somerset County, Pennsylvania, unfolded, and found myself postponing the interview yet again. I thought I could detect a tone of agitation in Signore Troncale's voice when I called. I was afraid his initial reluctance and all of the postponements might have soured him on the interview.

I finally arrived in Bisacquino later that same dreadful September week. I met with Nené on a beautiful late-summer day when the sky was perfectly blue and scattered with brilliant puffy white clouds. He was waiting for me at the gate to his home near the train station. He wore a blue-and-white-checkered long-sleeve shirt with the sleeves rolled up, the white of his shirt and hair matching with equal vibrancy.

He spoke with the gruff and raspy voice—much like his uncle's, I assumed, based on my conversation with Franco Maresco—it seemed to be a trait of the people from this region. I was relieved to learn it was that voice, and not his irritation, which I'd picked up on the phone.

I'd had an image of a much different man. I'd heard a rough tone; I met a smiling, docile grandfather who immediately introduced me to his wife of more than fifty years, Viola, a trim and attractive woman with a bright smile. I was invited into their home.

"One thing before we start," Nené said, as we settled into chairs around a large dining room table opposite a large and thankfully cold wood-burning oven. "I didn't want to talk with another journalist because I never heard back from the ones who have come here before. I've never seen their work."

I promised that I would send along a copy of my next book.

"Have there been many writers here before?" I asked. I had only heard about the Troncales through the Capra family.

"Oh, yes. Several over the years for articles here and there. My uncle was a very famous man. But I'm not sure I can really offer much. I didn't know him very well. He was only here one time."

"I know," I said, "I'm really here to learn about you, not your uncle." Nené seemed confused.

"I know about your uncle," I continued. "His life is well documented. It's your life that I'd like to talk about."

This seemed to surprise the Troncales.

"What is it you want to know?" they asked. I could sense the Sicilian suspicion.

"My family is originally from Abruzzo and Basilicata," I explained. "Only I didn't know very much about that until just a few years ago."

"Yes," Nené said, "your name is obviously Italian. The Basilicatans and Sicilians have much in common."

I was grateful once again for a name that meant a very different thing in this land than in my own. I went on to explain that I was learning about the Southern character, had started that education with my own family, and was very curious about the people who stayed and the ones who left. I told how much I was learning about the stories of the Italians and the Southerners, in particular, that I thought the Troncales' story would be an interesting contrast with their famous uncle's.

It took a while longer for Nené to develop a sense of comfort with me. At first he asked more questions than I. My answers must have satisfied him and, over time and, inevitably, a few coffees, he began to tell his family's story.

THE OTHER SIDE OF THE SEA

Life was far from the American ideal for Frank Capra's oldest sister, Ignatzia, and her family back in Bisacquino.

Ignatzia 's husband and Nené's father, Vincenzo Troncale, worked hard on the land, believed that if a man worked hard, there was no need to move across an ocean. He thought his father-in-law, Salvatore, was more interested in playing the guitar and singing than in hard work. Sal would be better off in America, Vincenzo thought, but he would stay in Bisacquino, safe on the familiar and known side of the ocean, and so would Ignatzia and their children.

True to his word, Vincenzo worked and prospered. In all, the couple had ten children, seven of whom survived into adulthood—a slightly higher than average survival rate for Southern Italy at the time. As each child was born, Vincenzo rented more and more land until he became one of the most respected and largest tenant farmers in the area. He eventually had so much land he had to hire fellow *contadini* to work for him. Troncale prided himself on being the first up and at work in the morning and the last to retire at night. He was a man who believed only in the religion of hard work, in back-bending struggle with the land, in sweat-stained clothing and calloused hands, and taught his children to respect the same.

All, that is, except for the baby of the family. Antonino, or Nené, as he has always been called.

Little Tony, the baby.

Nené didn't have to follow his brothers into the fields; he was pampered and, a rarity for young Sicilian men, he completed his elementary and secondary schooling and then the unthinkable—he went on to the university, the first of the Troncale or Capra clan in Bisacquino ever to achieve such high academic success.

"I could not hide in this region." Nené laughed. "I taught elementary school here for twenty-nine years. There isn't a person in this region who wasn't a student of mine, or a parent of a student, at one time or another." Nené's career is an understandable source of pride for him.

"Education just wasn't something that was common to people who worked the land," Nené continued. "Many thought that after learning reading, writing and enough math to figure out basic quantities and money, there wasn't much use for anything else the schools had to offer. It took a long time for the habit of formal education to develop here."

"Why is that?" I asked. "Was it a cultural opposition to formal schooling or was it the lack of resources, the lack of schools and teachers?"

"Both," Nené replied. "We have always been simple people here, working the fields for our existence. A long education meant losing your children from the fields, and the fewer children you had helping, the less work you could accomplish. The notion that children should go off to school is a difficult one in poor agricultural societies. I was very fortunate."

"So then, this changed during your lifetime?"

"Most definitely," said Nené. "If my uncle Frank hadn't gotten on that boat, he wouldn't have had much formal education, even though he, too, was the youngest. He would have had more than the others, probably, but there was only a very limited amount at that time."

"What happened when you got out of school?"

"Well, now that takes some explaining." Nené laughed. "Many things. But there was a war, there was no work at first. And I was in love. And then the war was over and I was going to Hollywood."

"Hollywood?"

"Yes," he laughed again. "But that comes later."

Nené told how he had met Viola. The first time he'd ever seen her, she was only thirteen years old. He was helping the local doctor inoculate the young villagers against an outbreak of *vaiolo*, or smallpox. Nené was seven years older than Viola and any romance would be out of the question until she was older.

So he waited.

A year and a half later he finally spoke to the young woman. It would be thirteen years from the time of that inoculation until they would marry. Six of those years would be a secret engagement; Viola's brothers would not have been happy if they knew of Nené's interest in their younger sister. This was still Sicily, after all.

"You know," added Viola, "this was a very different time. We met at church or in public. Nené used to hide letters to me in the wall near my house, carefully hidden under a stone, so no one would accidentally discover them. I would leave letters for him. We never spent a moment alone until the night before our wedding. That night, we went to confession together. My mother watched us walk to the church from her window. But Nené's parents also saw us going into the church and were horrified. They thought we were eloping. Young men and women in our generation did not spend time alone together.

"And we knew nothing about sex. When we first married, the only form of birth control we knew about was called prayer."

She sighed at the memory.

"We had no money," Viola continued. "Nené had no job. Yet we were very happy and completely innocent. Young people today have much more wealth, but I'm not sure they can be as carefree as we were then, no matter how bad those times seem now."

Nené said that there was no work or money because of the war. He was exempted from military service because of a heart condition. Palermo was being bombed, so he couldn't go there. And there was nothing in the village, except safety. So, like his many years of courtship, he waited things out. He tended a small garden, raised his own food.

The Allies made one bombing run on Bisacquino as they advanced on the Germans to the north. The train station, only a few hundred meters from where we sat that bright afternoon, had been hit. No one had been hurt.

"The Allies came right through this village on their way to Palermo," Nené explained. "The roads were too narrow for their tanks. They planned to knock down houses along the way to widen the road, but the local residents got wind of the plan and staged a big protest on the Corso Umberto, the main drag through town. The soldiers decided to go around."

"Have you ever seen your uncle's films, the *Why We Fight* series he made during the war?" I wondered. "You know, they were considered to

be extremely important at the time, and they've been released on video-
tape just a few years ago. Your uncle was more or less the chief propa-
gandist for the American and Allied cause in that war."

"I have heard about those films, but I never saw any of them."

"Was this village aware of your uncle's work?"

"They knew he was a famous American director. But his films were
hard to see. There are no cinemas here. My mother, of course, knew all
about her brother's success. And my grandmother and aunt came back
to Bisacquino once for three months. I loved talking with my grandmother and aunt and hearing the stories of America."

"Did your father ever see his brother-in-law's work? What was his
reaction?"

"My father never went to a movie," he said. "For one thing, the cinema was done in Italian, which my father didn't understand. Also, since
he awoke at dawn every day of his life, he would have fallen asleep and
would have been deeply embarrassed. He was a simple man, unfamiliar
with my uncle's world. I had to go to Palermo to see the films. The first
one I ever saw was *Arsenic and Old Lace*, after the war, but my parents
never saw any.

"You know," Nené went on, "we lived in a remote village and mostly
in poverty, but the poverty here was economic, not cultural. There were
many intelligent people here, but they had little opportunity to prove
that intelligence. But the Southerners *had* to be more intelligent because
they had more need, and need builds the mind as much as formal
schooling. My uncle went to Los Angeles and his first job was as a
shoeshine boy. But he knew an opportunity when it came. And his films
all had one central characteristic: the family and the character of the family. That comes from culture, not from a school."

The echoes, again, of culture trumping a formal schooling system.
The Sicilian and Southern Italian school of life that I'd been hearing
about constantly in my travels. Perhaps that explained the quick assim-

ilation when the Italians left remote places like Bisacquino and, in less than a generation, became prominent and often influential Americans.

"So what's this about you and Hollywood" I wondered aloud.

Viola interrupted.

"Before we go to Hollywood, we must eat something. Nené's had bypass surgery, his heart is not strong. He should eat."

"I've had three heart attacks now," Nené said quietly. "It's why I had to retire from my work."

I offered to return to town and come back on another day.

The Troncales would not hear of it. They said they set "a plain table," but that I was welcome to join them if I didn't mind a simple meal. Of course, I acquiesced. We ate penne in a simple tomato sauce, along with a small salad, Signora Troncale's bread and Nené's wine. Nené proudly said that the olive oil, the tomatoes and the wine had all been grown on his land and made in his house. It was, of course, a delicious meal, made even more enjoyable by the presence of this sensitive and lively couple. Their home and table were wonderfully comfortable.

During our meal Nené talked about his six children and nine grand-children. He was, understandably, proud of their accomplishments. All of his children had been or were still at the university. They all spoke several languages and had interesting work. All have stayed in Sicily, mostly in Palermo, though not in Bisacquino.

"Every penny I made as a teacher," Nené explained, "I put into this household. But I did lots of extra work—tutoring, whatever it took—and all of that money went to educate my children. It is a father's job to set up his children in life."

"Nené's father was the same way," Viola added. "Only, fathers were much more stern and strict when we were young."

"How do you mean?" I asked.

I thought about Nicola Zitara's comments in Gerace earlier that summer. Zitara believed that the Italian father had to serve as role model for the sons in a much more important way than in other cultures, since sons of Southerners had so few other role models to choose from. There were few or no political heroes, none in houses of royalty. Local nobility in the South was often a foreign group who had purchased their titles and basically stolen their land. According to Zitara, it was the Southern Italian father who held the family together, defined both the family and the culture. While the role of mother was extremely important, it was not as *symbolically* strong as that of the father.

"Our fathers were our heroes," Nené explained, echoing Zitara. "Their word was law. We used formal pronouns to address our fathers when I was young. When I saw my father in the evening, after he'd spent the entire day from the first rays of the sun working in the fields, I never said, 'Hello.' I said, *'Mi benedetto.'* I asked my father for his blessing. It wasn't enough just to say, *'Ti voglio bene'* or 'I wish you well,' 'I love you'; you had to prove your words by actions. A father had responsibilities to the family and a son had responsibilities to the father. The father in those days was like God, he was the center of everything; he was both the practical and the moral leader, our ultimate authority."

"And love?" I wondered. "How did he express his love?"

"By his actions. There wasn't time for hugging when there were fields to be tended. A father provided, worked hard. That's how he showed his love."

I was reminded of my grandfather, a remote man who would sit formally in tie and jacket in his parlor, smoke his ever-present cigar, and listen to grand opera. His relationship with us, his grandchildren, consisted of a mere few sentences on each visit. He was never the Norman Rockwell grandfather playing with us; wrestling, fishing, teasing, tickling. He oversaw from a distance. His job had been building his career, raising my mother and her brothers, building their homes. He was intelligent, could discuss politics, opera, business, his own thoughts and experiences; but he spoke in terse fragments. And he could not hug. As I learned the culture he was part of, I understood his actions more clearly.

"My parents were in love with each other," Nené recalled as he finished his penne and bread. "But love in those days meant a commitment to each other in the very hard work of raising a family. It wasn't living in a Hollywood movie, it was working the land and raising your children."

"Ah," I replied, "there's that word again. 'Hollywood.' What about Hollywood? You said earlier you were going there?"

"Well," Nené laughed, "when the war was over the main thing I wanted to do was get married. But I couldn't get married without a job. I was looking over my options. While I was deciding, a letter came."

"A letter?"

"Yes, a notarized letter. Wait."

Nené disappeared for a few moments, then returned to the table carrying a folder of documents. He retrieved a paper from the file and placed it in front of me. The letterhead read: "Columbia Studios, Liberty Films," Frank Capra's production company.

"My uncle sent me a letter telling me that he'd made arrangements for me to go to America and to work for him. This letter was for the Italian government."

The letter, dated December 26, 1946, was, in fact, an affidavit from Nené's famous uncle stating his income at $156,000 per year and his assets at another $500,000 and vouching for his nephew's character and ability to speak English. The letter went on to say that he could guarantee employment for Nené at the Columbia Studios and would be responsible for him. Another letter from Capra's bankers verified the income and investments in the first letter.

"This says you speak English," I said. Nené had not spoken a word of English all day.

"I know," he laughed. "I think he wrote that so that the Americans would grant me a visa."

"But you never went? Your uncle was one of the top directors in Hollywood—or the world, for that matter. You didn't go?"

"I couldn't go."

"Couldn't?"

"The Italian government wouldn't let me emigrate. My uncle was only a 'third-grade relative.' In order to emigrate in those days, you had to be sponsored by a first- or second-grade relative; a father or grandfather. An uncle wasn't close enough. It was the Fascist law. The new government in Rome hadn't gotten around to making any changes at that time. They were too busy with other things. I waited a year, but could never get my papers from the Italian government."

Nené shook his head and smiled.

"So I stayed in Bisacquino." He added simply.

Nené collected the letters and returned them to where he'd stored them.

"He got bad advice," Viola said quietly in an aside as Nené was out of the room. "The attorney he went to didn't know how to find a way around the law. But others left at the same time."

"Maybe he needed to pay someone some money?" I ventured.

"Probably," said Viola. "But Nené is quite innocent of those sorts of dealings."

"That's amazing," I said, after Nené returned. "You could have been a movie mogul, if it weren't for an outdated law. Weren't you upset?"

"I feel some anger I couldn't go to America. For a year after the war I was a big shot in the village, a movie star. But that was a long time ago, now. I was young and had my head full of dreams.

"But now it's forgotten. I married the woman I loved. We had no money, I had no job, but we had five hundred twenty people at our wedding. People came without invitations just to wish us well. We started our lives together with twelve chickens and ten eggs a day. We knew we wouldn't starve. And our friends had, in the Sicilian tradition, given us a year's worth of grain and salt. We knew somehow we'd be all right."

I was reminded of the scene in *It's a Wonderful Life*, Capra's favorite movie, when the Jimmy Stewart and Donna Reed characters gave wine and bread to a working-class Italian family as they moved into their first home they'd just financed through the "Bailey's Savings and Loan." A simple family starting a new life with the very basics, yet somehow fulfilled.

"I also decided at that time to forgo my *laurea* or formal university degree," Nené continued. "Instead, I applied for a teaching certificate. I made a mistake on my application and wound up having to wait an entire year before I could find a position. All of the teaching jobs, of course, were controlled by the government.

"After we were married, we decided to go to Rome on our honeymoon. On our way, we stopped at an aunt's house in Palermo. I expected to get my teaching appointment right away. While in Palermo I went to check on my status. That's when I learned about the mistake. So, there we were, on our way to Rome, and I had no money, no job, and no prospect of any job for quite some time. We stayed hidden at my aunt's home for the rest of the time, pretending we'd gone on to Rome. No one in the village ever knew we'd spent our entire honeymoon in a relative's guest room.

"*E questa è stata la nostra gira di nozze.*" Nené laughed. "And that was our honeymoon."

Viola had cleared the table. The woman moved with incredible speed. She placed a small espresso cup before me and poured another coffee before I could refuse. I was about to reach caffeine overdrive.

"You taught for twenty-nine years?" I asked.

"Yes. I finally got my first teaching appointment when Viola was seven months pregnant with our first child. I moved eighteen times in all. I worked on average of eighteen hours a day. I tutored when I wasn't in the classroom. We kept a small garden and grew much of our own food. That's how we saved enough to build our own house and educate our children."

"And," added Viola with a rare comment, "we didn't have to go to

Hollywood to make our life, after all. We made our life right here in Bisacquino."

Troncale's story was typical of many Italians on both sides of the Atlantic. A study released a few years ago by the Italian government placed the Italians second only to the Japanese in percentage of saved income. The first generation of Italian men to America saved most of what they made in order either to return to Italy, or to bring their families to their new country and buy their own home. Savings rates were especially high in the South, another Southern tradition of sorts.

"You set your children up in life," Nené said. "It's a father's job. You should live a life in which you are proud of your family, that's the most important value to pass along."

We were interrupted by a phone call. I could hear Nené telling the caller that I was asking about *his* life, not his uncle's. He seemed pleased about it.

"My daughter, the one you spoke with," he said after clicking off. "She wanted to make sure you'd arrived. All of my children look after me now." He seemed truly contented. "There's something else I wanted to show you," he said. He disappeared again into the back of the house and returned with another folder of photographs.

"These are the pictures of my uncle's visit here in 1977."

Nené and I leafed through a stack of old black-and-white photographs. In each, Nené was plainly visible, dressed formally in a dark Sunday suit and wearing the big black-frame glasses that were in style at that time. The whole village, it seemed, including the entire Troncale clan, had turned out in their Sunday best for the return of their native son. I wondered if Franco Maresco had been captured on film spotting his *contadino* hero, but didn't see any youths resembling him. Capra wore one of his trademark sport coats and looked distracted at times.

"My daughter," Nené said, "the one who just called, wrote a poem for him and he wrote her a thank-you note for that poem."

"He spoke Italian then?" I surmised.

"He understood everything, but he spoke only in English. I'm sure he didn't want to speak in dialect."

"Why is that?" I wondered for the umpteenth time. "What was their problem with the dialect?"

"I understood why he didn't want to speak. After all, he left here as a little boy and he never learned the proper forms of the language. Here, especially in Sicily, it is an embarrassment, a sign of weakness if one cannot speak properly. He knew that. So my uncle did what I would have done, he spoke the language he knew well. But he understood everything, I could tell. When my daughter read her poem to him, she used all of the titles of his films in her poem, but it was all in Italian. I watched his face; he smiled and reacted to all of the plays on words. He knew the language."

"I will never understand this embarrassment over dialects," I said.

Nené and I looked over the remaining pictures.

"I had the back of the house rebuilt for his stay," Nené explained, pointing to a photo of a large room, a huge table in its center filled with apparent delicacies. "We built a large room for him to stay here, with us, but he wasn't feeling well, he couldn't even eat anything. He stayed in Palermo at a hotel. We were disappointed. The room is now two rooms."

"How do you explain your uncle," I wondered aloud. "How do you explain a boy leaving this small place and making such a big mark in the world? Have you thought about that?" I asked.

Nené smiled.

"When Frank Capra left this village," he began, "he left here poor, ignorant, illiterate. That was the reality of this village when he was born. When he came back here as an old man, he wouldn't speak the language because by that point he couldn't demonstrate anything other than the great success he'd achieved. It would have been a disappointment to the villagers if he'd made grammatical mistakes. He knew that. After all those years, he remembered."

Nené paused for a moment, rearranged the photos in the yellowing folder as he gathered his thoughts.

"You know," he continued, "what the immigrants from Bisacquino, or anywhere in Sicily, brought with them to America were *values*, not valuables. Every one of my uncle's films were about the values that every boy in this village learned from his own father."

Nené had reached my question before I'd asked it.

"So you think then," I asked, "that Frank Capra represented the average man from this village?"

"He represented the *values* the average man from this village would have believed. They were poor, not stupid. They were illiterate, not uneducated. They were farmers who understood the land and human nature. Southerners had to be more intelligent than others, we had so much less. We had to work things out without the guidance of professionals or scholars. But there's only a limit to what you can do. Here we were limited to family and place. But once out of here, once there was actual opportunity...well, my uncle shined shoes, did menial work. But he knew an opportunity when it came. And he took it."

I was truly taken in by Nené's words and knew that he, too, had thought about the same question, probably for a very long time. Nené helped clarify many of my own thoughts about these people. Not just how they became famous movie directors, but all of them, the Sicilians, Basilicatans, Calabrians—all of them. There really was something to the "land of opportunity" we'd grown up believing in. And they really did bring something with them to their new lands beyond strong backs; they brought strong ideas of how to deal with the world and those ideas all started with their family.

"Things are different today," Nené added more quietly. "Today there are pensions, health care. Much has changed."

"Do you think your children are better off?"

"Yes. But not because they have *more*. Because they have *opportunity*. That's all we've ever needed here."

*   *   *

I left Nené and Viola with a promise to keep in touch. I drove back to Palermo, took the highway across the northern part of the island, then a ferry across the Strait of Messina.

I stood at the rail of the ship as it crossed the black water that night and watched the lights of Messina twinkle in the slight haze. A young couple was intertwined a few feet away, cooing and kissing from time to time, completely oblivious of the middle-aged man standing near them and gazing off into the Sicilian hills. Messina looked like a carnival from the water, its lights dancing in the mist, traffic on the highway splashed yellow, white and red lights onto the black canvas of the night.

I was thinking about a five-year-old boy who left this island so many years ago, and a seventy-five-year-old man who still lived there. And I knew that both of them represented the character, strength and vitality of the place. While one might be world-famous, he was like them—the ones who stayed. And they were like him.

It *was* all a question of values, after all.

Several months after my conversations with Nené Troncale, I was introduced to Dr. Fred Gardaphe, a professor at Stony Brook in New York. Gardaphe is considered one of the top scholars in the field of Italian-American studies. We met in the back room of Sam Patti's Pittsburgh coffee shop, where Gardaphe was reviewing a speech he was to deliver that afternoon at Duquesne University.

Patti's coffee shop is a gathering point for many in Pittsburgh's Italian-American community; eclectic conversations and topics are the nature of the place. Somehow, but not surprisingly, the subject of films came up. Gardaphe said offhandedly he taught Frank Capra's *It's a Wonderful Life* as an example of an *Italian-American* film.

I was surprised by the coincidence, it was the exact thought Nené had shared with me in Bisacquino. I told the professor of Nené's comments.

"I look at the film through the perspective of a 'born-again Italian,'" Gardaphe joked. He, like me, came to his sense of heritage as an adult. "But if you think about that film, the Italian values are obvious. *It's a Wonderful Life* is a story about how a community creates an identity. Without that community, and each individual's role in the community, there is no identity. It's George Bailey's [Jimmy Stewart's] involvement in the community that defines his life and actions."

"So, you believe, like Nené, that his films represent Southern Italian values?" I asked.

"Most definitely. Capra's films are about nobodies who are destroyed when they become somebodies," Gardaphe continued. "And Capra learned that from Southern Italian sensibilities where the community depends on contributions for survival. *Alone* in the Southern Italian culture is not a positive attribute. In fact, they have a couple of sayings, '*Chi beve solo muore solo*—He who drinks alone dies alone' and '*Chi non beve in compania, è un ladro o una spia*—He who drinks alone is either a thief or a spy.'

"Everything about Capra's films displays his Sicilian sense of the world transposed to America. But he created those images on film in an American way. Much more so than many later films which claim to have Italian-American themes but miss the mark."

In other words, Capra's films did represent the values every Sicilian boy learned from his own father, as Nené had said. And those same values had been passed down for countless centuries. Given the appeal *It's a Wonderful Life* has gained internationally, those values would seem to be enduring.

8

Amantea Adieu

RETURN TO THE MAINLAND

I had been in Palermo on September 11, 2001.

My cell phone went off as I checked my mail at an Internet shop. Enrico Borsetti called from Rome and excitedly told me what was happening. "Get to a television set," he said, "you must see for yourself."

I stumbled about the Castel Nuovo district of Palermo. People I passed on the street seemed to be going about their normal lives. I walked a couple of quick blocks through the upscale section near the Piazza Settimo, which reminded me again of exclusive shopping districts in Paris and Berlin. I had hoped to find an international hotel, but found instead a beauty parlor, the sound of a news report coming into the street.

A heavyset middle-aged man sat behind the cash register, staring across the room as if he were watching television. He pointed to a radio along the opposite wall. A woman beautician was working on a client in one of the shop's two large swivel chairs. Both women studied me cautiously, the now common reaction for Southerners and Sicilians hearing my foreign accent.

"*Sei americano?*" the man asked.

"*Sì,*" I replied, trying to hear the report.

"Come with me," he said. He rose, quickly crossed the floor and took my arm. "There is a television set next door."

We walked, his hand firmly holding my arm, a dozen paces or so to the adjoining shop, a general store. A male customer stood at the counter receiving change from the clerk. Without asking permission, my escort reached up on the top shelf opposite the cash register and turned on a small television set.

"There is trouble in America," he said to the clerk as he turned up the volume. "He is an American." He nodded in my direction.

The four of us stood motionless and silent for the next several minutes as the horrendous pictures flickered by on the screen.

Then I heard the word "Pittsburgh." The incomprehensible story went from horrific to personal. I pulled my cell phone out and dialed my sister's number. Marie and her family, along with countless other relatives, live in Pittsburgh and its suburbs. It was terrifying news. Surprisingly, the call went right through.

"My God," I said. "What's going on? Is everyone okay there?"

The other men in the store watched me closely. A few others entered the store and stood quietly about as I spoke to America. While none of them had spoken any English, they seemed to be hanging on every word of my end of the conversation.

"I can't believe what I'm seeing," my sister said in an unsteady voice. "The local TV stations are all trying to get to this airplane crash, it must have just happened. It looks to be over in Somerset County."

I breathed a sigh of guilty relief. While there was rampant horror occurring in New York, Pennsylvania and Washington, at least my family seemed to be safe. I clung to the illusion of at least that much security.

"I can't believe it," my sister repeated. "We were watching the morning news when they showed the pictures…"

"I know," I said. "We see them here in Palermo, too."

The technological wonders of our era didn't even register on us at that moment. A mass murder unprecedented in American history was being transmitted in mere seconds around the world in who knew how many languages. The events were seen by millions upon millions, live and in color and real time. I was discussing the event from a shop in Palermo via cell phone with my sister an ocean away in Pennsylvania.

Everything about the story was strange, mysterious, fantastic and utterly awful.

After switching off with my sister, I gave my companions in the general store a report on what she had told me. It didn't vary much from what we were hearing over the TV from the Italian national news from Rome, but through me my Palermo friends had a personal link to the tragedy. They extended their condolences, much as if there had been a death in the family and, in way, I guess there had.

The Italian network, RAI, was taking in the CNN signal and rebroadcasting it with a simultaneous translation. It made the event even more unreal as the English and Italian blended into a frustrating and nearly indecipherable cacophony of language. After several minutes of this additional aggravation I decided to return to my hotel. I escorted my companion back to his shop. The two ladies asked about what we had seen on the television set. The client sat under a gown as the beautician worked on her hair. She seemed very upset. "I have a cousin in Brooklyn," she said, voicing what many Italians must have been thinking at that moment.

The next several hours went by in a haze. I had spent the past several months talking with poets and paupers, professors and proprietors, anyone and everyone who could help me understand and dig deeper into the heritage and culture which had taken over my thoughts in recent years. Yet, on this day, all of that seemed almost irrelevant.

Real-time events had taken over and this digging into the past wasn't nearly as important. And, while the Sicilians I talked with were most sympathetic and supportive, I found myself feeling isolated. I yearned for the company of fellow Americans. I'd seen an American couple at breakfast that morning, and I searched unsuccessfully for them in the lobby and bar when I returned to my hotel. I wanted to be with someone from home; there was just no other way to describe it.

That evening I met Warren Blumberg at the Piazza Marina, about a mile's walk from my waterfront hotel. I had contacted Warren, an American jazz critic and fellow writer, to translate the Troncale interview I'd rescheduled for later in the week. Warren had been living in Palermo for the past year or so and had been married to an Italian woman in Umbria for nearly ten years before moving to Sicily.

I was grateful to have another American to share the evening with. As we sat in the piazza picking at a sandwich and having a drink, we were frequently interrupted by local youngsters who knew Warren and approached our table with the air of attending a funeral. They offered sympathy, wanted to know if we'd heard anything more, talked about death tolls and war. Warren and I shared our disbelief and sense of isolation.

Palermo was a long way from New York.

THE QUAKE AND THE MADONNA

A few days later I found myself back on the mainland heading toward Reggio di Calabria. It was hard to imagine the terror that had just occurred in the States and even harder to conceive of the minds who had planned this outrage. Yet, this same coast I was now driving along had been the scene of terror for century upon century as various marauders and terrorists—though that name would have never been used in the same context—came time and again to plunder, rape and dominate the region.

It was a common story of Southern Italy and, in its time, undoubtedly as horrifying as airplanes intentionally flown into office buildings. Did it maybe help explain the deeply religious nature of these people? They seemed to be religious in a more spiritual sense than we Americans were; references to God and the saints were constant. Great tragedy has a way of prompting the eternal questions, that much was certain.

For years I had been reading about the bronzes from Riace, ancient Greek statues now the pride of the main museum in Reggio. I wouldn't be getting back this way anytime soon. I intended not to miss this opportunity, despite my desire, my need, to get to a television set and watch the continuing, awful story of the terrorist attacks in America.

Reggio was certainly no stranger to disaster. The city, and the entire Strait of Messina, sits on a fault line, the convergence of plates where Africa and Europe come together. This land has been threatened by earthquakes and tidal waves since it was formed. But none was worse than the quake and subsequent tsunami that occurred at five-thirty in the morning on December 28, 1908.

I saw Reggio for the first time eighty-three years after that quake, but there are still signs and reminders of the tragedy almost everywhere. Every date on every building relates, somehow, to 1908.

At least a hundred thousand people died that morning in the deadliest natural disaster in European history. The quake in San Francisco two years before had destroyed most of the city, but the highest fatality estimate was placed at seven hundred, a tragic number, indeed, but significantly lower than that of the Italian quake two years later. The majority of the deaths were across the strait in Messina, the larger of the two cities. But both cities and every town and village throughout the area on

Sicily and all through southern Calabria were devastated. The aftereffects of the quake were felt as far away as Washington, D.C.

In one of the few positive stories of the House of Savoy in Southern Italy, the young King Vittorio Emanuele III, then thirty-nine years old, and his wife traveled to Reggio in the first week after the tragedy, placing themselves at risk. Just as in September of 2001, the entire civilized world was both shocked and sickened by the event, and volunteer relief efforts came from near and far.

It was, by every criterion, an extraordinary catastrophe; thousands were buried alive under rubble; all transportation and shipping was severely hampered by destroyed roads, rails and docks; medical supplies and food were scarce and nearly impossible to distribute; dead human and animal bodies polluted the water supply and threatened the health of survivors; the region was left in crushing poverty and with serious health concerns for decades afterward.

Every Calabrian family has some memory or story about that quake.

My own family is no exception.

My Uncle Dominic Falduto was from Trunca, a tiny spot on the map just outside Reggio in the steep mountains to the north of the town. He was fourteen years old that morning. He was still asleep when he was aroused by his mother just before dawn, calling anxiously to him and his brothers and sisters.

According to Uncle Dom, his mother said the Blessed Virgin had come to her in a dream and told her to awaken the family and get them out of the house. She managed to get all but one child outside before the quake hit. The daughter who remained indoors was killed, crushed in the rubble of collapsed ceilings and walls. Miraculously, everyone else—five children and both parents—survived the quake and its terrible aftermath.

Only one part of the house remained after the quake, a section of the bedroom wall that had stood behind his parent's bed. Uncle Dom said the portrait of the Blessed Mother remained on that wall fragment, hanging serenely as if nothing had happened. Until his death many years later, Uncle Dom had a special reverence for the Madonna, a picture of whom now hangs next to his crypt.

THE RIACE BRONZES

On August 16, 1972, Stefano Mariottini was sport-diving in the Ionian Sea about nine hundred yards off the shore of the small Calabrian town of Riace Marina. The youth spotted something mysterious on the seafloor and dived down thirty feet or so. What appeared to be a human arm was reaching up through the soft sandy bottom.

That thrusting arm pulled antiquity into the present and resulted in one of the most important archaeological and artistic finds of the latter twentieth century.

Two larger-than-life-sized bronze statues had lain on the seabed for around twenty-five hundred years, the apparent remains of an ancient Greek shipwreck. No one knows where the ship was bound or exactly when it went down. But one thing was sure: the statues were definitely Greek and from the Greek Classical period. The date of the wreck was set at sometime between 450 and 460 B.C.E., though the age of the statues places one of the bronze men at thirty to sixty years older than his companion.

After careful excavation, the statues were gently and lovingly restored in Tuscany. The highly technical work took five years. Of course, an inevitable political fight broke out over where they should be displayed. Florence kept the bronzes for all of 1980; Rome displayed them in 1981. The Tuscans and Romans argued for permanent display. Fortunately for Calabria, where the bronzes had been discovered and which was quite probably their ancient destination, the city of Reggio prevailed.

It was only fair that they return to Calabria. When the bronzes first settled on the floor of the Ionian, Rome was just an emerging city-state, still a long way from empire, and Florence didn't even exist, whereas Reggio and Messina were thriving Greek centers. Logic won out; Il Museo Archeologico Nazionale was to be their permanent home.

Bronze statuary from the Classical period is very rare, guaranteeing any museum a natural draw. Since Roman times, invading armies throughout Italy melted down bronze statues and reforged them mostly into weaponry. The few statues that survived have been found underwater, like Marcus Aurelius on horseback, which stands in the heart of ancient Rome in the Piazza Campidoglio. It is several hundred years younger than the Riace sculptures and survived only because it was thrown into the Tiber, where it remained for over a thousand years.

The Museo Archeologico Nazionale in Reggio was the brainchild of Paolo Orsi, the father of modern Italian archaeology. He had been the driving force behind its development following the 1908 earthquake, arguing that a modern structure was necessary to hold the priceless artifacts of so many years of Calabrian civilization. Many ruins and precious pieces had been destroyed in the quake. Orsi wanted a definitive quake-proof place in which to put the region's historical artifacts.

The initial plans for an archaeological museum were finally approved in 1932. Then came an economic depression, the Second World War and the massive postwar rebuilding. Reggio's museum didn't open its doors to a small display until 1954, and wasn't fully completed until 1981.

Il Museo was built to the most up-to-date engineering standards possible to prevent against future earthquakes. It stands at the end of Reggio's mile-long seafront promenade, which the *Abruzzese* poet Gabriele D'Annunzio called "the most beautiful mile in Italy." The promenade looks across the strait to the coast of Sicily and is lined with statues, fountains and palm trees. D'Annunzio didn't exaggerate.

The bronzes are displayed in a basement room of the museum especially designed to roll with any movement of the earth and in carefully controlled and conditioned air. When I finally found my way into the display, I couldn't help but feel I was in a very important place. The various catalogue descriptions can't do justice to the statues; one was described as "Bronze with copper lips and nipples, silver teeth and inlaid eyes."

The bronzes are breathtaking, so much more than a mere mixture of metals. Standing before the statues is like standing in front of your own ancestors. You feel you and they are somehow related. They stand as defiant survivors from a time and place when art, as we know it now, was literally being invented. They look as new today as they must have in their own time.

The inlaid eyes of *Il Vecchio,* or The Old One, stare out onto the horizon as if scanning it for danger. His hand is cupped to hold his missing weapon. He is a soldier, the physical ideal of his time and place. *Il Giovane,* or The Young One, stands a few feet away, his left arm and hand poised to hold a missing spear, his eyes empty bronze sockets, yet his face is somehow the face of every young man who must go to war. Both are bearded, the old one has ringlets of hair pouring out from under his helmet, the young one more close-cropped. They are completely absorbing in their silence and grandeur, representing a society that was technologically, artistically, militarily and culturally the defining one of its time, and one with direct ties to our current forms of politics, art and religion.

No one knows exactly whom these two statues were meant to represent. But in their time, *everyone* would have known. Literacy in Magna Graecia wasn't necessarily in books, but in the understanding of man and art. It was in the understanding that the representations of great warriors or gods told the stories of man's capabilities, hopes, dreams and *possibilities.* These bronze men represented the standards of the Greek, Sicilian and Southern Italian culture that for centuries would languish in the minds and hearts of the people, if not in books. How else could one explain churches in Sicily displaying small statues of Persephone, Demeter and even Aphrodite to this very day?

Looking at the bronzes, it was obvious to me how close we are to our collective past, how much we must be like the people who created and admired these statues. They've made art historians reassess the timing of man's artistic development, since they both represent the Classical period from an earlier date than was previously established. The people who would have seen these statues never heard of e-mail or airplanes, electricity or telephones. Yet they have communicated over thousands of years with technologically perfect castings that were constructed and transported throughout the then-known world.

Are we really that much more advanced today?

The bronzes cause such stirrings.

They have also increased tourism to Reggio, a long-delayed recognition of one of the ancient and modern worlds' most beautiful cities. If there is no other reason to celebrate the bronzes, traveling down the toe of Italy to see them is a reward enough.

NOTES ON ROCCO'S PLACE, ANCORA

I am at Rocco's for the last time. I drove most of the way from Reggio to Amantea on the old Route SS18 as it winds its way along the coast and beside the ever-present mountains, passing old castles and Norman towers and looking back over my shoulder to Sicily for a good deal of the way. It had been a beautiful day, the kind you see in Cary Grant movies; perfect cumulus clouds hanging above a blue-green sea; ancient castles crumbling picturesquely on the opposing cliffs.

I reached Amantea in late afternoon and sat in front of the Pensione Margarita on a plastic chair as Rocco and I decided world problems. We were joined by several men passing by: Roberto with his ever-present smile and newspaper talking about the day's events in Rome; Frank, who is from is from Ambridge, Pennsylvania, and is back for his yearly visit to his family; Giovanni on his yellow bicycle, who insists on speaking German with me and whose Calabrian dialect is so thick I actually prefer it; the young fellow from the men's clothing store across the street who always wears designer shirts and loves to try out his English; and two or three other elderly gentlemen who show up in the late afternoon for their card game accompanied by shouts and arguments.

As usual, none drink or smoke; Rocco never makes a single lire from these gatherings, but it doesn't seem to bother him as he seems to delight in the conversation and exchange of ideas.

"You know," he says, "I don't criticize Americans for how they live, but I don't want to live that way. You get up and go to work, come home, maybe talk to your wife and go to bed. I need to go out, to walk, to talk with people about what's going on, maybe eat something, have a coffee. Do you know your neighbors in the United States?"

I said I did, but in Ohio everyone disappears for six months a year during the winter.

"That's what I mean," he said. "I don't like to live like that."

Like or not, however, winter is coming on again. The season is over in Amantea for another year. A sunburned, bright red and very blond German couple who don't take their meals at Rocco's are the only other guests in the place. I dined alone in the big dining room, remembering the crowds of just a few weeks ago.

During the meal Rocco brought the plastic furniture inside.

"A little early to close up," I said.

"It's over now," said Rocco, "nobody comes anymore this year. They all go home at eight o'clock to eat and now they stay there. Not like in summer, when they come back out and stay late."

A few minutes later Rocco's brother-in-law showed up, coming through the beaded doorway and saying it felt like *inverno*—winter—outside.

Later, I sat on my balcony and watched the nearly deserted streets. There was something sad about the evening. I missed the incredible level of noise the summer had brought, the constant buzzing and whirring of the *motorini,* the shouts of youngsters, the loud voices of the card players below. Another season has passed by in this little town which has witnessed so many seasons before. Soon it would be time to leave and to put this place in memory. Here I had my place among the men discussing the world's events after the evening meal.

Amantea had treated me well.

AMANTEA ADIEU

Rocco seemed preoccupied with paperwork, not his ebullient self. I needed to find out the latest news and decided to go on the Internet where I could catch up on e-mail as well.

During my first visit to Amantea, I'd asked Rocco if he knew of an Internet café in town. He said he thought there was one about a mile away near the fountain at the foot of the mountain, a block from the neighborhood where Rocco had grown up. As I reached the corner on my way up the Via Margherita, I happened to glance over my shoulder. A sign for an Internet shop was halfway down the block on the main highway. Rocco was not into computers and hadn't even heard of the place, which was only a few hundred meters from his *pensione.* I couldn't have been more delighted and spent more than a little time there during that first and subsequent visits.

The little store was basically a shotgun arrangement: one long wall with three or four computer stands and an opposing counter for printing. The place was stifling hot, there was no ventilation. My shirt would be soaked through after only a few minutes at a terminal. The young Italian who ran the place was apologetic but had apparently never heard of electric fans.

When I went to pay for my time after my initial session, the shop owner spoke English with me. His name was Mark, he had lived in Arizona for a time and had an uncle still living there.

"Are your parents from here in Amantea?" I asked.

"They died," he said.

I was taken aback by his comment. The young man looked terribly sad.

"I'm sorry to hear that," I replied. "I didn't mean to pry."

"It was a surprise," he continued. "My father died suddenly. I think it was too much for my mother. She died a few months later."

"When was this?" I asked.

"Almost a year ago," he said.

Over the course of my visits that summer, I learned Mark was married and, in mid-summer, he and his wife celebrated the birth of their first child, a baby girl. I'd seen the infant briefly and met his wife and brother. He seemed happy about his child, but nonetheless had a palpable air of gloominess about him.

On my last visit to Amantea, I walked over to the Internet shop to catch up with Mark and my e-mail. It was cooler now, the lack of air circulation wouldn't be nearly as critical. I was curious about how Mark was adjusting to fatherhood.

The shop had gone out of business.

I wondered about Mark, his new baby, his life in Amantea without his parents. I wished him well.

I was, again, the only diner at Rocco's that evening. I told him I didn't want to disturb things and that I could eat in a restaurant if that would be easier for him and his family.

"You eat what we cook," he said with a smile. "You can always eat here." He served an early meal of *pesce spada,* or a broiled swordfish, so tender and light it all but floated into my mouth. The only seasoning was a little salt and pepper and some lemon and it tasted divine.

I wished I could always eat at Rocco's place.

After dinner, on that last evening, I sat in the long shadows at the front of the *pensione* and marveled again at the silence and solitude. Eventually, Rocco joined me. He asked, of course, about what I had heard from my family in the States.

"You know what this is really all about?" Rocco asked. "I'll tell you what I think. This is all about Lepanto. They're still trying to settle the score."

I laughed.

"Lepanto?" I said. "Do you realize that maybe four people within a range of maybe six hundred square miles would know what you're talking about?" I laughed again.

"You can laugh, but Berlusconi is right. These terrorists are people from another age. You Americans can't understand how they think."

Rocco was referring to the Battle of Lepanto, a naval engagement between the Holy League led by the pope and the Ottomans in the sixteenth century, in which the Turkish fleet was defeated. Some referred to it as the last Crusade because it was an alliance of Christians against Muslims. Miguel de Cervantes, the famous Spanish writer, was wounded in the battle and recounted some of his experiences in his famous novel *Don Quixote.* The Christians won decisively. The only reason I was aware of Lepanto was because of the Metro stop in Rome using the name. I'd had to look up the reference.

Just the evening before Rocco made his analogy with Lepanto, the Italian president Silvio Berlusconi had commented that the attacks against the United States were attacks on all Western civilization. He said the attacks were made essentially by people who still lived in an intellectual mind-set a thousand years behind the West. He'd been soundly criticized in the Italian and world press for his non-politically correct comments.

"Only the Italians could relate this to the Crusades," I said, "and mean it."

"Your own president used the word," Rocco countered.

"Yes, but he used it in the contemporary sense. When an American uses the term, he immediately thinks of Eisenhower, the Second World War, the cold war. Not many Americans picture knights on horseback running off to fight the 'infidels.' And he backed off the term the second his advisers suggested it might raise the wrong issues."

"Maybe," said Rocco, "but you can't erase history when it has caused such anger for so very long."

Giovanni came by on his bicycle.

Giovanni is a middle-aged man, very thin, completely bald on the top of his tanned head and with large tufts of gray-blond hair at the sides. Ever since he'd learned that I had been stationed in Germany as an American soldier, he insisted on speaking German with me.

"*Grüß Gott,*" he said as he chained his bike to a lamppost. The saying—"May God greet you"—is mostly used in Bavaria and Austria.

"*Guten Abend,*" I replied with the standard "Good evening."

"*Es tut mir leid—diese schrecklichen Vorfälle in Deinem Land.*" He was sorry for the terrible events in my country.

"*Danke,*" I thanked him.

He spoke German with an Italian accent, mine was heavy with Pittsburgh and American pronunciation. The sunburned, bright red German couple had gone out, again, for dinner someplace else. I can only imagine what they, as native speakers, would have thought of our babbling.

Giovanni had spent several years in Germany as a *Gastarbeiter,* or guest worker, in the construction trade. The country had imported thousands of workers from elsewhere in Europe and the Near East during its great rebuilding period of the sixties and seventies, with the largest number of workers coming from Southern Italy and especially Turkey. Many Turks had chosen to remain in Germany, while the Italians mostly returned home when their labors were done. The Turks had a difficult time gaining German citizenship; it was one of the factors in the current uneasiness between East and West.

The sun was setting earlier now. We were joined by a few other locals, but our group was substantially smaller than the summer groups had been. Roberto, Rocco, Giovanni, one or two others and I sat facing the empty street. Soon we were surrounded by oddly quiet long shadows as we chattered away.

"Das ist verrückt!" Giovanni insisted. "We are living in crazy times."

"Speak Italian or English," Rocco said, laughing. "Things are crazy enough."

"People expect too much today," said another man, a regular I recognized from the summer crowds. "We have too many things, so we expect too many things. Is it any wonder the people who have so little want more?"

"What do we have?" asked Giovanni.

"When I was a boy," Rocco said, "there was no such thing as two automobiles for one family. People didn't have such luxuries. Now people not only expect to have a car, they expect it to be air-conditioned. *Air-conditioned!*" he repeated, as if the phrase itself were self-explanatory. "Can you imagine? These little rental cars that run about the town all summer long, tiny cars with air conditioners. We were lucky to have enough food. Sometimes my mother had to make bread from chestnuts, from things we picked up in the woods, just to survive."

"Ah, chestnut bread," said Giovanni, sighing. "I love chestnut bread."

"This was no luxury," Rocco said. "This was survival. Today we take things for granted that only a few years ago would have been unbelievable."

"So the have-nots have a right to attack those who have?" I asked. I wasn't sure where Rocco was going with this.

"No. But they are bound to want what they don't have. Your CNN and all your movies have shown the world air-conditioned cars and hamburgers and beautiful women with perfect bodies who walk about freely and say what they think. If you live in a society with none of that, you either want it or are threatened by it. Don't you see, you've created the expectation and the fear?"

"Er hat recht," said Giovanni. He's right.

"No," I argued. "We didn't create the fear. We created the opportunity. Everyone in this town should know beyond a doubt what we've offered the world. We give people a chance to create themselves, to do it better. It was Italy that failed the Calabrians, not America. I don't know who failed these maniacs who hate us so much, but we would have given them opportunity."

Rocco smiled sadly. "I'm not sure there's an answer to this problem." He sighed.

"Gelegenheit," said Giovanni. Opportunity.

"Exactly," I said. "It's why you went to Germany to work. You couldn't find it here, you found it there. It's why Rocco went to South America and the States. To find work, to save some money, to come back home."

"Ah," said Rocco, "yes, but sadly things haven't changed all that much. The young here still have to go away to school. And the good jobs are up north. The work here is seasonal—fine for me, but for a young man starting off..."

I thought about Mark and his failed Internet shop. Most of the businesses along the main drag were tourist-oriented. I'd assumed that they made enough during the season to keep going the rest of the year.

"The future will be very different for all of us," I ventured. "For the United States, for Europe, for everybody."

"Yes," agreed Rocco, "as it has always been. Italy is changing every day. Air-conditioning, we're losing our dialects, the village life is dying and the young still go away."

On my last evening in Amantea, I stood by the seawall and watched the sunset across the oddly vacant beach and miles of empty sea. I wondered what it must have been like to stand there in ancient times and see the prow of a Carthaginian or Saracen or Byzantine or Norman bark round the distant cape. Men who came to conquer or plunder. I thought about the fear it must have caused, the continual panic that would have risen in these people as strangers came in creaking ships.

Today they came in airplanes.

And every time they came, things changed. The only difference was, when we could look backward, we knew what had happened.

9

The Sad Tango and Other Stories

MICHELE'S DRAWER

"Caro Paolo," Michele said, as I entered the Di Pedes' electric appliance shop. *"Come stai?"*

I was back in Matera in between adventures. Cosimo Di Pede sat in the deep shade at the back of the shop. He looked like a centenarian Roman senator accepting petitioners. There was the usual group of middle-aged men visiting Cosimo. One of the men shared my family name, he was a local banker. Though we could not establish any relationship, it made for an interesting conversation, since so few of my generation of Americans have ever found their way back to the city of the Sassi. I was always greeted with great courtesy and curiosity by the shop's other visitors. All quickly recognized my family name and accepted me as a welcome American cousin.

As we talked among ourselves in the back of the store, an English couple stopped by, shopping for a clock.

"*Papa,*" called Michele, "*per favore.*"

The old man got up and walked steadily and confidently with the aid of his cane to the bright sunlight in the front of the store. He explained the intricacies of a particular battery-operated clock to the couple. The woman asked about Cosimo's fluency in English and listened delightedly to his story of spending ten years in the New World.

"Might I ask how old you are?" the woman ventured in her polite British fashion. Cosimo's dates of 1918 to 1928 had apparently raised a mathematical interest.

"I'll be one hundred years in September," Cosimo said, in a strong and clear voice.

The couple fussed over the old man for the next several minutes, clearly enjoying his story and the vigor with which he told it. It was also evident that Cosimo enjoyed the exchange, though I was disappointed because I knew it would tire him and I'd have that much less time to dig into his memories before he'd start answering in fatigued and one-word responses.

The couple failed to purchase a clock. The old man returned to the cool at the back of the room. I leaned against a dishwashing machine. Cosimo sat surrounded by refrigerators, washers, dryers and electric fans; all but the fans nonexistent when Cosimo had been born a short distance, I assumed, from where we sat.

"Where you born in the Sassi?" I asked.

"Yes. Sure."

"Can you tell me, was the Sassi as unhealthy as Levi says it was in his book?"

"Yes. Sure," Cosimo repeated.

His conversation with the English couple must have tired him.

"I mean, I find it hard to believe it could have been as bad as Levi described. Especially since you're living proof of health and vitality and you came from a supposed unhealthy environment. Was it as bad as Levi said?" I asked again.

"There was work," Cosimo replied.

"Work?"

"Yes, work. There was construction work. We made things with stones. Built houses. I helped my father. We built our house. There was always work."

"So it wasn't as poor as Levi says?" I wasn't very clear about Cosimo's comments.

"Yes, of course. There has always been work for those who want to work. We built things, we kept busy. Hard work is always available."

"You mean," I attempted to clarify, "that you didn't feel the poverty the way others have described it?"

"Yes. Sure."

Cosimo's mind was starting to wander slightly. It was hard for him to focus on a specific question, though I doubt many of us could focus at all if we survived to his age. I marveled at the flush in his cheeks and the determination with which he spoke. I would have to wait for another day to probe his memory.

One morning, not long after the British couple's meeting with Cosimo, I spotted Michele sitting alone at the back of the store as I passed by. He waved for me to come in. He said he wanted to show me something. Cosimo had apparently already gone home for the day. Michele reached into his cluttered, overflowing drawer and pulled out a few papers.

"You have a computer and e-mail?" Michele asked.

"Yes."

"Here," he said. "Maybe you can answer this man. I did some research for him and here is the information."

Michele handed me the documents, a page of handwritten notes and a cover note from a certain Cosmo Di Pede of Aberdeen, New Jersey.

The American Di Pede was doing some genealogical research and had written Michele to see if the families were related.

"I went to the city hall and looked up the records for this man," said Michele. "You'll see that your family name is in this family's tree two generations back. A Paolicelli woman married into this family. The New Jersey Di Pedes might be a very distant relation to me but none that I could find."

I looked over the papers and Cosmo Di Pede's letter. Then I spotted the date.

"Michele, this letter was written over three years ago. Have you responded to the Di Pede in New Jersey?"

"No, not yet. I was hoping with your computer you could write."

I was struck once again by the Italian sense of time. Michele had waited three years and had spoken with me several times before rummaging in his drawer and bringing the American's request to light. And the timing didn't seem the least bit unusual to him. Michele seemed pleased by my interest in the papers and not the least bit troubled by three years of elapsed time. He'd certainly not neglected the request, he'd gone to the city hall and looked through the ledger books, but evidently felt no sense of pressure to respond.

Michele smiled contentedly and nodded when I promised I'd contact the New Jersey family. He didn't ask me *when* I planned on making that contact.

Later that day I e-mailed the New Jersey Di Pede and received a reply within a day. Cosmo Di Pede explained he had been making a family tree for his children and grandchildren and had found almost all of the information he'd been looking for in the Ellis Island document files. He still had a question about his grandfather Di Pede; he couldn't find a date of entry into the United States for this particular Cosimo, but he had everything else he needed. He now knew he wasn't related to the Matera centenarian, but had hoped the Matera Di Pedes could shed some light on his grandfather's story. He'd been given the name "Cosmo" after his grandfather, Cosimo, in an apparent attempt to Anglicize the name.

The New Jersey Di Pedes, now in their sixties, had made their first visit to Italy in 1999. Their letter to Michele had been in preparation for that visit, now made, photographed and a valued memory.

But they never made it to Matera.

"We took a package tour," Cosmo said, during a follow-up phone conversation, "but didn't know how to get from Sorrento to Matera and didn't really have the time. I don't speak Italian and it seemed fairly complicated."

The Di Pedes were typical of many second- and third-generation Italian-Americans who wanted to know more about their heritage. Many have the time and financial wherewithal for research and travel and are actively interested in their family origins. However, given that the overwhelming majority of Italian-Americans are from small villages in the South, most who take the package vacations never find their way back to the Mezzogiorno origins of their grand- and great-grandparents. The major tours never get there, though there is evidence of a growing determination of some hearty adventurers to find their way back to these remote places of origin.

I contacted Mario Perillo, who bills himself as "Mr. Italy," and runs what is probably the largest American travel agency and packager of Italian tours. Perillo's tours are mostly jaunts to the main tourist attractions of Florence, Rome, and the Amalfi coast.

"Most of our customers just want a taste of Italy," Perillo explained. "Those with a special purpose go back on their own."

I asked Perillo if there was any way travelers on his main tours could break away and go to the villages of their families of Southern Italian origin.

"They have a day or two near Naples when they can do that, but we have no way of offering any assistance with that sort of interest. It's really something they need to do on their own."

Another travel agent, Donna Franca of Boston, offers elaborate and luxurious tours of Rome and Florence. Through her agency you can obtain everything from a rented Mercedes to servants. Both Franca and Perillo agree that tourism to Italy has been increasing steadily since the mid-1980s and, while neither has statistics on just how many clients are of Italian origin, both suspect that Italian-Americans are a substantial part of their business.

Ms. Franca added that the greatest increase in her trade is among people who are putting together independent itineraries or are building separate itineraries onto tour packages.

All this must mean increased tourism and tourist dollars for the smaller towns and villages of il Mezzogiorno. All of the tourism offices I contacted in Southern Italy reported the same basic statistics, a yearly increase of around five percent in tourism in the past decade, but none had specific figures on the national origins of the tourists.

The National Italian American Foundation, headquartered in Washington, D.C., reported a sixty percent increase in travel to Italy in the jubilee year of 1999-2000. Paul Minolfo, a native Italian who immigrated to the United States after the Second World War, organizes tours and packages for the organization's membership. Minolfo says there's a greatly increased interest in the Italian heritage because "This generation feels it's losing its heritage with the crush of new immigrants and ethnic groups to the United States." Minolfo says his "mission" is to return Italian-Americans to Italy and specifically to the Southern provinces.

"I think it's now obvious," Minolfo continued, "that the grandparents and great-grandparents brought a very strong culture with them to the United States. Not an 'institutional' culture from Italy, but a family and village tradition which was and remains very appealing to this modern generation."

ENGLISH LESSONS

Not all of the towns throughout Southern Italy are completely ready for the increase of tourism. While English is the second language for all of Northern Italy and Northern Europe, it is not nearly as widely spoken in Southern Italy as in Rome or Florence.

"My friends don't want to learn English," one young woman explained to me in a Matera coffee bar. "We want to stay Italian here and not be like the rest of Europe." I assumed from her comments she meant the "rest of Europe" was becoming Americanized, and that Americanization was somehow threatening to her friends' sense of culture.

One evening, I spotted a young English couple who seemed to be struggling with both the menu and the waiter in a Matera trattoria. I offered to help.

"Too late," said the young man, somewhat frustrated. "I just ordered for us both. I have no idea of what I ordered, but the waiter seemed to approve."

The couple explained that they were touring in the Naples region and had read about the UNESCO designation of Matera as a "City for Humanity." Since they were driving a rental car and had no fixed itinerary, they had decided to drive to Matera on their own.

"But there's absolutely no way we can communicate here," the young man continued. "We checked into a hotel and the young woman behind the counter didn't know a word of English."

"We had to use a dictionary and hand signals to get a room," his companion continued. "I mean, it's very difficult if you don't know the language."

"Did the hotel clerk wrinkle her nose?" I asked.

They looked at me, somewhat puzzled. I explained my theory of the local discomfort at having to struggle in foreign languages.

"Well, they'd bloody well better take stock," the young man said. "We wanted to take a tour of the Sassi, but we couldn't even find a pamphlet in English to explain how to do that. I'm not sure we'll stay."

The few guidebooks that did include other languages offered superficial overviews in German, French and English—in poorly translated English, at that.

"Why do they do this?" the young man continued. "Is it their way of sticking the finger to the rest of the world?"

Their dinner arrived. The couple had ordered a *primo*, or first course—of *cavatelli*—a local type of macaroni made of very small dumplinglike shells—in a tomato sauce, and another local specialty of baked lamb for their entrée. I passed this information along to them. They seemed pleased with their choices.

I told the couple where to go to arrange for an English-speaking tour guide. I assured them they would find the Sassi most fascinating and felt obligated to defend Matera's lack of English speakers and publications. I did not see the couple again.

As I traveled about Southern Italy, I wondered about the lack of English. I prided myself on having learned to communicate without having to rely on my native tongue, but fully understood that few people had the time or inclination to study a language just for a vacation.

The use of English can be a problem for Italy in tourism. Even in Rome, there is abounding evidence of fractured English in both official and unofficial writing. In one of my favorite Trastevere restaurants the menu offers an English version of the choices, along with the standard Italian names. One has the option of *bruschetta*, or of "a fried bread which is treated in oil and tomatoes." Of course, *bruschetta* is neither "fried" nor "treated," but does involve the use of olive oil and tomatoes in a much more delectable concoction than the one described. Still another butchered menu item was the listing for *"supplì,"* a wonderfully tasty deep-fried mixture of rice, cheese and tomato sauce, described in English as "a supply of rice."

At a Rome art museum, a sign warns English-speaking visitors that "it is vehemently prohibited to expectorate." Great expectorations, I assume, can be the downfall of man.

On the autostrada to Reggio di Calabria, a sign warning drivers of possible traffic congestion reads: "Warning, Slow When Plant is Blinking," whatever that means.

The casual tourist can find dozens of such examples during a very short stay.

The literature offered to tourists can be equally confusing. Guidebooks sometimes translate sentences directly from the Italian and provide English readers with dense or incomprehensible word patterns. The following quotes two sentences, chosen at random, from one of only two guidebooks available with English translations for Matera:

> Moreover there is no other town where humans have shaped nature to the same extent to which nature has shaped the anthropic system in the "disconcerting" fusion of the human and the natural system, organic and inorganic, be (man, nature) and existence (environment, society, institutions).
>
> Nevertheless, the original values held by such a symbiotic society were gradually changed, as a result of the social and political events which led to (especially during the 19th and 20th centuries, during which choices were made which were not appropriate for their time, and which simulated a misunderstood "cultural" connotation, basically speculative in nature) the gradual fragmentation of such an identity, the progressive reduction of intensity of such a relationship, which has contributed to the adandonment [sic] of the old Sassi quarters.

This is clearly taken directly from a scholarly dissertation on the Sassi. It desperately needs a translation from the academic to the popular vernacular, if the intended reader is an ordinary English-speaking tourist. But even more important, it is obvious here and in the other examples that a native English speaker never looked at this text. There is something in the Italian bureaucracy opposed to finding native speakers and editing English text in order to to communicate beyond exact translation.

Aside from offering the traveler some unintended humor, the lack of foreign languages can also ultimately hurt development of tourism in the South—especially the lack of English, since it is the second language for virtually every other culture, worldwide.

Many times there are no translations, good or bad, available. The little town of Altamura sits only a dozen miles to the north of Matera. Like the Basilicatan town, Altamura is also on the western edge of the huge plain called the Murge, but is just over the provincial line into Puglia. The town was destroyed by the Saracens and rebuilt by the first Swabish king Frederick II. It was Frederick who was well loved for living in Sicily and speaking Italian, and who continued the Norman tradition of domination throughout the South.

Altamura is a little town frozen in the thirteenth century. The main cathedral, Santa Maria Assunta, was completed in 1232. It is the most beautiful and dominant structure of the long-ago rebuilding effort. A warren of alleys and streets run in several directions off the cathedral's main square, a legacy of the Arab influence.

There was an Internet café in Altamura, which I was delighted to find and became dependent on while waiting for my phone to be installed. I became familiar with the main section of the town and one night stopped by a very beautiful little four-star hotel, the Saint Nicholas, to ask if they had any tourist brochures or anything published in English.

Two clerks scurried about looking for something that might fulfill my request. Finally the desk clerk handed me an Italian brochure with very formal apologies and asked that I come back in a year or so. I stopped in at the town's largest bookstore across from my Internet bar and asked for any histories in English.

"Non c'è," said the proprietress, *"non abbiamo avuto una domanda per questa."* We haven't had any demand for this.

It seemed such a shame, the town was so historically and visually rich, yet only Italian speakers had access to the place and its history.

Tourism has been long in coming to the South of Italy since the fall of Rome. Places like Matera would be better prepared to handle the linguistic challenges with some additional schooling in vernacular English and publications in English! And there are other areas beyond mere language where tourism in the South might be lacking...

THE SAD TANGO

Rodolfo Guglielmi was born in 1895 in Castellaneta, Puglia, about thirty-five miles to the southeast of Matera.

The tango was born in Argentina in the early nineteen hundreds.

The dance and Guglielmi, its future icon, converged in New York City in 1913.

The tango became an international craze and Guglielmi, who would always claim a disdain for dancing, came to symbolize it. American women, in their nascent independence, found a freedom in the dance few American men could understand—and a sensuality and animal attraction in the swarthy stranger who taught them the steps.

It was a time of invention and reinvention in America. There were new machines like the automobile; telephones were in common usage in New York and other big cities; electric lighting was gaining in popularity and new electric gadgets like radios would soon appear; jazz music, an American invention, could now be recorded and played back on another American invention called the phonograph; dances like the tango became crazes, and new ways of looking at things popped into the culture on a daily basis. Thousands of immigrants arrived by the hour, wanting to be a part of the newness and excitement of America, to be a part of the future. They didn't want to be excluded from any of it. Many immigrants eliminated elements of their past and took part in another great American invention: re-creating themselves and inventing a history to fit in better.

Guglielmi was no exception.

After thinking long and hard about exactly the right name for himself in his new society, Rodolfo Guglielmi remade himself into Rudolph Valentino.

It's hard to imagine today how Valentino reconstructed the image of male sexuality in his time. American men in the early part of the last century were mostly inept at sophisticated dance steps, and extremely suspicious of men who weren't. Especially the swarthy "Latin" types represented by Valentino, who now were swarming into the United States in unprecedented numbers. Valentino symbolized a great threat to American manhood. For many at the time, the tango was the darkest and most sinister of dances, and Valentino, and his generation of immigrants, the darkest and most evil of forces.

Valentino didn't stay on the dance floor very long. He worked his way across the country with a small theater troupe, spent a little time in San Francisco and, almost without effort, moved south and became part of a relatively new community of filmmakers located in Hollywood, a district of Los Angeles. Within a few short years he was the very model of the Latin lover and matinee idol. His films were extraordinarily popular with women. His sensuous face and movements were seen all over the world, and he was soon one of the most recognized people anywhere, even better known than the pope.

Not bad for a kid from a small town in the middle of the Murge in the middle of Puglia, places Guglielmi knew, but places never heard of in Valentino's New York and Hollywood.

Of course, there was little to gain in the America of Valentino in being from Puglia or il Mezzogiorno. Valentino took to claiming Northern Italy as his origins. He told Louella Parsons, one of the first of the major Hollywood columnists writing for the Hearst syndicate, that he was from *Genoa*. The interview first appeared in the New York *Telegraph* on September 11, 1921.

"Please," he told Ms. Parsons, "do not talk much about my dancing. I never liked it, but it was the only thing I could do."

Valentino quickly distanced himself from the sleazy image of a taxi dancer. Though in fact he had never completed elementary school, now he became an educated Northerner.

Though one can't be sure from a distance of nearly a century, and without any firsthand accounting of the story, it would be relatively safe to say that Valentino claimed a Northern heritage for several reasons.

The North gave him a greater sense of legitimacy in America, a greater association with the developed economies.

By claiming Genoa as his hometown, one couldn't escape the comparison with Genoa's most famous son, Christopher Columbus, not yet demonized by the political correctness of the latter twentieth century. As Columbus was an international hero, so was Valentino of international stature.

During this same time, there was great concern over the ever-increasing influx of Southern Europeans, mostly Italians and Greeks. Several factions, including the United States Congress and Northern Italians themselves, wanted to limit the immigration to America from those Mediterranean areas. Many in official and unofficial America were overtly prejudiced against the natives of those regions. The U.S. Congress enacted legislation slowing down the flow of Southerners.

With Genoa as his origin, Valentino escaped such prejudice.

Valentino, thanks to his mother, spoke fluent French, a language always in vogue in upper-class American circles—yet also the lingua franca of Naples until the Italian unification just a few years before Valentino's birth. And despite his lack of formal education, his language, acting and dancing skills allowed him to claim a more advanced social status than a mere Puglian immigrant could have claimed at the time.

When pressed on the issue, Valentino claimed his father was a research scientist, a veterinarian, who had died trying to find the cure for malaria. Again, a social and intellectual prestige not common among Southern Italian immigrants at the time.

The American newspapers and the new genre of movie and fan magazines lapped this up. After all, how could the most famous American movie star (next to Charlie Chaplin, who was English, a comic, and not a leading man) be nothing more than a poorly educated rustic from some unpronounceable province in Southern Italy? A mere *paisano*? A barely literate young man from nowhere, a part of the very plague of Southerners the country was trying to avoid?

Rodolfo Guglielmi knew this would never fly. He invented and refined his new identity to the seeming delight of everyone involved.

In an issue of *Photoplay* magazine in February 1923, Valentino published his newly created "autobiography." He claimed he was descended from minor nobility—though, he humbly admitted, the title was in dispute. He described himself as the son of a daring and doomed research scientist, and a noble mother. He claimed degrees in elementary and secondary education, and said he had planned on a career in agriculture. He also asserted he had arrived in America with a fair amount of money; he had not been one of the starving immigrants crowded in on Ellis Island.

Valentino now had a background and history commensurate with his stature.

He was now far removed from a merely simple Puglian with a distinct talent for the tango and exaggerated sighings on the silent screen.

For those countrymen still in Castellaneta, there was little reminder of their native son. They'd never seen his movies; there was no cinema. And the newly formed Fascist government in Rome wasn't a big fan of tango-dancing fancies. Nor was the pope, still technically at war with both the nation of Italy and the democratized world which the Vatican saw as hedonist and sinful; at one point, the pope tried to ban the tango.

The Fascists, meanwhile, kept newly released American films out of Fascist Italy.

Valentino returned to Italy in late summer of 1923 and attempted to meet with Mussolini. Il Duce was busy; he declined Valentino's request.

According to Irving Shulman in his 1967 biography *Valentino*, the actor then decided to return to his hometown in Puglia for the first time since leaving for America more than a decade before. Shulman is the only major Valentino biographer who records the visit.

The journey was meant to be a nostalgic reunion.

It was a dreadful mistake.

Valentino set out for Castellaneta, interestingly, on September 11, 1923, the same date as the Parsons interview two years before. What he found was hardly the homecoming he'd envisioned.

Somehow a copy of *Photoplay* magazine had made its way to the small Puglian town. An English speaker had translated Valentino's fabricated story for the crowd at the town square. When Valentino arrived, they ridiculed him for having put on airs, for having claimed nobility and wealth. They were angry. Angry that he was too proud to tell the world who he really was, that he refused to tell the world who they were.

They were *Castellanetani*.

They were Puglians.

They were hardworking and honest people.

And they were tired of apologizing for who they were, tired of Southern Italians being thought of as "wretched refuse" washing up on the American shore.

The crowd threw dung at America's greatest film lover.

He quickly retreated to the safety of his fancy automobile and sped out of Castellaneta, never to return. It was rumored he told his female traveling companion he would hate the town and all of the entire South of Italy forever.

There's a Sicilian saying that sums up Valentino's reception; *"Truvasti Ameriga!"* You found America. Or, as Lina Insana, a professor at the University of Pittsburgh explained, "It means you've grown 'too big for your britches.' The saying warns others not to stray too far from the path most traveled and criticizes anyone whose life has become easier as a result of newly found riches." That certainly describes Valentino's circumstances in 1923; he had clearly "found America" and America had found him.

And for all the artifice and imagination Rodolfo Guglielmi used in making up the character of Rudolph Valentino, it doesn't appear to have brought him much happiness. Though known as a great screen lover, his personal life was anything but serene. He married twice, both wives claimed nonconsummation of their union as a reason for their subsequent divorce. Of course the standards of the times were quite different. People didn't speak openly of their sexual behavior. Divorces had to have cause.

Valentino's sexuality was consistently unclear. He lived in an age and time when only heterosexuality was acceptable for public discussion. A Chicago newspaper writer questioned Valentino's sexual inclination and was immediately challenged to a duel by the overly dramatic actor. This apparent challenge to his manhood and the stress it caused is said to have been one of the factors leading to his early death.

On August 16, 1926, Valentino collapsed from pain in a New York hotel. He was taken by ambulance to a hospital, where he underwent emergency surgery for "an acute gastric ulcer and ruptured appendix." He never recovered and died of an infection one week later.

He was thirty-one years old.

"A Rodolfo Valentino"

I arrived in the town of Castellaneta, for the third time, more than seventy-six years after Guglielmi/Valentino's last visit. Ironically, I, too, arrived a few days after September 11 that year. Only this September 11 was marked, and will be marked for years to come, as one of the saddest and most dreadful dates in American history.

I wanted to photograph the house where Valentino was born and visit the museum in Castellaneta now dedicated to his memory. Earlier that summer, I'd found the museum on the Internet and taken it as a sign that the town had forgiven Guglielmi his hubris. When he died young—almost a boy—at thirty-one, he immediately went from actor to legend in the world's imagination. He'd never made a talking motion picture, never had children, never—after his horrible experience in his hometown in 1923—returned to his native land. And even now in Castellaneta, as in his times, there were few who could claim to have seen his films. The image of Valentino lived on, but the man was difficult to find.

Crossing the Murge and approaching from the west, the town of Castellaneta is visible for miles before one reaches its boundaries. It sits on a rise of land dramatically different from the mountains and hilly terrain throughout most of Basilicata. The Murge is a broad and continuous plain that goes from the Matera-Altamura boundary on the west all the way to Bari in the east, Canosa in the north, and Taranto in the south. The city sits atop a gentle elevation and shines bright white in the afternoon sun, contrasting greatly with the surrounding brown and green fields.

As I drove through the main street of the town I saw the modern sculpture along the side of the road across from the Centro district, the oldest part of the city. It is a monument to Valentino. The sculpture sits on a large flat white marble platform overlooking the Murge Plain as it flows toward Taranto and the Ionian Sea. In the middle of the platform stands a bronze sculpture of an Arab "sheik," the actor's most famous role. At the side of the platform a bronze-and-ceramic tile depiction of a movie set adorns a semicircular wall, and a plain marble tablet at the back of the stand bears the simple inscription, "*A Rodolfo Valentino,* 1961."

Even the *Castellanetani* seemed to have abandoned the Guglielmi name.

Each time I'd visited the town, the monument stood silent and vacant. I'd never seen any signs of tourists or activity at the site.

On my first visit earlier in the year, I'd pulled into a nearby gas station and asked the attendant, an older man with a balding head and a big belly, if he knew where the Valentino museum was.

"You see that house right there?" He pointed to a row of houses across the street built on a cliff overlooking the main highway.

I nodded.

"That's it."

"The museum?" I asked.

"No, his house," he replied. "The museum is there." He moved his finger about ten degrees to his right.

"Do you get many visitors for this museum?" I asked.

The man shrugged and walked back into the station office.

According to its Web site, the Valentino museum had been built in 1995 and held evening summer hours from 4 P.M. to 7 P.M. I arrived just after 3 P.M. with nearly an hour to kill. I drove into the Centro and parked and walked about the warren of streets in the oldest part of Castellaneta.

It was interesting that Valentino's most famous role and his statute was of the "Sheik." Castellaneta had never been a Saracen town, some say its name comes from "Castellum Munitum," a fortified castle built in Byzantine times as a defense against the Arabs. But despite its apparent success in defending against the Saracens, the town's winding streets and the dark eyes and sultry air of the local women still held an Eastern aura.

According to the town's official Web site, the original village was founded in 1280 B.C.E. at the top of a hill called Archinto "and was a center of the lands of ancient Greece." It then goes on to say, "We have information about the history...starting with the eleventh century." It doesn't explain the gap of nearly 2,400 years.

The museum, built much more recently, is in a building that once housed the convent of San Domenico. While waiting for it to open, I walked into the church and sat in the cool for a while as workmen moved about rigging the statue of San Domenico. I assumed there was to be a festival in the near future.

When the appointed hour of four arrived, I walked back to the museum.

The door was locked.

I waited for over twenty minutes, standing alone in the little alley in the cooling afternoon shade.

No one came.

An elderly couple walked by, the woman bent over and holding on to the arm of her only slightly more erect husband. She looked up at me, recognized an unmistakable tourist. The camera dangling from my neck was a definite giveaway.

"*Non c'è*" She shook her head. "*Più tardi.*" "No one's there. A little later."

"Do you know when?" I asked.

"*Alle cinque,*" she replied as she rocked and wobbled her way by me. "At five."

"*Grazie, signora.*" I watched the couple teeter up the slight incline and wondered how long they'd been walking these streets together.

It was several very hot blocks and down a large staircase over to 116 Via Roma, where the actor had been born. I moved slowly, trying to keep cool. When I arrived at the short street I took a few photographs of the house, which was virtually indistinguishable from any of the other row houses along the street. The buildings were all from the nineteenth century and were rather plain, the basic, solid houses from that era, now as then middle-class quarters. There were no markings, no plaque or indication anywhere that a native son had gone from here to Hollywood and international fame.

I returned to the museum a few minutes before five.

I waited again for nearly a half hour.

No one came.

I knocked on the door frame of what looked like a woodworking shop. A heavyset woman with a bright red bandana covering her hair and a plain white apron came to the open country door. I asked about the museum.

She shrugged. "Many times they don't open in the evening," she said. "Come back in the morning."

I returned to Matera that evening and tried calling the number listed for the museum on the Web site several times after that, all without success. I returned one morning in the hopes of finding the museum open. It remained closed, and no one in the area of San Domenico or at the gas station seemed to know anything about it. I never saw anyone at the memorial on the road below, either.

In the belief that "the third time's a charm," I returned to Castellaneta one morning in September, determined to find someone who could talk with me about the museum.

It remained closed.

I walked into the Centro, found a sign indicating the local tourism office and rang the bell. A young man with a bright blue shirt and those fancy tiny European eyeglasses came to the door. He told me I'd made a mistake, the tourist office was across the courtyard, but the sign was on his building, which housed a group of local architects.

I apologized and started off for the building.

"But you won't find anyone there," he said. "I haven't seen them here today."

"These aren't normal office hours?" I asked. I wondered if Castellaneta was on some time system that was even stranger than the normal Italian time system, which is only a suggestion at best.

"Yes, it is the business hour," the young man said, "but sometimes they don't come. What was it you wanted?"

"I was looking for information on the town and hoping to learn when the Valentino museum would be open. I've tried several times to visit, but it is never open and they don't answer the phone."

"You're American?" he asked.

"Yes."

"How are things in New York?" He was referring to the horrible events of the previous week. "This was terrible," he added. "Is your family well?"

"Thank you." I said. "Yes, everyone in my family is well, but frightened."

"These are frightening times." He seemed a sympathetic young man.

"Do you have any idea of how I can reach your tourism people?"

"Wait a minute," he said.

He pulled a miniscule phone out of his pocket and tapped out numbers on the tiny keyboard. It was evident from his glasses and phone that we were living in an age of miniaturization. He reached his party. Whoever he was speaking with asked him several questions. I overheard him say, "of course he speaks Italian." I waved my hand back and forth to qualify his statement, but he smiled and plowed on. He clicked off the tiny gadget, pulled a pad from his shirt pocket and wrote down a phone number.

"Call this man," he said, "he will help you."

I thanked him.

"*Salutami gli Stati Uniti.*" It was almost a mantra during the days immediately following September 11, "Say hello to your country for me." The Italians seemed to be taking the events in the United States personally. Of course, with a man named Giuliani at the center of things, and hundreds of Italian-American names on the fatality lists, they could readily identify with the situation.

I called the number on my own, now somewhat bulky-looking, cell phone. The fellow on the other end seemed greatly agitated and interrupted me, saying he'd call me back. I started to give him the number, but he interrupted again and said he had the number and hung up. The rules of courtesy in these cellular times are unclear. I had no idea of just when or if the man would return my call, nor did I have any idea of his identity or how he fit into the Valentino picture.

By now it was noon and I was in the center of town. I decided to do what everyone does in Italy when you don't know what to do: *eat something*. I walked about the Centro looking for a place. There was no trattoria or pizzeria; no bars; nothing.

I made my way to the main square in the center of town by the Municipio. The building sat opposite a large rectangular green with a fountain at its center. I assumed this was the square where Valentino had been confronted by his outraged compatriots after learning of his "autobiography."

Three elderly men sat on a bench near the fountain. I approached them and asked if they could recommend a place to eat lunch.

I know better than to ask three elderly men in Italy, with time on their hands, for any opinion, on any subject. My decision to do so indicated my level of hunger. I was sure the question would start a long and detailed argument. My expectations were fulfilled.

First of all, two of the men wanted to know if I intended to dine alone, or if I had family with me. I had no idea what difference that would have made. I told them I was alone.

One fellow, a heavyset man with a small gray straw fedora who looked remarkably like the American boxer Jake LaMotta, said I should go to the end of the street, turn left, and find a hotel on the outskirts of town. He told me the hotel didn't have a very elaborate menu, and the food wasn't particularly good, but they would be open for *un pranzo*, or a midday meal.

Another fellow, a very thin man in a short-sleeve white shirt and suspenders, said that was a terrible idea. He said if I wanted to eat well, not pay a lot, have my choice of French, Russian or Italian food (an interesting combination), I should go to the end of the street, turn right, and go several kilometers near the town of Gioia del Colle (the Stallone family's hometown), where I would find a sensational place.

The third fellow, the smallest of the three, bald and wearing a bright blue-and-red-plaid shirt, said nothing until the other two had finished. He then explained in a very soft voice and apologetic manner that everyone in Castellaneta took vacations in September, though, he admitted, it was hard to understand why.

"It's not like we have a tourist season here like Rome," he said.

He suggested that I come back to Castellaneta another time.

"Do you gentlemen know anything about the Valentino museum?"

It was worth a try, I thought.

"It's near the church," the fellow in the suspenders said. "Up there." He pointed in the direction of the San Domenico.

"I mean, do any of you know who runs it? Why no one is ever there?"

"They are open in the evenings," said the man in the gray hat. "It's new. They have some movies there sometimes."

"Have you ever seen them?" I asked.

"Everyone has seen Valentino. He's very famous," the man in the hat continued.

"But have you ever seen the films at the museum?"

"No, I've never been there," he said. His friends all nodded, indicating they hadn't visited the site either.

"Do many people come here to see the museum?"

The three men shrugged silently.

I thanked them for their time.

At least I'd had a better reception in the town square than Valentino. I drove back toward Matera. On the outskirts of town I found a little place called La Caffetteria. Normally anything with caffè in the title means coffee bar or snack bar, and that's just what this place was. I bought the only sandwich they offered and, for the first time ever in Italy, had something on white bread with mayonnaise—in Castellaneta! It was awful. As I sat down to endure the sandwich and some tea *alla pesca*, my cell phone went off.

"*Dove è?* Where are you?" the voice demanded, without any sort of pretension of politeness or a "hello."

I assumed it was the same fellow who had brusquely cut me off a half hour or so before. He started giving me directions to where he was, though I still didn't know *who* he was, or why I should find him. And I couldn't possibly follow either his speed or his dialect. When he finished I told him I was sorry for my poor Italian, but could he please repeat the directions much more slowly.

"Wait," he barked, "I get someone who can speak better."

"Here," I heard him say, "speak *inglese*."

"*Inglese?*" I heard another man's voice moan. "I can't speak English... hello?"

I answered him. He continued in the same rapid Italian as the first man to say, I assume, exactly the same thing, which I wasn't getting very well. Finally he asked where I was again. I told him the name of the café.

"Stay there," he said, "we'll come to you."

I ate the terrible sandwich, finished my tea, and was on my second mineral water when a fellow finally showed up carrying a bundle of books and literature, all in Italian, of course. He was the brusque one from the phone, and he couldn't have been nicer.

"What is it you want to know?" he asked.

He gave me his card. He worked for the city in what was vaguely described as "domestic affairs."

I gave him a general thumbnail: an overview of the town's history, some statistics regarding tourism, anything at all he could tell me about the immigrants to America from this town and their current relationship with the town, and someone who could tell me about the story of Valentino from the town's perspective.

"Ah," he sighed, "that is difficult. It is a very long time since anyone lived here who knew this man."

"I know," I said, "I don't care if they knew him, just anything they might know about him—the family, that sort of thing."

He sighed again.

"How about the mayor?" he asked. "He's been to America and knows our history well."

"I'd love to meet your mayor," I replied, "but only if I can have someone help me with translation since I would be embarrassed to do an interview with your mayor without precise and proper Italian."

"I will find someone for you and call you. What do you want to know about Valentino?"

"Well, for openers, why did it take thirty-five years after his death for a memorial to be erected? Why did it take another thirty-four years after that to establish a museum? Has the memorial or museum resulted in increased tourism? How many visitors do you think come here every year because of the link to Valentino? Did many years have to pass before the local people could feel comfortable claiming him as a native son—how else can anyone explain the long time between his death and the formal markings here of his life?"

I ran through all of these questions that had been brewing in my brain in a matter of seconds.

The young man from city hall sat mute, returning my gaze. He shrugged his shoulders.

"What do you know about Valentino?" I asked.

He shrugged again. "This was a very long time ago," he repeated.

"Yes, but just a few days ago I drove by Cicero's tomb. He was killed after Caesar's assassination, about forty years before Christ was born.

Everyone I spoke with asked me if I'd been to his tomb. This is a country with a very long memory for its local heroes."

The young man's cell phone beeped. I heard the brusqueness return as he spoke quickly and firmly to his caller. He flipped the phone closed with a one-handed sweeping motion. He appeared practiced in cell phone etiquette and dexterity.

"I will see what I can do," he said. "I am afraid I must go, but I will call you soon."

I thanked him for the literature on the city, the map and the paperback history book.

I never heard from the man again.

I never got an answer to the several messages I'd left on my mysterious friend's cell-phone mailbox, never received any replies to my e-mails to the tourist office, the city or the museum.

I cursed myself for not stopping the old couple who had passed by me as I stood waiting at the museum door. I should have asked them what they remembered about the actor. They were the only people I'd seen in the town who would have been old enough to know Valentino's reputation, if not his movies. And I'd have bet anything they didn't carry a cell phone.

I had a feeling it was going to be a while before tourism would be adding many dollars to Castellaneta coffers.

A DYING PAESE

"Gamberale is dying," Theresa DiIulius said.

She was talking about the little Abruzzo mountaintop village in the Apennines where my maternal grandfather's and Theresa's family had originated. "Claudio still runs the hotel there, but nobody comes. It's sad, but it's dying."

I had made many visits to the village during my time in Rome a decade before. It was a place that I'd often heard about during my childhood in Pittsburgh. Every family in that village had someone who had emigrated to Pittsburgh, there had been an entire colony from Gamberale living in that city's Oakland section where I was born.

The DiIulius clan was one of the first to leave Abruzzo. My great-grandfather, Gaetano DiIulius, found work in the construction trades in Pittsburgh during the closing years of the nineteenth century. That began a tradition that remains to this day. Theresa and I were distant cousins; we had exchanged news of her hometown at a family gathering in Pittsburgh. Her brother Claudio had remained in Gamberale, where he ran the village's only hotel and restaurant.

As a child, I'd never been told the stories of the Second World War's effect on that little place. Ten years ago, I'd gone up into those hills where I learned about the awful toll on the people living there during World War II. Gamberale had been the temporary headquarters of the German Field Marshal Albert Kesselring, the man in charge of the Nazi defense of Italy. Over thirty percent of the village never survived the winter of 1943-44. The Germans executed or murdered several *paesani*, destroyed crops, killed farm and work animals and burned the place when they left, destroying records and homes.

According to Richard Lamb, the true story of Kesselring's atrocities in Italy during that war is only now fully coming to light. In *War in Italy 1943-1945, A Brutal Story*, Lamb argues that Kesselring's brutality was overlooked at his war-crimes trial. The author details the bloody and illegal revenge the field marshal exacted on the Italian civilians as a result of the Italian government's overthrow of Mussolini and its subsequent alignment with the Allied forces. Lamb says Kesselring made it known procedure to look the other way from his subordinates' behavior in exerting control over the Italian population, and firmly insisted that any resistance from them be met by overwhelming and deadly force.

Gamberale is an all-too-explicit example of Kesselring's malicious and monstrous policy. He had thirteen men, all English speakers, executed in the public square on the day his forces arrived. This unlucky thirteen—most with work experience in America—had been rounded up and murdered by German soldiers posing as Englishmen. They had been flushed out to prevent them from communicating with the English forces on the opposing mountain. During the course of their occupation of the village, Kesselring's soldiers routed all the villagers from their homes, used the beautiful little church of San Lorenzo as their stable, despoiled the local graveyard and shot and killed entire families scavenging for food. Many *paesani* starved to death while living in the woods that terrible winter, including Theresa and Claudio's mother. Others eventually returned home to burned-out shells, their crops and animals gone.

After the war, Marshall Plan money eventually found its way up the mountainside to the survivors. The village rebuilt as best it could, in the hopes of becoming a skiing and recreation attraction. Claudio DiIulius built the town's only hotel in the hope of cornering the tourist market.

But the skiing never happened, the tourists came only in dribs and drabs, there was no rush to climb that steep hill or vacation in the village. There were far too many other places in Italy less remote and equally as beautiful and charming. Gamberale struggled to define itself, a medieval village searching for a function in modern Europe.

In late summer of 2001, I went back up that hill for the yearly festival of San Lorenzo. I wanted to see if the tiny place had found a role for itself. While driving through the Valle di Sangro and up into the mountains, I was struck, once again, with the almost indescribable beauty of the place. Tiny villages dot distant mountaintops in an almost dreamlike juxtaposition of village against sky. The mountains scrape the heavens and are filled with lush forests and the greenest of pastures. The sun paints brilliant yellow streaks between the trees and splashes on fields of waving grass. Small torrents gush white from the hillsides and splatter against the ancient rocks as the road twists and turns up into the sky.

At the end of the asphalt, a turret indicates an ancient castle that once protected what is now merely forgotten.

Theresa was right; the place was dying.

Claudio had just returned from the hospital in Ancona, in the north along the Adriatic seacoast. He was suffering from severe complications of diabetes, he'd been battling an infection, and had great difficulty walking and moving about. His sad dark eyes were sunken, he was pale white and obviously ill, his speech a little slow, but his smile and warmth were just as quick.

Surprisingly, there was only a handful of other guests, despite the festival. It was the one time of year the place should have been busy.

"They stay with families here," Claudio explained. "Many Pitts-burghers have built little summer homes now, or stay with their relatives. They don't need my hotel." He seemed calmly resigned to the situation. Stefano, Claudio's son, kept the restaurant going and had opened a small pizzeria-discotheque in the lower part of the building, hoping to draw local and visiting youngsters. Business was far from booming.

In my grandfather's day, the little spot on the map had been a farming community. People either worked the fields or tended sheep. The town is miles from any industrial centers and the nearest big city is Pescara, which sits about fifty miles away on the Adriatic coast at the bottom of the mountain and at the eastern end of the Valle di Sangro, the Valley of Blood. The highest point in all the Apennines sits directly across from Gamberale, which is itself the highest point in the province of Chieti.

More than a thousand years ago, when the place was first settled, it provided protection and defense against the ever-roaming hordes of invaders into the Italian peninsula. Today's spectacular view was yester-day's advance-warning system. The community was self-sustaining. An enemy would have had to climb a nine-thousand-foot mountain and be prepared to storm defensive walls in order to capture the place. And the question would have to be asked: Why would they want it in the first place, given its remoteness and lack of any real wealth?

It was one of the great ironies of history that Kesselring was the first, and apparently the only, invader to find the village militarily advantageous.

Its purpose for being is now part of that long-ago history. None of Gamberale's few offspring hope to become a shepherd. While its fields remain fertile, there's no reason in modern-day Italy's wealthy economy to work that hard at that altitude. Italy is one of the world's richest lands; it can feed all its people without problem. There are no marauders stalking along the Apennines. If Gamberale survives another thousand years, it will be as a result of economic and social changes that aren't now apparent.

It is not just Gamberale that faces this modern dilemma. As Rocco had said in Amantea, the village life in Italy, especially Southern Italy, was disappearing at an alarming rate. Hundreds of small fishing villages along the coasts that for years sent their men to the sea each day now dine on fish caught by huge commercial fleets. Mountain villages which sustained a few hundred people were scattered with great frequency throughout the Apennines' Aspromonte and Pollino ranges in the South. There were literally thousands of such villages, all now giving their few children to the big cities. They've become, in large part, retirement communities for those who remember another way of life, and they worry about the town's future when they're gone.

Italy maintains the lowest birthrate in the world. Italians are not reproducing themselves, marriage is being delayed into later years for both men and women. Italian national statistics report an estimated 1.18 births per woman as of 2001—well below the 2.1 birthrate needed to keep a population even with itself. The few children who are being raised will probably go off to the cities for their educations, and speak the language they learn on television and radio, not the local dialects.

And in Abruzzo, which already claims the lowest population density of any region in Italy, the situation is even more pronounced. There are fewer children, and they are leaving in greater numbers.

The winds of change are unstoppable.

FACING THE FUTURE

In the Sangro valley below, it was still summer. Up in Gamberale, it was jacket weather. I stood at the concert in the cold wind at the village festival. I'd been to this same festival ten years before. There were half as many people this time. The band blared out a variety of traditional Italian songs, the audience moved about, more out of a desire to keep warm than to keep tempo.

The bandstand stood opposite the Pollice house, as it had a decade before. But the ancient signora who owned the house, and who had so eloquently told me about her time in that village, was now in the cemetery below. It was in that house that Kesselring spent his brief but lethal time there.

"Are you the one who wrote that book?" an American woman asked. She was, predictably, from Pittsburgh. A member of the populous Sciulli clan, she was staying with relatives in the village annex a few miles down the road. A small group, we talked about the Second World War's effects on the village.

"A German officer came to my mother and told her to get their animals and get out of town for a couple of days," another Sciulli cousin said. "The next day, they rounded up all the farm animals and put them in a house and burned the place down. My family was able to spend the time in the woods and stayed safe."

"I still don't understand their need to punish poor peasants," I said.

"It was war," she replied. "They had to obey their orders."

I'd heard that defense before. It always amazed me how these people could accept their history with such equanimity, just one more event in the long and eternal saga of human suffering.

I returned to the square the following evening for the last night of the festival. This night it was past cool into cold. The winds had picked up considerably and it must have been in the low forties or high thirties. I was unprepared for this kind of weather, it had been in the nineties when I started up the hill, and I had only an inadequate light windbreaker to hold back the chill.

This night a rock band was performing in a louder version of the previous evening's entertainment. Artificial smoke poured out of the speakers and a female duet was singing. But the weather's effect was evident. There were no more than a couple of dozen people milling about in the cold.

I wondered if the festival would survive for another generation.

I was preparing to leave Gamberale.

While waiting for Claudio, I stood opposite the hotel's main door and watched the water run from the small fountain from which the hotel, La Fonte, took its name. I imagined this source of water had been a determining factor in the establishment of the village so many centuries ago. I'd always marveled that water could be found at so high an elevation. I watched as the small stream splashed into a semicircular retaining pool.

Suddenly, my eye spotted something along the steep embankment leading up to the village's only road.

Amid the dirt and ground cover, a small but clearly visible sculpture was poking through the earth. It was a stone carving in the shape of a man's head and looked as if it were from the buttress of some ancient church. To my untrained eye it resembled other carvings I'd seen on fourteenth- and fifteenth-century edifices.

A few moments later, Claudio came out of the hotel to say good-bye.

"Claudio," I said, "I never noticed that sculpture in the ground here before."

"Ah." Claudio sighed. *"Quel cretino,"* he said. "That idiot."

"The sculpture?"

"No, my neighbor. He wanted to rebuild his garage. In Italy one must have a work permit for this sort of thing. And before you can get a work permit, someone from the government must come and do an inspection for antiquities. If something historical might become damaged, they will not issue the permit. But my neighbor wouldn't wait, he went ahead and did the work without permission."

"But what is it that I'm looking at?"

"Something very old," he said.

The source of water would have been a protected site in antiquity. There was so little written about this place, there were no formal histories that I had been able to find, no formal documentation on the village's age or origins. It was assumed that the Longobards had settled the place around the ninth century and the first tax record from the village showed up a few hundred years later in the register of the baronies, the first official documentation of Gamberale's existence. It could be that the fountain was the core of the original settlement.

"Maybe this was some sort of religious structure?" I asked.

"Maybe," agreed Claudio. "Or something that might have been a part of the original village. Or something that was here before that." He waved in the direction of his neighbor. "If that *cretino* hadn't been in such a hurry and would have had the state come in and do their inspection, we might have found out. Who knows? Maybe it would be a tourist attraction now."

A few months later I received the news that Claudio had passed away, finally overcome by the battle he'd been fighting for a very long time. I like to think of Claudio now—dying, yet standing defiantly erect in an old and dying village while cursing his neighbor's folly. Our last conversation was about his eternal hope that things would turn around. That the stone face peeking through the hillside from hundreds of years ago might somehow be the future.

In a village where the past is marked with historical irony, maybe Claudio's dream is still possible.

10

Ceremonies and Festivals

LA FESTA DEL SANT' EUSTACHIO

One twilight in mid-September, I stood on the small balcony off the kitchen of my Matera apartment and looked over the Piazza Veneto, awash in the soft evening light reflected from the white stones. A neighbor in the building across the way poked her head out of the window.

"La tua famiglia sta bene?" she asked. Is your family all right? We'd seen each other before in passing, but had never exchanged a word. She somehow knew I was an American.

"Sì, grazie," I replied. *"Tutti stanno bene, grazie a Dio."* Everyone was okay, thank God.

"Abiti a New York?" she asked. Do you live in New York?

"No," I said, but explained I had many friends there and had thankfully heard from them all. *"E uno sacco di guai,"* I said. We've got a sackful of trouble.

"Che è successo nel mondo?" What's going on in the world? She fretted. I wished I'd had an answer for her.

It was festival time in Matera.

The streets were lined with portable arches, thousands of small colored lights swept up alongside and over the cobblestoned *via*s. The arches illuminated the main passages to and from the Piazza Veneto, in the town's center, and the Piazza Ridola near the lookout over Sassi. A bandstand stood at each end. The normal business of the evenings— entire families moving about, greeting neighbors, sharing a sweet—was even more electric, children a little noisier. The old men sitting on the circular bench in the corner of the plaza by the death notices seemed a little more alive, more animated.

During the afternoon, several competing marching bands had paraded on an hourly basis through the streets, playing stirring martial music or traditional Italian sacred songs.

Now, with the lights on, vendors had set up their stands at the fringe of the square hawking their lupini beans and varieties of nuts and candies or religious icons and votive candles. A few Chinese, whole families, had set up tables with cigarette lighters, binoculars, cameras and a host of household goods. Business was brisk as people munched and shopped throughout the town. It seemed as if Matera's entire 55,000 inhabitants had dressed up and turned out for the event.

The theoretical focus of all this activity comes on September 20, the feast day of Sant' Eustachio, the second patron saint of Matera, sharing almost equal billing with Santa Maria della Bruna, whose feast day is in July. Three days of bands and parades build up to the procession of the life-size Sant' Eustachio statue through the streets on the back of a pickup truck.

The Cathedral of Santa Maria della Bruna was built in the thirteenth century on a bluff overlooking the Sassi. It was constructed on top of the remains of an ancient church dedicated to Sant' Eustachio, thus the dual patrons for the city. Except on his feast day, the life-size image of Sant' Eustachio stands regally by the rear of the church, adorned with beautiful flowing red robes, a warrior's helmet on its head and a spear in its hand.

Eustachio was a Roman general under the Emperor Trajan. According to the *Catholic Encyclopedia*, Eustachio's original name was Placidus. He was a renowned warrior and hunter. One day while stalking a stag he saw a crucifix between the animal's horns and converted to Christianity. He renounced the Roman gods and was martyred in 188 C.E.

I could find no evidence of a direct relationship between the saint and Matera, but the first martyrs were widely revered in the early Church, especially during the period when the Church was replacing other gods, temples or forms of worship. Given Matera's age, it would not be too far a stretch to guess that Eustachio's church in Matera had been on top of still another, older place of worship. Replacing a temple with a church dedicated to a Christian martyr made a strong political statement, as well as a religious one.

I watched as the statue was removed from its platform and gently carried down the main steps in front of the cathedral and respectfully placed on the back of the truck. It was then slowly driven through the ancient streets, followed by a group dressed in medieval costumes singing sacred songs. A marching band accompanied the singers. Many in the crowd joined in the singing and still others followed behind the band as Sant' Eustachio wobbled over the cobblestones through the entire upper old town above the Sassi. I followed along with the crowd; it was like a walk through the centuries.

THE LIVES OF THE SAINTS

Religious processions and the veneration of saints are as old as the South of Italy itself. Before Christ, the Greek and Roman gods were widely worshipped throughout the South, undoubtedly in Matera as well. Entire cults were dedicated to an array of Greek religious figures. The strongest in Southern Italy were the representations of Athena, her half-sister Persephone, and Persephone's mother, Demeter. The latter two were the most revered gods in Magna Graecia. Small statues of them are found in ruins or digs throughout the area, an interesting contradiction in a land where women were never fully incorporated into full citizenship until modern times, yet female gods seemed to dominate in antiquity. The relationship between the people of Southern Italy and their gods, or saints, has been, and remains, a strong and mystical bond.

Even today there is a strong movement throughout the area venerating one of the Church's newest saints, Padre Pio.

It is virtually impossible to travel in Southern Italy and not see images of the Capuchin priest who died in 1968. A life-size statue of Pio stands opposite the boardwalk in Amantea, another in a small sanctuary across from a city park in the newer section of Matera. Fresh flowers always adorn the pediments. Several corner grottoes in Rome also hold his image. A fountain in Siderno is dedicated to him. Every town, village or city I visited had some marking of this holy priest.

My little *alimentari*, or corner market, near my Matera apartment offered votive candles with Pio's picture for the equivalent of less than a quarter. His photos or portraits are enclosed in cheap to very expensive frames, are imprinted on leather, laminated on wood, sealed in plastic key chains, embroidered on pillows and adorn dozens of other articles sold at street fairs, grocery stores and festivals.

There is a sort of Piomania going on in the South, part pop art, part piety.

Francesco Forgione was born in Pietrocina in 1887, the son of peasant farmers. As a child he tended sheep, worked the farm, but always felt a special calling to the priesthood. His father went off to America to earn the money for his son to enter the seminary. He took the name Padre Pio and, despite his ongoing battle with tuberculosis, began limited spiritual duties.

In 1918, when Pio was thirty-one years old, five strange marks appeared on his body; both hands, both feet and his chest bled from wounds that had not been physically inflicted, wounds that replicated the wounds of Christ at His crucifixion—the stigmata. Pio is the only known contemporary priest to have ever been marked in this fashion. No one has ever been able to explain the phenomenon scientifically, but those who have suffered the stigmata have always been revered by Catholics and considered to have been chosen by God for their piety and devotion.

Pio was a stern man who demanded prayer and who didn't coddle penitents. He was also a healer. He is credited with helping save hundreds of medical lost causes through his prayers. Canonized a saint in June of 2002, he can now be the object of prayer; Catholics call on saints to intervene with God for special causes.

"It's not surprising that Pio is a Southerner," Father Dominic Sturino told me one afternoon in Cosenza. "The Southerners have always held a special reverence for religious heroes; political heroes are not the norm." Father Sturino is an American, born in the Midwest, now teaching at the University in Cosenza. "The people need heroes and saints. Pio represents the fundamentals of piety and prayer. He represents a spirit uncorrupted by politics or greed or ego. And most of the Italian saints are Southerners. Not surprising, since humility is a basic part of the culture."

Pio is one of the most recent in a long string of pious men and women who either lived or found sanctuary in the South.

During the early days of the Christian Church, after Rome fell and Italy was racked and sacked by constant invaders and marauders, an entire colony of religious wanderers and exiles found life and devotion in the caves and tufa dugouts in and around Matera. The warring armies of the time tended to move up and down the coasts, leaving the mountainous and isolated middle section, Basilicata, the perfect place for free religious expression. These people painted the walls of their elaborate rock-walled sanctuaries in what were probably the first major depictions of holy icons in Christianity.

Michele Di Pede's brother, Franco, and his daughter, Mariagrazia, have made a study of these primitive artworks. Franco's artwork has been displayed internationally, and he has published several books reproducing his work. Mariagrazia has photographed and written extensively about the significance of the cave paintings and their depictions of saints and the life of Christ. The people who practiced their faith in this rough and early fashion were credited with keeping the fundamental faith alive during difficult political times.

WAYFARERS

Religion, of course, was only one cause for people to roam about in the search for freedom of expression. The great emigration wave to the west was another extension of this same principle. Since the concept of free expression of faith was so basic in the Southern culture, it should come as no surprise that many centuries later, western movement replaced what had once been an internal wandering.

In his beautiful book, *I Quattro Camminanti,* or the English translation, *Wayfarers Four,* Rodolfo Di Biasio explores this wandering and its toll on those who stayed behind.

I caught up with Di Biasio in Rome between trains. He was returning to his hometown of Scauri, just outside Gaeta. I found him at the appointed track number at the appointed hour; he wore a light coat over his shoulders in cape fashion. A tall man in his fifties, he had the sensitive eyes so common in Southern Italy—large, curious brown eyes that dominated his gentle features. Di Biasio was thin and slightly lanky, and had a definite elegance and stylish air about him. Over a long coffee in the Termini café, he talked about the loss to Southern Italy, the sacrifice of its sons to the New World.

"The land couldn't give them any more," he explained, "we had been isolated from the North and the industrial economy. From 1860 to 1915 we watched thirty million leave. But it had to be done. Parents at that time watched their children go off across the sea. They felt they were delivering a child to the world and it was for the better, though, in many cases, they never saw that child again. It wasn't easy for any of them, but it was necessary."

"Was the Church a positive factor in their lives, did it help during this great migration?" I wondered.

"For a peasant in the South," he said, "the only moment of society was the Church, its rituals and festivals. It was the only recurrent thing in their life. It's no wonder they kept their festivals and processions in the New World. But politically, the Church always backed the status quo. So even the Church couldn't solve the economic problems of the South; only a great migration could help."

I had been fascinated with Di Biasio's perspective in *Wayfarers Four*. He wrote eloquently and poignantly about four boys who had gone off to America and the effects on the family and little village they'd left. It was the other side of the story we'd known so well in the States.

"The one thing I remember most clearly as a child," the author recalled, "were the photos from America. Every little house in Southern Italy had at least one photo from America. It was the first thing the immigrants did when they arrived: they went and had a photo taken and sent that back home. It was proof of the right decision, as if to say, 'Look how well I am, how rich I am.'

"And they all sent money home. So much money. And since they'd left these tiny villages their vision of the world got so much bigger, you could see it in their eyes in the photos they sent back. Everything changed—their perspectives, ideas, knowledge, hopes; their lives. Only the connection to the Church stayed the same."

"So you think the Southerners changed from who they were when they went to America?"

Di Biasio studied the table with his soft eyes as he considered my question.

"They were almost ashamed of their roots," he replied. "They wanted to be more American than the Americans because they had been so poor. Only the Church remained unchanged for them. And the food."

"*Macaroni?*" I asked.

"Exactly," Di Biasio replied. "Food is culture. They kept their religion and food and a hidden nostalgia for the Old Country that they cooked and prayed away, yet it always stayed a part of them. Why else would you be here asking me these questions?"

I laughed. "Maybe I'm just a little off."

"No, we see your generation showing up more and more now. There's a legacy you're obviously concerned about. And do you know the first place they all go, all the grandsons and granddaughters who return here now?"

I shook my head.

"The cemetery. All over Southern Italy you can see your generation standing in the cemeteries studying tombstones. You seem to be searching for something."

MATERA'S WAR

On September 22, 1943, American forces came through Matera on their way north, one day behind the retreating Germans. John Durante, a son of Sala Consilina emigrants, was a dogface with the advancing American infantry.

"My father talked about the murder of the Italians by the Germans in that town. It was one of the few things he talked about from his war experiences," Tommy Durante said. "He often said how much what he saw in that town affected him. You mean, that was your grandfather's hometown?"

The Matera uprising that made a deep impression on the young Sergeant Durante is still remembered. To this day, the date of September 21,

1943, is commemorated in Matera with parades, speeches, military honor guards, flags and bunting on every post and pillar. It falls on the heels of the Sant' Eustachio festival and caps off a very busy week. A plaque on the wall of the city administration building reads:

> On the tragic day
> 21 IX 1943
> during the German execution
> of a devastating slaughter
> of innocent hostages,
> the population of Matera
> rose up in arms
> hunted its ferocious enemy
> and with the sacrifice
> of their righteous sons
> recaptured liberty.
>
> Warning to the oppressors
> Incitement to the oppressed.
>
> 21 September 1944

Strangely, I could find no literature in Matera in either Italian or English on the uprising. Matera's two main bookstores carried nothing specific about this event from World War II, despite the plaque in the square and the annual ceremonies, possibly because the Sant' Eustachio festival is their main focus.

I contacted Giovanni Scandiffio, the press spokesman for the president of the region. He gave me literature in Italian with some background information, including a short piece Carlo Levi had written about the incident. From that pamphlet and several locals I spoke with at Michele's shop, a fascinating story emerged about Matera's role during the transition of the Italian government from Fascism to the Allied side, including, once again, an interesting coincidental date....

On September 11, 1943, a battalion of the German army arrived in Matera, in retreat to the north where they would eventually re-form into the "Gustav Line" under the command of Field Marshal Albert Kesselring. The strategy called for the Nazis to write off Southern Italy and delay the Allies' advance to the more industrialized and easier supplied northern section of the peninsula. (Three days later the concentration camp at Ferramonti would be liberated by the British forces following quickly on the heels of the north-bound Germans. A month later Kesselring would set up shop in Gamberale.) The Germans stopped in Matera to regroup and resupply.

Matera, at this point in the war, was full of refugees: men who had left the ranks and were hidden by relatives or friends, others in hiding from Fascist officials for various offenses to the state, and still others in flight from the poverty and dislocation of war. The German occupation was a turning point in the ancient town's history. Though the Nazi stay was short, it represented, once again, the boot of foreign oppression in Southern Italy. It brought back living memories of feudalism, the constant and consistent exploitation of the area by outsiders and the use of violence and military control against the people.

Shortly after the Germans' arrival, a young girl doing housework unthinkingly tossed a bucket of dirty water out into the street. It nearly hit a passing German soldier, who assumed she had intended to insult and humiliate him. The frightened girl ran into the house and hid under a bed with her terrified siblings as the soldier followed into the building, firing his pistol. Although no one was hurt, news of this near tragedy spread quickly through the town.

On the afternoon of September 21, 1943, two German soldiers entered a Matera jewelry shop, probably in search of souvenirs. The surviving soldier claimed they intended to pay for their purchases. However, mistrust and hatred of the Germans was so strong that, when a passerby saw the soldiers in the shop, he assumed they were robbing the place. The man ran to a pair of nearby Italian policemen with his inaccurate report. The police shot and killed one of the soldiers; the second escaped unharmed and returned to his company.

That shooting was the flash point for many of the men in the town, fed up with the Fascist domination of the South, fed up with the failure of the Mussolini government, and now, after a summer of indecision, frustrated with the ineptitude of the new Italian government, which couldn't communicate with the Italian people.

In the minds of many, it was time to take matters in their own hands. One such man was Emanuele Manicone. He saw a German lieutenant sitting in a local barbershop. The sight of the gray uniform apparently set him off. He entered the shop and stabbed and killed the soldier, then ran through the streets and alleys like an Italian Paul Revere, shouting to the Materani to arm themselves and get out into the streets. This was the start of the first insurrection in all of Italy against their former allies and now clear oppressors. Men all over the town took to the balconies and rooftops, bearing carbines and pistols and anything else that would shoot.

Manicone was an electrician and a member of the electricians' union. He set up a headquarters of sorts at the electric society's main building and was soon joined by other likeminded insurrectionists armed and barricaded in the union's courtyard.

The Germans reacted by placing a cannon in the street a few hundred meters away from the union hall and blasting away until the place could be stormed by infantry soldiers. Several men were killed in the courtyard. The Germans then began collecting hostages and corralled them in the local barracks, which they had mined. At eight o'clock that evening, the Germans began pulling out of Matera. They detonated the mines in the area where the prisoners were being held, killing eleven men in the process.

In all, twenty-one were dead at the end of the bloody day, including Manicone.

The next day Sergeant John Durante and the rest of the Allies, who had been in nearby Montescaglioso, arrived in the City of the Sassi. They were greeted with hugs and shouts. The Materani had accomplished what few other Italians could claim; they had forced the early departure of their German occupiers and had made a loud and bloody sacrifice for Italian honor.

According to Carlo Levi, this uprising represented the essential character of the people of this land who for so long had been without a voice in government or self-determination. It had been more than merely a small skirmish in a war costing millions of lives; it was a defining moment for the Southern Italians. It was the moment they finally said, "*Basta*. Enough!"

It was the moment change finally came.

Sofas, Not Sons

Giovanni Scandiffio and I sat in the piazza by the Duni Conservatory, away from the marching bands and chanting parishioners. I had been trying for over a month to meet personally with the former journalist and now government spokesman. Our schedules finally coincided just days before I was scheduled to return home.

"You look like Materani," Scandiffio joked as we ordered drinks at the sidewalk café. "You have the face of this town."

"I've been told that before," I said. "I've seen the few pictures of my grandfather and know how much I look like him. So I guess I look like here. It's too bad for Matera. You'd have done better with Robert De Niro."

Giovanni laughed. "But we have better, we have the man who directed De Niro, Francis Ford Coppola."

"His family is from Matera?"

"No, Bernalda, just down the road. He's Lucani. Same face."

"I love the way all of Italy seems to claim their American sons when they've become famous."

"That's because too often we don't know our sons. We have no idea of just who left this place a hundred years ago. Every family had sons leaving. Thousands never returned. Many changed their names. You're one of the few who have found their way back. You have never found your grandfather's family here?"

"No," I said. "But I've found enough to be interested in the general story, not just my family's. The cost of bad economy to Southern Italy was enormous. It's taken a while for me to fully realize that cost in human terms. It must be hard for this town to realize that much of its lifeblood is off in another country helping making it successful."

Scandiffio was a man my own age, of similar coloring and, of course, carrying an ever-beeping cell phone. In between calls he brought me up to date on Matera's changing economy.

"1970 was the big year for us," he said. "We found a way to bring industry and employment to the area without pollution. The answer was furniture production. We are now one of the largest furniture manufacturers both nationally and internationally. We send sofas to America now, not our sons."

Scandiffio went on to explain that because there had never been any organized crime in the area—it had been too poor for the mobsters to bother with it—businesses had been able to develop in a normal way. Labor costs hadn't gone through the roof and the furniture market was allowed to develop on market needs, not social needs. It was one case where the remoteness of the region was to its benefit, and Rome stayed out.

"We had the right mix of geography, people and resources. For too long, Rome had been trying to develop heavy industry in the South, which runs contrary to both the nature and the skills of the place. The furniture business was perfect for us; we had no chemical pollution problems, we were able to attract EU dollars because we offered a safe environment to artisans. It's the future of Europe, too. It was a perfect fit."

A man strolled by walking a big white dog on a leash. Giovanni called out to him. He came over to our little table. I was introduced to Francesco Paolo Paolicelli.

"That was my grandfather's name," I said.

"We might be cousins," Francesco joked. "You look like you belong here." He was a tall, thin man with a full head of prematurely gray hair.

"I know; so I've been told."

"Do you know what branch of the family your grandfather came from? *Il suo soprannome?* His nickname?"

It was the nickname in these places which determined the relationship. In villages and towns with so many similar surnames, a distinctive characteristic was generally awarded a nickname, and it was that name by which people were known.

"No," I said. "Our Francesco Paolo left here almost a hundred years ago. I don't think they ever used those names in the States. If they did, no one can recall them."

"It's such a shame," Francesco said. "It is a name from here."

Giovanni and Francesco exchanged a few words and then the tall man went off with the white dog in the direction of the old castle guarding the Sassi.

"Would you care to walk a bit?" asked Giovanni.

We strolled across the bridge over the Sassi Caveosa toward the large piazza and lookout in front of the Cathedral of Santa Maria della Bruna.

"So, Carlo Levi's picture of the disease-ridden Sassi from the Second World War is finally being replaced by healthy, smiling furniture makers?" I asked, returning to our previous conversation.

"More or less. Levi saw this place at the worst time in its entire history. Three and four families had been living in dwellings meant for single families. Animals, too. Part of that overcrowding was from the trade wars Rome had declared with France and England. The farmers didn't have the market anymore, so they went to America or moved into the cities. Then there were depressions, wars—you name it. But the worst of it was in wartime. It always is."

"You've had a bad couple of centuries," I said.

"But the worst is over."

We'd reached the piazza and stood at the waist-high wall overlooking the Sassi.

"Look at this place," Giovanni said, waving in the direction of the Sassi. "Isn't this a truly magnificent sight?" We looked back in the direction of the Piazza Veneto. The stone houses below were bathed in a gentle yellow-white light.

"There is no other place in Italy or the world with this combination of color and architecture," Giovanni added. "The worst is over. What was once wealth, then poverty, will again be wealth."

"Are you speaking as a spokesman for the province, or as a native of the province?"

"Both," he laughed. "You can't grow up here and not be proud of what you've seen accomplished.

"And that's not all," Giovanni continued. "We might be sitting on top of something that could become the most profound change to Basilicata, ever."

"Sitting on top of?" I asked.

"*Oil!*" He paused. "Lots of it."

"That would be a first for Italy," I said.

"Exactly," Giovanni replied. "Right now there is no oil produced in Italy, all of our fossil fuel comes from someplace else and costs a great deal. But our scientists and engineers now say they've found a large deposit of petroleum in Basilicata. They're currently experimenting, producing seven thousand five hundred barrels a day, but say they can bring that figure up to between a hundred and twenty-five and two hundred fifty thousand. Some say we've got as much as twenty-five percent of all of Italy's demand right here, underfoot."

Giovanni Scandiffio seemed a happy man.

It wouldn't surprise me at all if the ancient past—this time the remains of a pre-human age—became the source of wealth for what had been the poorest of all of Italy for so many years. The past in Southern Italy had a way of becoming the future, of that much I was sure.

It was easy to understand Scandiffio's grin.

LAST NIGHT IN MATERA

I stopped by the electronics store to say good-bye to Cosimo and Michele Di Pede. The old man sat leaning on his cane in the deep shade; Michele was at his desk and smiled as I came in.

"*Buona sera, Signori Di Pede,*" I said, feeling clever about combining my greeting.

"Hello," the old man replied in his clear English.

"Paolo," Michele said, "I didn't know where to send this." He handed me an envelope.

It was an invitation to his father's hundredth birthday party to be held the next week at a local hall. The card was a photograph of Cosimo's birthplace in the Sassi.

"This was your home?" I asked the old man.

"My father's house," he replied. "I built my home in the upper town. But that's where I was born, in the Sassi. That's where we were all born."

"*Mi dispiace.* I'm so sorry I can't be here," I told Michele. "I very much want to, but it's time to go home."

"This is your home, too, Paolo."

I don't know if Michele will ever know how much those words meant to me.

Later that evening, I went down into the Sassi, down to where gener-

ations had lived in both good and bad times, and surrounded myself
with the ghosts of Matera....

My last night in Matera I spent walking on the smooth white stones,
in the section of Matera—the Sassi—where it all started so many centuries ago.

There are pockets of dead air as stairways and walls converge into
damp corridors. The humidity, even in September, hangs in vaporous,
barely visible clouds. Easy to see how Dr. Levi would find the place so
unhealthy. One gets a strange feeling walking about this ancient mixture
of stone and rock and heavy air. There really isn't any other place like
it, and words are so ineffective in attempting to capture its mystery, the
meandering walkways, the feel of the stones underfoot, the smell of
the place.

The surrounding colors of the walls and walks, depending on the time
of day, are mostly a dirty yellow or gray mixed with the oranges of roof
tiles and bright whites and light yellows of the newly refurbished walls.
These new colors will undoubtedly darken with age and this place with
return to its grayish nature. After sunset, the colors fade into the soft
shades of Italy. Walking about the Sassi at night, it's easy to remember
the monk's description of candlelight washing the walls and streets in its
soft yellow-white glow, the ancient and eternal color of men blocking
out the black of night, perhaps praying against the black of ignorance
and despair.

The sounds in the Sassi are also very different from the usual city
noises of the South. The shouts of children and the chatter of adults
come to the ear in an echo, voices enhanced by the reverberation from
aged and worn facades. Conversations, the clinking of dishes, the chattering of families, all bounce along the narrow corridors and off the uneven
walls; their origins either from above or below, and the almost musical
cacophony adds to the strange feel and mystery of the place.

It has come, once more, to the last night; another leave-taking.

"You look like the people from here," so many have said so many times.

"I am from here, in a way," I'd say.

Who knows? Ten thousand years of life in the Sassi, less than a hundred in Pittsburgh. A code deeply embedded in the genes and in the soul, the reason I had to search this place out, live here, try to understand.

A local newspaper reporter wrote that my Italian is heavily American-accented, but at least he called it "Italian." I was pleased with that much; I've ceased to worry about how bad I must sound. We have communicated here, and that is more important than language or dialect. I have learned much about this all-but-forgotten ancient, ancient place. Now some here claim me as their own, a definition I won't dispute.

Though I am an American and will always remain one, a part of me will always want to be in Matera. Or with Rocco over in Calabria, or down in Sicily, or over in Puglia, or up in Molise. Or in Abruzzo.

I wish Matera well with its UNESCO adventures, its humanity and heritage ratings. I wish it well with increased tourism and oil exploration and with defining a future that will be wealthier than its past. I wish it well in raising beautiful bilingual children, now ready to show the world what our grandparents knew all along, now able to stay here in their own culture rather than carry that culture with them to other places.

11

The Garden of the
Joe Commissos

It was time to leave Matera and Southern Italy and return to my American life. I thought about all of the adventures I'd had during the summer, the lessons learned, the wonderful and colorful cast of characters I'd met, once again, in a land beyond beautiful.

I had been blessed, indeed, by good fortune and health. I had learned much and been fascinated by compassionate and caring people.

But one conversation, above all others, remained in my memory....

Prior to leaving for Italy, friends had given me the name of an American artist living in the ancient town of Gerace, Joe Commisso. Early in my roaming about the South, I'd driven down the toe of Italy to the very end of the peninsula and taken a room in Siderno prior to my first interview with the Italian writer and activist Nicola Zitara. We had scheduling conflicts that took a few days to resolve.

To kill time, I drove over to Locri, the ancient Greek settlement only a few miles to the southwest. I went through the dig, marveling at the level of civilization that had been in this part of the world for so very long.

It was a bright, hot, typically Ionian day—too hot to spend much time walking about a shadeless archaeological site. I decided to look up the artist in Gerace, a hill fortification overlooking Locri as well as miles upon miles of the Ionian coast. I drove up the winding mountain road to the old town and parked the car in a large lot at the very top of the mountain opposite the ruins of what appeared to be a Norman castle, then walked down a steep cobblestoned street in search of Joe Commisso's studio.

I didn't have to search very hard; a large yellow arrow with the name of the studio pointed in the direction I was walking. The studio was a few dozen meters farther down the hill.

The place was open, but empty. It was housed in a reconstructed building that I estimated to be at least two or three hundred years old. I walked about the large room looking at the various paintings, all scenes of Gerace, and all capturing the unique patterns and texture of an ancient Italian hill town.

I called out to see if anyone was there.

A woman's voice replied from the back of the room. *"Vieni qua,"* she said. Come here.

I walked through a door at the rear of the studio and up a few steps into what was clearly the Commissos' living quarters. Signora Commisso was working in the kitchen, preparing vegetables. She was dressed darkly in what my mother used to call a "house coat," and appeared to be the traditional Italian *casalinga.*

"Sì," she said. *"Vuole qualcosa?"*

I explained that I was looking for Joe and had been given his address by friends in the States.

"Un attimo," she said, just a sec. She walked over to an adjoining room and called to her husband through a closed door, saying an American was here to see him. In a few moments Joe came into the room looking

slightly disheveled and apologizing for it; he wore shorts and a T-shirt and looked every bit like an American suburbanite. He said he'd been doing paperwork and hadn't heard me enter the shop.

"You'd like to buy something?" he asked.

Anyone with the desire could have stolen every painting in the place, but this didn't seem to concern the Commissos.

"No," I said. "Not right now. I've been given your name as someone to talk with here in Gerace."

"Talk with? Talk with concerning…"

"I'm sorry," I said. I took a card from my wallet. "Let me introduce myself." I handed him my card. "I'm an American journalist and am…"

Commisso glanced at my card.

"Are you the fellow who is going to speak with Nicola Zitara tomorrow?" he interrupted.

How on earth could this man know about an appointment with a writer in a neighboring town I'd only made the night before?

"Yes," I said, showing my surprise. "You know Signor Zitara?"

Signora Commisso laughed. *"Lui è più brutto che bello,"* she joked from the kitchen. He is more ugly than beautiful.

"Prego?" I was completely confused.

Signora Commisso laughed again. "We were schoolmates," she explained. "I spoke with him last evening and he said he'd spoken with you. He said you are interested in how we think here in the South."

"Guilty as charged," I said.

"You might not find that such an easy task," Joe said, smiling. "Many think we are a difficult group to understand."

"Well, I really wanted to talk with you about your own experiences here if you have a few moments."

"Come," said Joe. "We will go out to the garden and sit. Let's have a coffee, or maybe some wine?" He was a soft-spoken man. He seemed interested in my quest. I heard a slight accent in his English.

Joe left the studio completely unattended and led me through the back of the house and outdoors into an enclosed courtyard shaded by orange trees and tall leafy bushes. We sat on a bench along the garden wall and exchanged pleasantries about the garden and the weather until we were joined by Signora Commisso bearing cake and coffee.

"You're an American?" I asked.

"Yes," he said. "But I was born here in Locri. My family moved to America when I was young. I went to school there and fought in Korea in the U.S. army. I studied language at a university in Michigan, but then found painting and decided to move back to my native country. This town is my inspiration, so to speak."

"Your work is beautiful," I said honestly. "You seem to have found where you belong."

"Yes," he smiled. "I think so. And you, where do you belong?"

"I'm working on that," I said. It was an interesting question.

"Nicola says you're interested in our history," Signora Commisso said. "Why here, why this culture?"

I told the Commissos I had written a book about my family and, after the book had been published, I'd been all but overwhelmed by the response from readers who shared my feelings. Many had gone or wanted to go on a similar quest. I'd found it quite amazing. There was something to this Italian heritage I still hadn't understood, something that was undoubtedly quite important to many people who felt the same way. I explained I wanted to examine the reasons for the importance people placed on their heritage. And since the majority of us had origins in Southern Italy, I assumed the South had something to do with it, and I wanted to try and find whatever it was.

"I know that I'm looking for something that may not exist," I said. "I know you can't quantify an idea or belief, but I do believe there's something here in the South that is important for me to find."

"I know what you mean," Joe said. "I came back because I couldn't find what I wanted in the States."

I was comfortable in that garden with the Commissos. They seemed serene, at peace with themselves. In mere seconds we were discussing matters as friends.

Signora Commisso explained that she had grown up in the area and gone to school with Nicola Zitara, who remained close. It was a small community in her generation, and still was. Joe was an artist; she was a writer. She gave me a few of her short stories to read, apologizing that they weren't in English. I read them as I traveled about that summer and found her writing to be a good exercise in Italian. The stories were also fascinating, especially one about a visit with family in Southern California, where she compared the beliefs she held as important to those she saw in her American cousins.

"What led you to this quest?" Joe asked.

I explained how my grandfather's dying words had affected me so much that I'd gone off in search of my family, and that search had led to my first book. Then, when so many people contacted me and shared so many things about their own families, I wanted to learn more about the culture I'd overlooked and all but ignored for most of my life.

"What was it your grandfather said?" Joe asked.

" '*Povri figli miei.*' 'My poor kids.' Those are the only words I know he said; he died many years before I was born. My father didn't tell me that story until I was a grown man, but when he did, I realized in that instant that the people I'd always thought of as ancient and unrelated to my life had an entire character that I'd never understood. If an illiterate peasant can die with responsibility to his children as his last thought, he had far more character and depth than I'd ever thought about. I wanted to learn how much of that character was formed here. How was it formed. It's not just my story, it's a story about so many Italian-Americans with Southern origins."

I studied their faces. It was a long speech and the words had almost involuntarily poured out of me. My *straniero*'s story had apparently pleased the Commissos.

"It's all but taken over my life," I added.

The Commissos smiled.

Joe talked softly about life in the South of Italy: how different it was here from Rome or the North; how the people had such different and more ancient influences than any other Italians, how poor the region had been for so very long, yet how connected most felt to the land and landscape. It was the landscape and the ancient sense of the place that had called Joe back to where he had been born. It had been possible to return in his generation, impossible in my grandfather's.

"We have been a part of this land for so long and in so many ways, it might be very difficult to explain," Joe said. "But one thing is certain—we've never lacked character. We might have been poor and repressed, but we've always been creative and have always found a way to express ourselves."

"How do you mean?" I asked.

"Look how powerfully your grandfather has communicated with you. Here was a man, as you say, without reading or writing or wealth, and whose voice you'd never heard spoken. Yet his mere three words have moved you and guided your life. We Southerners understand the power of such words."

In the garden of the Commissos on that summer afternoon, sitting in the shade and away from the blazing Southern sun, I heard an important truth.

Joe was right.

As Nené Troncale would say, our people brought values with them to America, not valuables. I had almost missed the difference, and now my work and life were about that difference.

It *was* a most powerful message, after all, delivered by an illiterate peasant departed from life many years before I was born, whose gift to me was far greater than anything I could ever repay. We, those of us with roots in Southern Italy, were all the children, grandchildren and great-grandchildren of such men.

They had been formed in a unique place.

They came from an ancient and vigorous culture which they carried with them intuitively, not in books.

And now, in the delightful irony of progress, many of us were writing books they couldn't have read, in an attempt to define them.

ACKNOWLEDGMENTS

The road leading to this book has been long and fascinating. It has been filled with supportive, captivating and informative friends and associates who have all contributed in a variety of ways to the life of this text. Its errors are mine. If there are strengths, they belong to those who gave me their time and insights.

There were many.

In Pittsburgh...

This book started with **Sam Patti** challenging my hyphenation. His passion for the subject and consistent energy helped push me along. **Joseph D'Andrea**, the gentle and dignified former Italian Consul for Pittsburgh, has been truly *un amico molto gentile*. **Nick Ciotola** has been an exceptional sounding board, a very bright young man in charge of the Italian-American section of a marvelous Pittsburgh resource, the Heinz History Museum. **John McIntyre**, a friend and former colleague, bucked broadcasting trends and did an author interview on his lively evening program on the Pittsburgh Cable News Channel, a rare event in modern news programming and for which I am indebted. **Dr. Lina Insana**, of the University of Pittsburgh, shared her Sicilian mother's marvelous sayings and graciously amplified their meaning. **Fred Sargent**, a friend from way back, has provided breakfast, encouragement, and cheerleading—a slight step away from the marching band in which we once played together on Friday nights in high school. **Joe Rovitto**, one of the nicest newsmen I've ever known, gave guidance and advice, made phone calls, and served as my unofficial Pittsburgh agent. **Helen Castaldo** sent maps, made notes, offered hospitality in Rome. **Bill**

Keslar, a friend from childhood, provided an open ear which I've been bending for most of our lives.

Elsewhere in the United States...

Dr. James Mancuso, now professor emeritus from SUNY in Albany, is a prolific writer and thoughtful contributor on the entire gamut of the Italian-American experience. His generosity, kindness, consistent feedback and honesty are deeply appreciated. Dr. Ken Scambray was my West Coast Sam Patti, both a challenge to my assumptions of ethnicity and a cheerleader for this continuing project. Dr. Fred Gardaphe of Stony Brook in New York has been a reliable guide and has become a friend as a result of this quest. Anna Ionta, an Italian instructor from Chicago, contacted me after reading *Dances with Luigi* and has been a friend and resource ever since, leading me to her friend, Rodolfo Di Biasio and his marvelous poetry and novel. Another Chicagoan, Lionel Bottari, and I sat on the benches in Matera talking of our love of Italy and fascination with its many mysteries. His insights into the regional music of Italy should be the basis for his own book. And Paul Cioe shared his experiences and support from Chicago. Jan Pate from Chicago helped with the original Nicola Zitara interview and connected me to the YMCA in Siderno. My fellow writer, colleague and friend, John Keahey in Salt Lake City, has provided his eye and instinct and consistent encouragement. Tommy Durante remains a quintessential New Yorker with an optimist's laugh and striking sense of humor. His father's story and our trip to Sala Consilina remains one of my life's great experiences. And, speaking of a father's story, Tom Capra in Palm Springs provided me with insights into his famous father's thinking that I could have never found in books, and with references to his cousins in Bisacquino, the Troncales. Aaron Breitbart at the Simon Weisenthal Foundation in Los Angeles was extremely helpful and eventually led me to one of the most remarkable people I've ever interviewed, Walter Wolff.

In Italy...

Enrico Borsetti was tour guide, translator and spell checker and, as always, an extraordinary resource and friend. Fausto Oricchio was a tremendous help in nailing down Rodolfo Di Biasio for our hurried interview in Rome, and provided the translation for that interview. Lina and Pino Filice, Rocco Musi, and Roberto Musi are all new Calabrian friends whose knowledge, passion and insights into their native land helped guide me through it. Sharon Cowan in

Rome is my touchstone in that wonderful city, her sympathetic ear and thoughtful suggestions are as keen as her exceptional editor's eye. Amy Weideman, an American married to a Materano, was of great help in Matera, helping negotiate an apartment, phone and other necessities of life. Dr. Carmine Colacino, Aldo Chietera, Michele Di Pede, Franco Di Pede, Giovanni Scandiffio, Carmine Sciulli, Father Dominic Sturino, and Dr. Nicola Zitara all took time from busy lives and busy schedules to help guide, teach, inform and enlighten me. Their insights, knowledge and love of the South of Italy can never be accurately recorded in mere words, their passion for their subject will remain with me for always.

In Ohio...

John and Jane McCormick's tales of their Gerace experiences and excitement with all things Italian was infectious. John's addiction to the Internet found not only relatives, but also Joe and Maria Commisso. Sam Fata and Richard DiPaolo from the Columbus Sons of Italy chapter, and Tony Spazianni from the state level, finally shamed me into joining the organization I once thought was only for my father. I am now proud to be associated with such conscientious and gentle men and am deeply appreciative for all the support and help they've offered in so many areas.

Thanks, too, to my editor and friend, Carolyn Chu at St. Martin's Press, for her sharp eye, hard work, always being there, and finding time for my interminable questions and requests.

A LIST OF SOURCES AND READING MATERIALS

Alexander, Paul J. *The Ancient World to A.D. 300* (Second Edition). New York: The Macmillan Company, 1968.

Breuer, William B. *Drop Zone Sicily, Allied Airborne Strike—July 1943.* Novato, CA: Presidio Press, 1997.

Capra, Frank. *The Name Above the Title, An Autobiography.* New York: Da Capo Press, 1997.

Carroll, James. *Constantine's Sword, The Church and the Jews.* New York: Houghton Mifflin Co., 2001.

Clark, Martin. *Modern Italy 1871-1982.* London and New York: Longman, Inc., 1984.

Colacino, Carmine; Grasso, Alfonso; Molett, Andrea; Pagano, Antonio; Ressa, Giuseppe; Romano, Alessandro; Russo, Maria; Salvadore, Marina; Sarcinell, Maria. *La Storia Proibita, Quando I Piemontesi Invasero il Sud.* Naples, Italy: Controcorrente, 2001.

Di Biasio, Rodolfo. *Wayfarers Four* (Translated by Justin Vitiello). West Lafayette, IN: Bordighera, Inc., 1998.

Di Biasio, Rodolfo. *I Quattro Camminanti.* Florence: Sansori Editore, 1991.

Dickie, John. *Darkest Italy, The Nation and Stereotypes of the Mezzogiorno, 1860-1900.* New York: St. Martin's Press, 1999.

Di Franco, Philip J. *The Italian Americans (The Peoples of North America)*. New York and Philadelphia: Chelsea House, 1988.

Di Pede, Franco. *Il Segno Rifatto*. Milano, Italy: Gabriele Mazzotta, 1992.

Douglas, Norman. *Old Calabria*. Evanston, IL: The Marlboro Press/Northwestern, 1998.

Folino, Francesco. *Ebrei Destinazione Calabria* (1940-1943). Palermo, Italy: Sellerio Editore, 1988.

Forrest, W. G. *The Emergence of Greek Democracy, 800-400 B.C.* New York: McGraw Hill, 1966.

Gambino, Richard. *Blood of My Blood, The Dilemma of the Italian Americans.* Toronto: Guernica Editions, Inc., 1974.

Geary, Patrick J. *The Myth of Nations, The Medieval Origins of Europe*. Princeton, NJ: Princeton University Press, 2002.

Gilbert, Felix. *The End of the European Era, 1890 to the Present* (Third Edition). New York: W. W. Norton & Company, Inc., 1984.

Ginsborg, Paul. *A History of Contemporary Italy, Society and Politics 1943-1988.* London: The Penguin Group, 1990.

Gissing, George. *By the Ionian Sea*. London: Century Hutchinson, Ltd., Brookmount House, 1986.

Camaiti Hostert, Camaiti; Tamburri, Anna and Anthony. *Screening Ethnicity: Cinematographic Representations of Italian Americans in the United States.* (Ben Lawton, "The Mafia and the Movies," pp. 69-91.) Boca Raton: Bordighera Press, 2002.

Hume, David D. *About Sicily, Travellers in an Ancient Island*. Exeter, NH: J.N. Townsend Publishing, 1999.

Keahey, John. *A Sweet and Glorious Land, Revisiting the Ionian Sea*. New York: Thomas Dunne Books/St. Martin's Press, 2000.

Lamb, Richard. *War in Italy 1943-1945, A Brutal Story*. New York: Da Capo Press, 1996.

Levi, Carlo. *Christ Stopped at Eboli* (Translated by Frances Frenaye). New York: Farrar, Straus and Company, 1947, 1963.

Lloyd, Susan Caperna. *No Pictures in My Grave, A Spiritual Journey in Sicily.* San Francisco: Mercury House, 1992.

Longo, R. Giura. *Sassi e Secoli.* Matera, Italy: BMG, 1986.

Mangione, Jerre, and Morreale, Ben. *La Storia, Five Centuries of the Italian American Experience.* New York: HarperCollins, 1992.

McBride, Joseph. *Frank Capra, The Catastrophe of Success.* New York: St. Martin's Griffin, 1992.

McGinniss, Joe. *The Miracle of Castel di Sangro, A Tale of Passion and Folly in the Heart of Italy.* New York: Broadway Books, 1999.

McLean, Maria Coletta. *My Father Came from Italy.* Vancouver, BC: Raincoast Books, 2000.

Motta, Antonio. *Oltre Eboli, Uomini e Avvenimenti Lungo le Vie di Basilicata.* Potenza, Italy: Casa Editrice, 1998.

Murray, William. *The Last Italian.* New York: Simon & Schuster, 1991.

Musi, Roberto. *Casanova in Calabria.* Amantea, Italy: Tipografia Grafiche Calabrie, 1999.

Patruno, Lino. *Una Vita in Jazz e Non Solo.* Rome: Editoriale Pantheon. 2000.

Perrone, Mauro Cav. *Storia Documentata della Città di Castellaneta e Sua Descrizione.* Bari: Stab. Tipografico E. Cressati & C., 1896.

Riccardi, Teodoro. *Notizie Storiche di Miglionico.* Napoli: Stamperia Dell' Iride, 1867.

Richards, Charles. *The New Italians.* London: Penguin Books, 1994.

Robb, Peter. *Midnight in Sicily.* New York: Vintage Books, 1998.

Sammartino, Peter, and Roberts, William. *Sicily, An Informal History.* Cranbury, New York: Cornwall Books, 1992.

Schoener, Allon. *Gli Italo Americani*. Rizzoli Libri S.p.A., 1988.

Sciulli, Aniceto. *Gamberale, Il Comune Più Alto Della Provincia di Chieti*. Pro Loco di Gamberale, 1986.

Shulman, Irving. *Valentino*. New York: Trident Press, 1967.

Simeti, Mary Taylor. *On Persephone's Island, A Sicilian Journal*. San Francisco: North Point Press, 1987.

Smith, Dennis Mack. *Mussolini*. London: George Weidenfeld and Nicholson, Ltd., 1981.

Sowell, Thomas. *Migrations and Cultures, A World View*. New York: Basic Books, 1996.

Stille, Alexander. *Benevolence and Betrayal, Five Italian Jewish Families Under Fascism*. New York: Summit Books, 1991.

Talese, Gay. *Unto the Sons*. New York: Alfred A. Knopf, Inc., 1992.

Toscano, Giorgio, and Basile, Pina. *La Storia di Oriolo*. Rome: Tip. Olimpica di C. Sterpi, 1985.

Walker, Alexander. *Rudolph Valentino*. New York: Stein and Day, 1976.

Wolff, Walter. *Bad Times, Good People*. Long Beach, New York: Whittier Publications, 1999.

Zitara, Nicola. *Negare la Negazione*. Reggio Calabria: Città del Sole Edizione, 2001.

Zitara, Nicola. *L'Unità d'Italia: Nascita di una Colonia*. Siderno, Italy: Dell'autore. 1995.

RELATED FICTION

Ardizzone, Tony. *In the Garden of Papa Santuzzu*. New York: Picador, 1999.

De Bernières, Louis. *Corelli's Mandolin*. New York: Vintage International, 1994.

Di Rosa, Tina. *Paper Fish*. New York: The Feminist Press, 1996.

Clifton, Harry. *On the Spine of Italy, A Year in the Abruzzi.* London: Macmillan, 1999.

Valerio, Anthony. *Valentino and the Great Italians.* Toronto: Guernica Editions, Inc., 1994.

Zitara, Nicola. *Memorie di quand'ero italiano.* Siderno, Italy: Dell'autore. 1994.